STORYTELLING
as Art and Craftsmanship

DENNIS M. CLAUSEN

Practical Strategies for Screenwriters and Creative Writers

Kendall-Hunt Publishing Company previously published this book under the title *Screenwriting and Literature*

Copyright © 2019 by Dennis M. Clausen

All rights reserved
No part of this book may be reproduced in any form or by any means including electronic reproduction and photocopying without written permission of the author.

ISBN-Print: 9781674967844

Interior design by booknook.biz

TABLE OF CONTENTS

Acknowledgements   ix
Preface   xi

1   The Elements of Storytelling   1
    Some Stories Never Die   1
    Know the Historical Background to Your Story   6
    A Story Needs a Strong Central Character—Complete With Flaws   7
    An Antagonist Must Be Worthy of the Central Character   10
    Minor Characters Help Create Great Stories   12
    Irony Adds Richness and Depth to a Story   13
    Ambiguity Also Adds Richness and Depth to a Story   16
    Great Stories Never Seem to End   17

2   Finding a Story   20
    Storytelling Starts With a Story Worth Telling   21
    Writers Must Be Emotionally Committed to Their Stories   23

Using People You Know as Models   27
Historical Subjects   29
Times of Transition   30
Stories from Film and Literary Genres   33
The Place is the Story   35
The One-Sentence Summary or Logline   37
Final Thoughts on Choosing a Story   38

3   Developing Characters in Screenplays and Novels   42
Screenplays and Novels are Character-Driven Stories   42
Classic Film Characters   46
One-Sentence Character Descriptions   48
Using Clothing and Objects to Build Characters   49
Distinguishing Physical Characteristics   50
Names of Characters   51
Exploring a Character's Weaknesses   53
When Characters Do the Unexpected   54
Character Relationships   55
Building Strong Antagonists   57
A Character's Internal Conflicts   58
Irony in Character Building   61
Character Growth   64
Some Books on Character Building   66

4   Structuring Screenplays and Novels   70
If You Build It, He Will Come   70
The Classic Film Paradigm   73
Pulling the Reader into the Story   75
Plot Points   76
Plot Points in Plays and Novels   77
Plot Points in Films   78
The Hero's Journey   79

Use and Misuse of the Paradigms   84
The Rule of Threes   84
Structure and Voice in Literary Classics   87

5   Beginnings and Endings   92
    The End is the Beginning   92
    Beginnings and Endings as Bookends   94
    The Endings Behind the Ending   98
    The Scarlet Letter   101
    K-PAX   102
    Cast Away   105
    The Hidden Story Behind the Story   109
    Apocalypse Now   110
    The Great Gatsby   112
    The Parallax View   114
    The Sixth Sense (1999)   117
    Write the Ending Early   119

6   Screenplay Adaptations of Novels   123
    Know the Inner Spirit of the Literary Work   123
    Know the Dramatic Conflict in Each Scene   130
    The Scarlet Letter: Original First Scaffold Scene in the Novel   131
    Scaffold Scene: Screenplay Form   133
    Scaffold Scene: Novel versus Screenplay   136
    Dramatic Conflict and Intensity in *The Scarlet Letter* Scene   138
    The Red Badge of Courage: Original Battlefield Scene in the Novel   139
    Battlefield Scene: Screenplay Form   141
    Battlefield Scene: Novel versus Screenplay   143

Dramatic Conflict and Intensity in *The Red Badge of Courage* 144
My Antonia: Original Scene from the Novel 145
My Antonia: Screenplay Treatment of the Same Scene 149
My Antonia: Novel versus Screenplay Treatment of the Scene 152
The Last Detail: Screenplay Scene 153
The Last Detail: Scene from the Shooting Script 154
Dramatic Conflict and Intensity in *The Last Detail* 156
Conclusions about Screenplay Adaptations and Formatting 157
Screenwriting Software 158

7 Reading Scripts and Shooting Scripts 162
Introduction 162
Final Scene: *The Turn of the Screw* 164
Final Scene: Reading Script 165
Final Scene: Another Reading Script 167
Final Scene: Overly Technical Reading Script 170
Final Scene: Shooting Script 173
Good Will Hunting: An Exemplary Reading Script 176

8 Screenwriting Terms and Techniques 182
Glossary of Screenwriting Terms 182
Examples of Technical Terms in a Screenplay 185
  The Sins of Rachel Sims (Scene 1) 185
    Shifting Headers (EXT. and INT.) 187
  The Sins of Rachel Sims (Scene 2) 188
    Flashbacks 190
  The Sins of Rachel Sims (Scene 3) 190
    Montages 191

  The Sins of Rachel Sims (Scene 4) 192
    Off Screen 195
  The Sins of Rachel Sims (Scene 5) 195
    Angles and Close Shots 197
  The Sins of Rachel Sims (Scene 6) 198
    Flashback Sequence 201
  Conclusions about Screenplay Terms and Techniques 201

9 Scenes and Sequences 204
  Introduction 204
  Scene 1 in a Novel Sequence 206
  Scene 2 in a Novel Sequence 209
  Scene 3 in a Novel Sequence 210
  Scene 4 in a Novel Sequence 210
  Screenplay Sequence from *The Age of Innocence* 211
  Tips on Developing Effective Scenes and Sequences 217
  Pacing Scenes in a Sequence: *Cat Ballou* 221
  A Final Note Regarding Scenes and Sequences 225

10 Writing Dialogue 229
  Introduction 229
  What is Bad Dialogue? 232
  Dialogue Scene: *The Deerslayer* 233
  What is Effective Dialogue? 235
  Dialogue Scene: *The Adventures of Huckleberry Finn* 237
  Mark Twain's Principles Regarding Dialogue 240
  Dialogue in Stage Plays 241
  Dialogue from Classic Films 244
  Dialogue Scene: *Butch Cassidy and the Sundance Kid* 245
  Dialogue Scene: *Casablanca* 247
  Write Dialogue with the Ear 251
  Write When You Are Not Writing 251

    Freewriting Dialogue   252
    Sometimes People Just Don't Communicate   254
    Avoid Long, Complete Sentences   254
    Other Tips for Writing Dialogue   256

11 From Screenwriting to Novel Writing   262
    Introduction   262
    Screenplay Version: *The Search for Judd McCarthy*   *267*
    Novel Version: *The Search for Judd McCarthy*   *273*
    Screenwriting Strategies Used To Write the Novel   282

Afterword   293
About the Author   295

ACKNOWLEDGEMENTS

When professors teach a subject for many years, they often forget the sources of their original insights and inspirations. So it is for me in writing this book. So much of what I have read, thought about, heard as a student in high school and college classes, and discussed with my colleagues during my many years of teaching has blended together and become a single unified vision regarding storytelling. I wish I could acknowledge all those who contributed to this vision, but that would be impossible. Too much time has passed, and too many people have helped create that vision. For those who did contribute to my understanding of storytelling over the years, even if I can no longer recall their specific contributions, I am most grateful.

There are other sources that are more accessible, and I would like to acknowledge their contributions. Project Gutenberg has been a rich source of publications that have been useful in the writing of *Storytelling as Art and Craftsmanship*. Project Gutenberg, which was founded by Michael Hart in 1971, is an on-going effort to produce and distribute free electronic editions of literary classics that are in the public domain. I am deeply grateful to the members of Project Gutenberg for making these resources available in such a convenient form.

Syd Field's book, *Screenplay, the Foundations of Screenwriting*, has deeply influenced my teaching and writing since I first read it in the early 1980s. Joseph Campbell's book, *The Hero with a Thousand Faces*, and Christopher Vogler's book, *The Writer's Journey*, have also taught me much about screenwriting, especially character development. There are other books on screenwriting and creative writing that are too numerous to mention, but they have also influenced my thinking over the years.

Many talented film directors, screenwriters, and actors—far too many to mention or acknowledge here—have taught me so very much just by watching their films and marveling at their talents and skills. I never tire of those films. I watch them over and over again until I know the plots as well as the events in my own life. They have given me many valuable insights into screenwriting as a form of storytelling. I often utilized those insights in my screenwriting courses and in the writing of this book.

The University of San Diego and my colleagues have provided support and insights during the writing of *Storytelling as Art and Craftsmanship*. My wife Alexa has provided a sounding board for many of the ideas I discuss in these pages. My son Derl, a talented young writer and actor, has offered numerous insights into films and literature that appeal to his generation. Those insights have motivated me to rethink several sections of this book. I would also like to thank my students at the University of San Diego who have provided so many exciting and insightful moments in my classrooms. They inspired and encouraged me to write this book so the next generation of college students could explore the relationships between screenwriting, creative writing, and novel writing.

–Dennis M. Clausen–

PREFACE

Storytelling as Art and Craftsmanship is a compendium of practical advice for writers who want to become more effective storytellers. The major point emphasized throughout this book is that the techniques of screenwriting are refined storytelling devices that are invaluable tools for all writers. Screenwriting should not be treated as something that is separate and distinct from other forms of creative writing, albeit there are differences. Rather, it should be considered a central component in literature and creative writing courses. As Sue Grafton, the hugely successful author of the alphabet series of mystery novels, said in an interview with *The Seattle Times* in 2017: "Hollywood taught me how to write dialogue. I learned how to get into a scene and out of it. I learned to do action sequences, and I learned how to structure a story, and those things have served me well."[1]

Storytelling as Art and Craftsmanship was inspired by my own experiences converting screenplay outlines into several traditionally published novels and works of nonfiction. I had the advantage

---

[1] Macdonald, Moira. "With 'Y is for Yesterday,' Sue Grafton prepares for the alphabet series' end." The Seattle Times 10 September 2017.

of having taught screenwriting for many years at the university level, so integrating screenwriting techniques with novel writing techniques was a natural extension of what I teach in creative writing courses. In the early 1980s, I first began experimenting with using screenplays as outlines for writing novels. Since then, I have published four novels—*The Search for Judd McCarthy*, *The Sins of Rachel Sims*, *The Accountant's Apprentice*, and *My Christmas Attic*—that were written first as screenplays. I have also published two works of nonfiction—*Prairie Son* and *Goodbye to Main Street*— that benefited from what I learned practicing and teaching screenwriting. To be sure, screenwriting techniques apply more to writing fiction than nonfiction. Still, writers of nonfiction can also benefit by learning screenwriting techniques regarding cuts, tying beginnings and endings together, and creating strong visual images for the reader when it is appropriate.

The Search for Judd McCarthy was a best-selling paperback when it was first published in 1982 under a different title. At the time, virtually no one was writing stories as screenplays and then converting them into novels. The technique worked quite well, and the storytelling elements in the novel received excellent reviews. (See Chapter 11 of this book for a more detailed discussion of the specific screenwriting techniques I used in writing this novel.)

Prairie Son, a work of creative nonfiction published in 1999, was not written as a screenplay since it was based on a true story. However, what I learned from writing screenplays helped me enormously in structuring the story, deciding where it should begin and end, organizing individual chapters using screenplay "sequencing" techniques, and other elements of storytelling practiced by screenwriters. *Prairie Son* received significant national attention when it focused a spotlight on the early twentieth century practice of adopting children and raising them more as indentured servants than sons or daughters. I do not believe I could have done justice to my father's story without the skills and techniques I had acquired teaching, evaluating, and writing screenplays.

Storytelling as Art and Craftsmanship would also be a useful resource and guide in any screenwriting, creative writing, film, or literature class where the emphasis is on storytelling. This includes interdisciplinary "narrative studies" courses that focus on storytelling rather than theoretical or scholarly pedagogies. To facilitate instruction in these courses, every chapter in *Storytelling as Art and Craftsmanship* has a set of creative, classroom-tested exercises.

What specifically can writers learn from this kind of screenwriting experience? The best screenwriters are masters of structure. A screenplay is primarily a structural device that unites a story from beginning to middle to end. Screenwriters can thus teach other creative writers much about structuring novels so they are freer to concentrate on voice and the other elements of storytelling. In another interview with *Publisher's Weekly* in 1998, Sue Grafton said, "There's nothing like a film script to teach you structure."[2]

Writing a story as a screenplay provides a structural foundation that is vastly superior to other outlines. A screenplay outline enables the writer to find and integrate the *inner spirit* of the story throughout the early drafts, thus improving storytelling elements like foreshadowing and false foreshadowing. The flaws in any plot are also more apparent in screenplay form because everything is on the surface and not buried in the descriptive, expository, and other verbiage of a novel. Simultaneously, a screenplay outline exposes the areas where revisions in the storyline can more easily be made without squandering precious time and creative energies.

---

2   Bing, Jonathan. "Sue Grafton: Death and the Maiden." Publisher's Weekly 20 April 1998.

A screenplay outline can help most writers overcome the many challenges of writing a longer work of fiction.

As a writer, I have benefited greatly from studying the relationships between screenwriting and more traditional forms of creative writing. I invite readers of ***Storytelling as Art and Craftsmanship*** to explore those relationships with me.

CHAPTER 1

THE ELEMENTS OF STORYTELLING

Some Stories Never Die

What makes a great story? There is probably no one answer to that question. Still, if we look at real-life stories, some do stand out because they never seem to die. They seem instead to grow in stature over the years as each new generation tries to find a unique pathway into their elusive secrets, or some new revelation that has yet to be exposed that will explain everything that happened.

Custer's Last Stand at the Little Bighorn in 1876 is one such story. Why does it live on when so many other stories about the conquest of the American West have faded into oblivion? As historians have pointed out, there was a similar story that occurred ten years earlier in Wyoming. Another impetuous, headstrong military leader, Captain William J. Fetterman, got caught up in the myth of his own invincibility and led his troops into a Native American ambush in which everyone under his command was killed. Yet, very few people remember that story.[3]

There is something about Custer's Last Stand, however, which lives on, rekindled by the hundreds of books that have been published over the years and the thirty to forty films that have either recreated the battle at the Little Bighorn or featured Custer as a central character. So what is it about this story that makes it so special? Why is it a story that never dies, but seems instead to grow in stature?

Let's examine some of the natural storytelling elements that came together in this isolated corner of Montana on that hot June day in 1876. In the process, I think we will see that it is a cornucopia of great storytelling techniques that fictional writers struggle to master. Yet, unless one believes in Divine Intervention and is convinced that the forces that govern this universe are also great storytellers, everything that creates a great story somehow just came together on Last Stand Hill.

I have used the story of Custer's Last Stand so often in my screenwriting courses to illustrate basic storytelling techniques that I know the history quite well. So I will be using this wealth of information—gleaned over several decades from many different sources too numerous to name or remember, film documentaries, and a visit to the Little Bighorn—to illustrate various elements of storytelling in this chapter. First, a little plot summary. Many of the facts that preceded Custer's defeat are not disputed. He graduated last in his class at West Point and became the youngest general in the Union Army. During the Civil War,

---

[3] Custer's story appears in most textbooks on American history. Fetterman's story is omitted from many of them and has never captured the public's imagination. Perhaps it is because Fetterman's story lacks some of the elements of storytelling discussed throughout this book.

Storytelling as Art and Craftsmanship

he demonstrated a remarkable courage that often bordered on foolhardiness because, although he usually led his men from the front whenever they charged Confederate strongholds, he was never seriously wounded. Others soldiers on both sides of him were shot off their horses and killed, but he survived the entire conflict unscathed.

After the Civil War, the military sent him out west to fight in what became known as the Indian Wars, where he led a number of attacks on Native American encampments often comprised mostly of women and children. He eventually fell into disgrace for failing to follow orders and other charges, and he was demoted in rank. Later, he was given another opportunity to redeem himself when the government learned that large numbers of Native Americans were leaving the reservations and journeying out west to Montana. Custer was chosen as one of the three military commanders—General Terry and General Crook were the others—to find and bring the Native Americans back to their reservations.

General Terry descended on the Little Bighorn from the north, General Crook led his men to the Little Bighorn from the south, and Custer approached from the east. The plan was that all three of the military commands would arrive at the Little Bighorn at about the same time, and, with such a great show of force, the Native Americans would peacefully surrender and return to their reservations. However, for reasons that are debated to this day, Custer put his men on somewhat of a forced march. He seemed determined to get to the Little Bighorn first. What his motives were is a matter of conjecture. Some historians argue that he was given considerable leeway in how fast or slow he would march his men toward the Little Bighorn. Others insist he was determined to get there first, win a decisive battle, and return to the east as a conquering military hero who could then thrust himself into that year's presidential campaign.

Whatever the case, at the Little Bighorn Custer made a series of mistakes that doomed himself and his troops. His first mistake was when he decided to attack the encampment before Terry and Crook had arrived. Another mistake was that he decided to divide his six-hundred men into three groups, further weakening his ability to fight an adversary that was far superior in numbers. Major Reno was ordered to attack the encampment from the south. Captain Benteen and his men were ordered to travel farther west to stop any Native Americans who managed to escape after the attack on their encampment had started. Custer and his two-hundred men then journeyed north to attack the encampment from that direction.

At some point Custer apparently realized that it was a very big encampment, and he sent one of his soldiers to Benteen with a message to "Come on and be quick." Whether Benteen didn't take the message too seriously, or whether he was content to let Custer, whom he loathed, take what he thought was coming to him, Benteen did not exactly rush to Custer's aid. Instead, he joined Reno and his men who had failed in their attack from the south and had fled into the hills overlooking the Little Bighorn, where they set up a defensive position and held off the warriors who attacked them persistently.

Two days later Reno and Benteen looked down into the valley and saw that the Native Americans were breaking their encampment and leaving the area. Shortly afterwards, they saw Terry and his troops approaching the Little Bighorn from the north. When the besieged soldiers under Reno's and Benteen's command joined Terry, they explained that they were not sure what had happened to Custer and his men. When they rode over to Last Stand Hill, it became immediately clear that Custer and the two-hundred men under his command had all been killed. How had it happened? They did not know. It was only painfully

Storytelling as Art and Craftsmanship

clear that Custer had blundered badly when he decided to attack a Native American encampment that was much bigger than he had first thought.

The troops under the command of Terry, Reno, and Benteen quickly dug shallow graves for the many bodies that were scattered across Last Stand Hill. Then they too departed the area, fearful that perhaps the Native American warriors had plans to double back and do to the soldiers under their commands what they had already done to Custer and the Seventh Calvary.

One can only imagine what that forlorn part of the Montana prairie must have looked like that night as the moon rose high in the sky, and not a single living person remained behind. There was only the carnage of the previous day's battle, and the mounds of soil covering the shallow graves of those who died on Last Stand Hill. As the moonlight filtered across the battlefield, it must have been eerie beyond belief.

No one returned to the site of the battle for another year. When the government finally sent out a contingent of soldiers to survey the battlefield, they found some of the bones of those under Custer's command who had been killed on Last Stand Hill scattered across the prairie, apparently unearthed by predators. Custer's bones were still buried somewhere in that carnage. The man, who probably had grandiose ambitions to win a decisive military victory and return to the east as a conquering hero, was instead reduced to one more pile of bones buried beneath a few inches of dirt on the Montana prairie.

So what are some of the natural storytelling techniques that seem to feed the legend of the Battle of the Little Bighorn? Let's examine a few and see what they can teach us about all forms of storytelling, whether it be an historical incident, fictional work, or speculative screenplay.

Know the Historical Background to Your Story

Not every story should be Custer's Last Stand, of course. There are an infinitive variety of stories that are worth telling. Still, there is much we can learn about storytelling by taking a closer look at the enduring appeal of what happened on that remote little section of the Montana prairie in June of 1876.

Anyone writing about the Battle of the Little Bighorn has access to a wealth of historical research on the subject. Most stories a screenwriter or novelist might decide to write are not that well researched or documented, and the writer must conduct the research himself or herself. In either case, the storyteller must know the historical background to any story if it is to achieve a more universal appeal and richness. That does not mean all of the historical research a storyteller engages in needs to be integrated into the storyline. Screenplays are intended to be lean and sparse, and that would unnecessarily clutter up the storyline. Still, the reader of a screenplay or novel needs to sense that behind every story, no matter how localized it might appear to be, there is a larger history somewhere in the background.

Behind the story of Custer's defeat at the hands of the Native Americans, there is definitely a much bigger story. The battle occurred in June of 1876, a few weeks before the centennial celebration of the nation's Declaration of Independence and near the very end of the frontier phase in American history. Most historians agree that the period of westward expansion effectively came to an end in the early 1890s. So at the Little Bighorn, what we are witnessing in hindsight is the inevitable final chapter of the Native American dominance of the North American continent. The Battle of the Little Bighorn was the last great battle of the Indian Wars and the last time the Native Americans would be victorious in defending their lands. After their victory at the Little Bighorn, their only choices were to return to their reservations or be hunted down by Union troops and killed. Their resistance against the great white horde that had invaded their lands was over. The continent now belonged to white civilization.

It is this historical background that enables the story of Custer's Last Stand to transcend the brutality and violence of what happened on Last Stand Hill. The story achieves a kind of poignant sympathy, not only for those soldiers who were killed, but also for the Native Americans who probably sensed that this was their last great victory. They probably knew their time as the dominant force in the American West was over, and there was no hope of reclaiming it.

With this historical perspective lingering behind the events at the Little Bighorn, the story assumes a depth and richness it otherwise would not have achieved. (Incidentally, much of this historical perspective was lost in many of the early films of the battle, and they were weaker as a result.) Without this historical perspective, the events on Last Stand Hill become just another superficial tale of human brutality in warfare. The storyteller does not have to belabor this historical perspective. However, the inner spirit of what happened at the Little Bighorn, and what it symbolized—the end of the Native American influence on this continent—needs to inform and guide the storyline from beginning to end.

A Story Needs a Strong Central Character—Complete With Flaws

General George Armstrong Custer was born to be on a Shakespearean stage. He wasn't a military commander so much as he was an actor posing as a military commander. He was a preening, self-obsessed, narcissistic superstar long before the term "superstar" was invented. If he had been born a hundred years later into a world with television cameras, the internet, and all the other electronic gadgetry that enables mere mortals to pose and pose until they transcend the smallness of their inner selves and become bigger than life, he would have fit right in. He probably would have developed a public persona that was even more grandiose than the one he managed to create in a nineteenth-century world with limited access to self-promotional opportunities.

Still, he played the limited media opportunities of his own time—mostly newspaper reporters and photographers—like a master politician-actor. We sense in every photograph of Custer that he spent hours preening in front of a mirror, making certain he had just the right pose to present to his adoring public. We know he was dissatisfied with the military uniforms of his time, so he designed his own uniform. Each of the changes he made to conventional military dress was designed to upstage everyone around him, and it did. This was a man who reeked of very little humanity and considerable megalomania. He was always on stage, always posing, always infatuated with himself and his public persona. Like the great kings in Shakespeare's tragedies, he was a celebrity—and he knew it.

The Shakespearean actor analogy will go only so far, however. Many of Shakespeare's heroes, as we learned in high school, were potentially great men who had tragic flaws. King Claudius in Hamlet was overly ambitious as was Macbeth. Hamlet was unusually intelligent and would probably have made a great King of Denmark, but we are told he was also too sensitive. Othello was a strong and effective ruler, but he allowed his jealously to destroy himself and his wife. Each of these characters had something redeeming about his personality. Had it not been for their tragic flaws, all of them would probably have been effective rulers of their countries. Custer was different. One shudders to think

Storytelling as Art and Craftsmanship

what America would have become under a Custer presidency, something that some historians have suggested was possibly in the back of his mind when he attacked the Native American encampment at the Little Bighorn.

Custer was the epitome of virtually every flaw Shakespeare imagined in all of his tragic heroes combined. Custer was dangerously ambitious, ruthlessly indifferent to both the men under his command and the Native American women and children he killed, and much too selfish to even consider the needs of anyone else. Yes, he was brave, even courageous, but his courage had more than a little tinge of foolhardiness and indifference to the soldiers who died around him. One senses that all of those lives were expendable to him. They only existed in his mind to the extent that they could serve his personal ambitions and grandiose self-image. Other than that, the rest of humanity mattered very little to Custer—except, perhaps, his adoring wife "Libbie" who created a far more positive image of her husband after the tragedy at the Little Bighorn. (As we shall see later, his relationship with her might have also been somewhat fraudulent.)

For our purposes as storytellers, however, the absence of any virtues in our main character, General George Armstrong Custer, matters very little. What matters more are his "flaws." The very things we often despise in much of humanity are the very things that make him an attractive central character for a screenplay or literary work. A film character *must be flawed*, even deeply flawed. Too much virtue destroys a central character. A little virtue might make him or her somewhat sympathetic. But if push comes to shove, and all a storyteller has is a choice between a deeply virtuous central character or a permanently flawed one with few if any noticeable virtues, most professional writers would probably choose the latter.

Custer's many flaws are a major reason why curiosity about him has never waned since he died on that hot June day in 1876. If storytellers are still not convinced that flawed characters get more attention and film treatments, all they need to do is go on the internet and count the number of films and television series that have featured General George Armstrong Custer. There are very few virtuous historical figures who had their names listed in so many film and television titles.

An Antagonist Must Be Worthy of the Central Character

The central characters in any story worth telling and retelling must have an antagonist (adversary!) worthy of their own skills and powers. Custer certainly had such an adversary on Last Stand Hill. Unbeknownst to him, the Native Americans who participated in the battle had learned military tactics from their white counterparts, and they did not go into the battle as individuals. Instead, they worked as a carefully coordinated military unit, surrounding and gradually converging on the besieged solders on Last Stand Hill. Then they overpowered Custer and the Seventh Calvary through the sheer strength of their numbers. Chief Crazy Horse had taught them well. It was he who studied these military tactics and integrated them into Native American warfare. Custer did not stand a chance. He was greatly outnumbered and outmaneuvered, and there was no possibility of escape.

Everyone who watches one of the film versions of Custer's Last Stand knows this, and yet we are all drawn into the sheer drama of watching soldier after soldier fall until only Custer is left standing. He has faced and lost to an adversary that is far superior to his own powers—and he will pay for that mistake with his life. We all know the end is coming for him, and yet we watch it again and again, mesmerized by a character we know is doomed. Why? One

Storytelling as Art and Craftsmanship

of the reasons may be that we are all mesmerized by what author Ernest Hemingway will later call "the undefeated, defeated man." This character is certain to be destroyed, but he refuses to quit even when he knows he is doomed or has no weapons or strategies left to engage his enemy. Custer's actions on Last Stand Hill, if he was indeed the last person standing, are an early example of this idea.

Still, there is yet another way of looking at the relationship between the protagonist and antagonist in this historical event. More recent film versions like **Son of the Morning Star** see the Native Americans as the central characters in this story. They still defeat Custer on Last Stand Hill. However, it is also their own "Last Stand," because Custer and his troops are merely the symbol of all of white civilization that is converging on their homelands and destroying their way of life. The Native Americans may have won the skirmish at the Little Bighorn, but they know their days are numbered. They realize there will not be too many battles left, and they will soon be defeated.

However one spins the story, and it has certainly been spun many ways, it is still important to note that the antagonist must be strong enough to be worthy of the central character or characters. A weak antagonist ends all drama. A powerful antagonist, even one that is impossible to defeat, heightens the drama and brings audiences back into the theaters, even though they know how the story will end. Custer has a powerful adversary in the Native American warriors who converge on Last Stand Hill. They also have a powerful adversary in white civilization that is converging on their lands. Either way, the protagonists have adversaries that are equal to their skills and powers.

Storytellers should remember that the antagonists in any film or novel are often more important than the main character. (Disbelievers should spend an evening watching the many wonderful villains in the Batman movies.) Yet, the antagonists in many amateur screenplays or novels are often underdeveloped and much too weak. Create strong antagonists. They are often the most important elements in any story.

Minor Characters Help Create Great Stories

Many storytellers insist that some writers place too much emphasis on the major characters in any literary text. They argue that the true test of any story is to be found (or not found) in the supporting cast of minor characters. If so, we have a treasure trove of these richly complex minor characters with their own motives and reasons for acting as they do at the Battle of the Little Bighorn.

Major Reno was branded by many as a coward for failing to carry out his orders to attack the Native American encampment from the south. These critics argue that once Reno fled into the hills to adopt a defensive position, he all but doomed Custer to his fate. The Native Americans could then direct virtually all of their overpowering strength on Custer's group. Reno's defenders, however, argue just the opposite. They claim it would have been foolhardy for him to keep attacking the encampment from the south once he realized he was hopelessly outnumbered. To his defenders, Reno did the only thing he could do: escape into the hills and save as many of the men under his command as possible. Had he continued the attack as ordered, he would probably have lost every soldier in his command. Still, the debate as to whether Reno acted appropriately or inappropriately continues to this very day.

Another richly complex character is Benteen. Did he betray Custer by deliberately failing to heed the urgent note that he return to the battlefield immediately? Or were there other reasons why it took him so long to get back to the Little Bighorn?

Storytelling as Art and Craftsmanship

Betrayal, envy, hatred for a superior officer he loathed—Benteen's motives are worthy of a minor character in a Shakespearean play.

Other minor characters also add rich elements to the plot. The Native American scouts who led Custer to the Little Bighorn knew from the pony droppings and other evidence that Custer was taking on an enemy he could not possibly defeat. They must also have had mixed feelings about their own roles in attacking a Native American encampment that was trying to restore some semblance of the life they once enjoyed on the prairie before the white man's arrival. Custer's brothers Tom and Boston, along with three other close family members, also died on Last Stand Hill, making it a family tragedy. Crazy Horse had learned the white man's strategies of engaging in warfare, and he led his group of warriors around to the other side of Last Stand Hill so Custer's men were surrounded on all sides and could not possibly escape. In that respect Custer was "hoisted on his own petard." All of these minor characters add considerable depth and richness to the storyline.

Often less experienced writers will build minor characters who are shallow and stereotyped because these characters play lesser roles in their stories. The great writers throughout the ages do not make this mistake. They create fully developed characters with their own external and internal conflicts that feed into and enhance the storylines. The master storyteller, or the accidents of history that created the last great battle of the Indian Wars, could not have created a richer, more complex cast of minor characters than the ones who came into conflict with one another at the Battle of the Little Bighorn.

Irony Adds Richness and Depth to a Story

The power of irony is everywhere at Custer's Last Stand, as it is in every great story. Irony creates depth and richness in human experiences, probably because we all know that our expectations in life almost never come out as we hoped. Often they are the very opposite of what we expect to happen—and that is the very definition of irony.

The ultimate irony at the Little Bighorn is that Custer probably expected he would have an easy victory over a Native American village of mostly women and children. He might have expected that this victory would allow him to return to the east as a conquering military hero. Instead, within a few short minutes, certainly less than an hour, his life's ambitions were destroyed, and he was reduced to a battle-scarred corpse lying on an obscure Montana plain. The contrast between the powerful national leader he probably hoped to become, and the corpse on the Montana plains that he became, would be the cruelest of ironies except, as many believe, "Perhaps he had it coming."

The other major irony, of course, was that the Native Americans may have won the Battle of the Little Bighorn, but they knew they would lose the larger war. They did not leave the Little Bighorn as a victorious army. They left knowing they would be defeated—and they soon *were* defeated in the few remaining battles that were fought before the end of the nineteenth century.

There were so many other ironies in play during and after this battle: Custer, who survived the Civil War without being wounded, suffered several gunshot wounds and died violently at the Little Bighorn; Major Reno, who courageously followed Custer's orders and led a charge against an overwhelming adversary, was later branded a "coward" and held by many to be responsible for Custer's death; and the Native Americans, who usually had inferior weapons in any battle with government troops, had superior weapons in this battle because they had apparently confiscated superior weapons from Crook's troops and elsewhere.

Storytelling as Art and Craftsmanship

Furthermore, Custer had led so many attacks on small, defenseless Native American villages populated mostly by women and children that he undoubtedly expected to meet little resistance at the Little Bighorn. Little did he know if that same village had existed in the latter decades of the twentieth century, as some historians have estimated, it would have been one of the largest cities in Montana. There were also at least two-thousand well-armed braves at the Little Bighorn, something Custer had certainly not expected.

There is something almost Shakespearean about the many ironies that envelope this story. William Shakespeare, arguably the greatest of all authors, knew that life was not simple, human motives go astray, and we often become the very thing we despise. Hamlet, for example, came to appreciate the awful irony that even as he sought revenge against a king who had killed his father, he (Hamlet) inadvertently killed Polonius, the father of his friend Laertes. Hamlet thus became the very thing he too despised.

It is impossible to know if Custer ever had a moment during the climactic events at the Battle of the Little Bighorn to ponder the many ironies in his own life and inevitable demise. Probably not. He was much too busy defending himself and would not have appreciated those ironies even if he had survived the battle. However, for those of us who have the luxury of looking back on this historical event, the ironies are inescapable. They are also what help to make this story far more powerful, and its effects more lingering, than the Fetterman Massacre and other such battles fought during the Indian Wars.

Irony is one of the most powerful tools in a storyteller's toolbox. It often elevates mundane, overly simplistic stories to the status of truly penetrating, insightful storylines.

Ambiguity Also Adds Richness and Depth to a Story

The Battle of the Little Bighorn left behind many lingering questions that simply could not be answered. Did Custer's presidential ambitions motivate him to put his men on a grueling forced march to the Little Bighorn to get there first and win a decisive military victory? Did he die early in the battle, as some Native Americans insisted, or did he make it to the top of Last Stand Hill where, as most of the movie accounts depict him, he was the last of his command to die? Did Benteen leave Custer to his fate, or was there some other reason why he did not seem in any hurry to return to the Little Bighorn after he received Custer's last message? Probably most intriguing, were there any survivors who escaped from the battlefield and fled back east to civilization? Years later, several men insisted they did escape from the battlefield. At least one of them had a fairly convincing account that he had been with Custer at the Little Bighorn, but for years he did not say anything for fear that he would be executed as a deserter.

These and other questions about Custer's Last Stand can never be fully answered. They are frustratingly just out of reach for inquiring historians, other researchers, and average readers. In real life, we all want answers to perplexing questions. In good stories, however, the questions that can never be answered are often the ones that keep the story alive for years after the actual events and those who participated in them are long gone.

So it is with Custer's story. We like to think of him standing on Last Stand Hill, facing the end with courage, the ultimate undefeated defeated man, raising his revolver in his bloody hand as the Native American warriors slowly converge on him from all directions. Yet, the reality might very well be that he was shot and killed early in the battle, when he tried to ford the Little Bighorn River to attack the encampment, and his body was carried to the top of Last Stand Hill. Or even more humiliating, since he had a bullet hole in his head, did he take his own life when he knew it was over, and he was fearful of what awaited him if he were captured?

We will never know. But that is often the power of great stories. We can never know everything we might want to know. The power of ambiguity is not that it creates more confusion in an already much too confusing world. Its power is that it presents readers or viewers of films with several choices, none of which answers all the questions. Yet, all are possibilities. That is the richness ambiguity brings to storytelling. It is what keeps those stories alive long after the simpler tales with simpler morals and simpler endings have been swept into the dust bins of storytelling history.

Great Stories Never Seem to End

A great story has more than one ending. In these stories, the endings come in succession, one after another, placing the reader or viewer on a roller coaster of unexpected twists and turns—until there is a final ending, and even that one may not answer all the questions. These endings behind the ending are almost always found in great stories. They are seldom found in stories with simplistic plots and one entirely predictable ending. Such is certainly the case with the Custer story. The ending of Custer's Last Stand could be defined as the moment when Custer himself died on Last Stand Hill, if he was indeed the last to fall. In the years that followed, however, a number of endings behind that ending breathed new life into the story.

The first ending behind the ending would occur on July 3, 1877, when federal troops returned to the Little Bighorn to retrieve the bodies of Custer and the other officers. They recovered what they took to be Custer's remains, although some skeptics questioned how they could be certain that any of the remains in the shallow graves were identifiable. The bones of the enlisted men were left behind to be uncovered by heavy rains and dragged across the hillside by predators. Photographs of Last Stand Hill taken in 1879 show a hillside littered with human bones. It calls to mind the Gravedigger in Shakespeare's *Hamlet*, as he peered at a skull he had just exposed in a grave and commented on the futility of all human activities. Yes, Shakespeare would have recognized the deeply poignant drama of a hillside littered with the bones of men who were once brave and courageous soldiers engaged in battle for glory and honor, or so they thought. Those bones scattered across Last Stand Hill are a poignant final ending to the tragedy that occurred there a few years earlier.

But we are still not done with this story. Another ending behind the ending was quietly discussed a few years later when Native Americans spoke of the possibility that Custer had a Cheyenne mistress named Meotzi who had given birth to his son. The boy's hair had streaks of yellow, just like Custer, and Meotzi and those close to her all apparently insisted he was Custer's son. How's that for another ending behind the ending? Now we may have a love story, together with Custer's possible betrayal of his wife Libbie, intertwined in the brutal and violent events that occurred at the Little Bighorn. It also reveals more of Custer's own brutality because he was not averse to killing Native Americans at the Little Bighorn who were probably relatives of his mistress and his own son. The troops under his command might have even killed his own son. (Now that subplot would grab any reader's or film viewer's attention.) Is the story true? There is considerable evidence that suggests it is true. If not, it was certainly the invention of some gifted Native American storyteller, for it combines the powerful elements of irony, betrayal, lust—and, yes, perhaps love.

Storytelling as Art and Craftsmanship

Then there is the story of Frank Finkel who late in his life insisted he had escaped from Custer's Last Stand on a horse that bolted and carried him away, gravely wounded, from the battlefield. Other imposters had come forth over the years with similar stories, but they were quickly debunked. In Finkel's case, however, the Native Americans who fought at the Little Bighorn spoke of a man who got away in precisely the way Finkel described. Finkel had other corroborating evidence as well, including battle scars. Still, there are researchers who dismiss his story. Was he the lone survivor of Last Stand Hill? The case is very strong that he just might be telling the truth. Another ending behind the ending? Maybe![4]

We could certainly use Custer's Last Stand to illustrate many other elements of storytelling. The one thing we can definitely conclude from all of these events that occurred during the Battle at the Little Bighorn is that the entire story and its aftermath seem almost to be the creation of some divinely gifted supernatural storyteller. For sheer drama, it would be hard to surpass the events that occurred at the Little Bighorn in June of 1876. This storyteller decided to show the rest of us human wannabes how it should be done—and whoever or whatever it was chose an isolated corner of Montana as the stage on which to tell that story.

---

4 Frank Finkel's story has appeared in many newspapers and academic journals. It was also the subject of a 2011 television movie, "Custer's Last Man: I Survived Little Big Horn." Of all the accounts from those who claim to have survived Custer's Last Stand, Finkel's story seems to be the most plausible.

CHAPTER 2

FINDING A STORY

So much for Custer. He was hardly a gifted military commander, albeit he did create a story that has lived on for almost two centuries after he died. Sadly, many innocent lives had to be sacrificed to create that story. If Custer had merely waited for Crook and Terry to arrive at the Little Bighorn, perhaps they could have avoided all that bloodshed by convincing the Native Americans to return to their reservations. However, that is a moral issue best left to the historians and others to decide. The focus in this book is on storytelling techniques—what works or does not work when putting a longer story together.

In the next chapters, I will be concentrating mostly on screenplay storytelling techniques, using other literary genres like novels and drama as supplemental examples. In the last chapters of this book, I will reverse the focus and discuss the many ways screenwriting techniques can strengthen novels. The emphasis throughout the book will be on strengthening storytelling skills regardless of genre or what the writer plans to do with the story after it is finished.

Storytelling Starts With a Story Worth Telling

One of the first questions the students in my screenwriting class often ask is, "What kind of story will work best as a screenplay?" They have seen movies that make them laugh, cry, and feel every conceivable human emotion. Yet, when it comes to choosing a story for their own screenplays, they are often stymied.

Is there one type of story that is so inherently inspiring it will inevitably produce a great screenplay and film? Probably not! The crucifixion of Jesus Christ, for example, has all the elements we would associate with a great story: a strong main character, supernatural intervention in human affairs, love, betrayal, intense and brutal suffering, and virtually every other human emotion. The story of the crucifixion has produced some splendid films like *Jesus Christ Superstar*, but it has also provided the foundation for many uninspired, forgettable films.

Likewise, science fiction has been around for decades, and it has produced some tediously predictable plots, characters, and storylines. Then George Lucas came on the scene in the early 1970s and added some new twists to the old Buck Rogers space flicks. Lucas grounded the characters in ancient mythology, and suddenly everyone flocked to the theaters to see *Star Wars*. The same is true for Stanley Kubrick's *2001: A Space Odyssey*. Kubrick's inspired rendition of a deep space probe, connected as it is to the evolution of intelligent life and hints of reincarnation, overcame the old science fiction stereotypes and motivated viewers to return to the theaters in droves. The movie also provided an intellectual foundation that was at the time often lacking in science fiction films.

The same can be said for every film genre. The detective genre has produced some very forgettable low-budget films, but Robert Towne produced a screenplay that took the same cast of characters one might find in a standard 1940s detective film and created a masterpiece with his 1974 movie, ***Chinatown.*** Most people in my generation saw so many bad westerns, often at free Saturday afternoon matinees in the early 1950s, that we knew the plots after the first few scenes. Then John Ford directed ***The Searchers*** (1956), which involved Ethan Edwards' (John Wayne) attempts to free his two nieces who were captured by Comanche, and the genre was revitalized. Clint Eastwood did likewise with ***Unforgiven (1992),*** a western based on a fairly traditional conflict between an aging, retired gunfighter (Eastwood) and a small town sheriff (Gene Hackman). The horror genre probably produced more bad films than all the other genres combined. Yet, ***The Exorcist*** (1973) packed the theaters by vividly providing new twists to the horrors of demonic possession.

Even a cursory glance at film history demonstrates that the story is important, but it is not as important as the treatment of the story. Some films, if they are reduced to brief plot summaries, may have elements that seem guaranteed to pull the reader into the story. But as we shall see throughout this book, it is the treatment of the story that distinguishes a mediocre film (and screenplay) from an excellent one.

There is no story that is so inherently appealing that it will always make a great film. Some stories that have appeared on the surface to be great have failed as films. Other stories that seem to have little appeal have become film classics. Perhaps a screenwriter cannot turn the telephone book into a great screenplay, but great writing can transform unorthodox stories or conventional stories into little gems.

Writers Must Be Emotionally Committed to Their Stories

The most important thing all writers must feel is a strong sense of purpose and emotional commitment in writing a particular story. Screenwriters must care about their stories, or script readers and film audiences are unlikely to care about them either. Conversely, if screenwriters care deeply and passionately about their stories, those who read their scripts or watch their films are likely to feel the strength of the writers' commitment behind the words on the printed page. Screenwriters must feel the same personal emotional commitments to their screenplays that successful novelists and playwrights have always felt for their stories.

Sometimes the choice of a story is an accident, not a well-thought out decision. I don't mean to be glib when I say, "Authors don't always choose stories. Sometimes stories chose authors." I can speak from some personal experiences with respect to this issue. I do feel a little awkward using my own published writings as examples, but they are the only ones I have experienced with such intimacy that I can use them to demonstrate one truism. When searching for a story worth telling, writers need to keep their eyes, their minds, and especially their hearts open to the immediate world around them.

My own personal epiphany started from just such an innocuous, seemingly meaningless and random decision to kill a few hours doing something I seldom did. At the time, I had no desire at the time to write the Great American Novel (and I still don't). My wife Alexa and I were back in my hometown of Morris, Minnesota, in the summer of 1978, and we had run out of relatives to visit or things to do. I don't know what motivated me to make the suggestion that perhaps we should "drive over to Dawson and ask people over there what they knew about my father's biological father." My father had already provided me with some of the background information regarding his adoption and subsequent quest later in life to locate his biological parents, but I sensed there was more to the story. I knew that both his biological parents were now deceased, but I figured there might be people in the area who still remembered them. Perhaps it would be nice to know my own biological grandparents as their friends and acquaintances knew them—if there were any still left living in the area.

So my wife and I set off on a forty-five mile journey that was to turn into a four decades search for my own roots. I simply trolled Dawson's Main Street and asked older shop owners if they remembered "Judd Thompson," my biological grandfather. Fortunately, he had worked as Dawson's lone police officer for a number of years, and he had a reputation as a "wrestler" who organized wrestling tournaments, so some people remembered him well. One local resident, a newspaper editor, started to cry when he recounted his memories of my grandfather. Yet another took us out to the cemetery where my grandfather is buried.

Alexa and I were so inspired by our first visit that we proceeded to drive to Dawson every day for the next few weeks that we were in Minnesota. On one visit, a local historian insisted on calling my biological grandmother's brother (my great uncle) who was still living in the area. He immediately told the historian to "send them over." When we arrived at his home, he was waiting for us on his porch. As soon as I approached him, he grabbed my hand and repeated several times, "I never wanted them to give you up. I never wanted them to give you up." At first, I had no idea what he was talking about. Then it dawned on me that he had mistaken me for my father. I explained to him who I was, and he chuckled and led us inside, where he proceeded to tell us everything he knew about the family's decision to force my Grandmother Clara to give my father up for adoption. He even gave us directions to the cemetery where she is buried, and we visited that gravesite as well.

Storytelling as Art and Craftsmanship

There is so much more to the story, but suffice it to say that by the time I returned to California my focus in life had changed considerably. That random decision to visit Dawson led to several traditionally published novels and works of nonfiction I researched and wrote over the next four decades. *Prairie Son* chronicles my father's life during the Great Depression and his determined efforts to locate his biological mother and father. *The Sins of Rachel Sims* was inspired by what I continued to learn about my biological Grandmother Clara, who was forced by other relatives to keep her child hidden on the family farm before giving him up for adoption. *The Search for Judd McCarthy* features a main character who, like my biological grandfather, was a legendary wrestler in the small community where he lived. *Goodbye to Main Street* was my attempt to complete my father's journey to learn more about the extended family he wanted to meet before lung cancer took his life prematurely.

As a Professor of American Literature, I had certainly thought about writing a novel before any of this happened. I had even made a botched attempt at writing a novel based on the academic world I inhabited. But it took a random, seemingly innocuous trip to a Minnesota small town that held the secrets to my ancestry before I felt the sense of purpose and emotional commitment I needed to research and write those four books over the next forty years.

Yes, I do think stories sometimes choose authors.

Does every family have the ancestral intrigue I found in my past? Probably not. But other authors, far more successful than me, have had similar experiences, often involving deeply felt, often unresolved emotional experiences. In *The Adventures of Huckleberry Finn,* Mark Twain explored his early traumatic memories of slavery when he was growing up in Hannibal, Missouri. Nathaniel Hawthorne explored his own early memories in many short stories and novels. Hawthorne's childhood in Salem, Massachusetts, home of the infamous Salem Witch Trials of 1692, was further traumatized by the knowledge that one of his ancestors had been a judge who helped send these innocent victims to their deaths. Hawthorne felt deeply and personally committed to the innocent victims who died in Salem, something that is readily apparent in his writings.

In the twentieth century, playwright Arthur Miller tapped into his early memories of his Uncle Manny Newman to write *Death of a Salesman.* Whenever Miller visited his Uncle Manny, a loudmouthed braggart who inspired the character of Willy Loman, he was made to feel inferior to Manny's two athletic sons.[5] Miller transformed those feelings into art when he wrote *Death of a Salesman,* one of the most powerful and successful plays in the history of American theater.

Another American playwright, Tennessee Williams, explored his own deeply traumatic childhood and teenage years in *The Glass Menagerie.* Tom Wingfield's restless, wandering desire to escape from a domineering mother, mentally and physically challenged sister, and dead-end life in St. Louis parallels Williams's early experiences and unresolved memories.[6]

Like novelists and playwrights, screenwriters often do their best work when they write about experiences that have affected them at some deeper emotional level. In *Citizen Kane,* Orson Welles created a film character, Charles Foster Kane, whom most film historians believe was modeled after Howard Hughes and William Randolph Hearst. Welles acknowledged these influences, but the character of Kane enabled him to explore the unresolved

---

5   John Tierney, "The Big City; Willy Loman: Revenge of a Nephew," *New York Times* 8 Feb. 1999 <www.nytimes.com>

6   George McMichael and James Leonard, eds., *Anthology of American Literature*, vol. II, 9th ed. (Upper Saddle River, NJ: Pearson Prentice Hall, 2007) 1684.

flaws and weaknesses he also saw in himself.[7] In **On the Waterfront**, screenwriter Budd Schulberg revisited his experiences on the New Jersey waterfront to write one of the great film scripts of all time. Elia Kazan, who directed the film, integrated his own experiences during the McCarthy hearings to add richer, even more compelling layers to the original screenplay.[8] More recently, Matt Damon and Ben Affleck wrote the screenplay **Good Will Hunting**, which was inspired by their early experiences in Boston. Many of the film's characters are based on their early personal relationships, including Damon's former girlfriend.[9]

In each of these stories, the novelists, playwrights, and screenwriters did their best work when they wrote about the experiences in their lives that had affected them at some deeper emotional level. These experiences gave them a strong sense of purpose and an emotional commitment to their stories that script readers and film audiences felt immediately.

Using People You Know as Models

Another question beginning screenwriters often ask is, "Should I use people I know as models for the characters in my screenplays and other creative writings?" My answer is, "Yes, but there are unique considerations when you model your characters on people you know." Obviously, there are legal issues. I had to consider those issues in the previous discussion in this chapter, especially for characters who are still alive. If a character turns out to be a popular movie villain, the writer might find himself or herself on the wrong side of a lawsuit.

---

7   James Naremore, *The Magic World of Orson Welles* (Dallas: Southern Methodist University Press, 1989) 81-82.
8   Elia Kazan, *A Life* (New York: Alfred A. Knopf, 1988) 487-89.
9   "Matt Damon Biography," *Pop Stars Plus* <www.popstarsplus.com>

Earlier generations of writers did not have to worry quite so much about the legal consequences of basing literary characters on people they know. Today, that is a concern. There are also the obvious ethical issues involving people who are deceased and cannot sue. I won't go into the other legal ramifications because those are better left to the lawyers who specialize in such issues. Let me just say the internet has many articles with helpful suggestions on how to avoid potential legal problems in this area. This is especially troublesome for authors because we all know that writers do their best work when they write about people and events they have personally experienced.

The legal issues aside, basing characters on the people a screenwriter knows can make it easier or more difficult to write the story. These characters are already living, breathing human beings, so half the job of bringing them to life in the screenplay is already over. The downside is that many beginning writers find it difficult to bend and shape characters based on people they know so they fit into the storyline. These characters can be rigid and inflexible in the writer's mind. They can also be incapable of growth—and growth is an indispensable quality in all literary characters. If characters do not grow through the course of the story, the story is probably dead on arrival.

There is a creative compromise that is possible. Rigidly basing screenplay characters on real-life models can create writer's block and be an impediment to the development of the story. However, creating characters *who are inspired by real-life people, but not rigidly grounded in them,* often enables the screenwriter to have the best of both worlds. They can be stronger characters because the writer has already known them in real life—so it is easier to bring them to life on the printed page. However, since they are not precise replicas of these people, but only inspired by them, there is still creative room for the character to evolve and grow within the story.

The short answer is, writers should not be afraid to be inspired by real-life models for their characters, but they should also not feel obligated to rigidly reproduce every nuance and detail about these people. One of the best examples of this in American literature is F. Scott Fitzgerald's ***The Great Gatsby,*** which is always included near the top of any list of the best novels ever written by American authors. Anyone familiar with both the plot of *The Great Gatsby* and Fitzgerald's life, especially his relationship with Zelda Sayre, would immediately recognize the powerful personal forces that motivated Fitzgerald to write this novel. It was a story that was already inside of Fitzgerald, and the power of Jay Gatsby's love for Daisy throbs behind every sentence. Still, Fitzgerald did not produce the story exactly as it happened in his personal life. He shaded and colored it to conform to his fictional plot. But the novel achieved its immense power largely because Fitzgerald had already lived through most of the emotions he presented in the novel.

Writers usually do their best work when they are inspired by the things they understand—including the people in their lives.

Historical Subjects

Obviously, not all screenplays are based on personal stories. History has been a rich source of screenplays ever since films were invented in the early decades of the twentieth century. Films like ***Apollo 13, Braveheart, Bonnie and Clyde,*** and countless others usually appear on lists of must-see movies.

However, the problem with basing a screenplay on historical characters and incidents is that unless the student has already done the research in other courses, the project involves research more than writing. Generally, numerous books on the subject must be read and contemplated. Divergent professional opinions must be reconciled. Meanwhile, the rudimentary tasks of learning how to create screenplay characters, write meaningful dialogue, structure the story, develop plot points, and learn the other formal elements of screenwriting must be placed on the backburner while the research is being conducted. For all of these reasons, students should probably learn the techniques of screenwriting before embarking on the even more ambitious task of researching and writing about historical characters and subjects.

This is not to say that historical subjects are strictly off-limits. One of the best student screenplays I have ever received was based on the love affair between Robert Browning and Elizabeth Barrett Browning. It was a splendid screenplay. The reader identified completely with Robert Browning after the premature death of his wife Elizabeth in 1861. However, the young man who wrote the screenplay was a graduate student who had devoted several years to researching the historical relationship between these two Victorian poets before he attempted to retell their story in screenplay form.

Times of Transition

During my graduate school days at the University of Minnesota, I attended a lecture by a professor from another college. I don't remember the professor's name, the subject of his talk, or where on campus the event was held. The only thing I remember are nine words from his lecture, when he said, "All great stories take place during times of transition." I not only remember those nine words: I often think about them when I teach my own college-level courses in American literature or screenwriting. I cannot claim to have read "all" the great stories. But I have read enough of those stories to know that his words regarding the importance of "times of transition" in storytelling resonate in most of them.

We have already discussed Custer's defeat at the Little Bighorn, which occurred during a time of great historical transition in our country. As described previously, this historical event took place as our nation was transitioning from the frontier phase of its history to the more modern phase of American civilization. Furthermore, the events at the Little Bighorn reflect the Native American transition as the dominant force in the West to a reservation-bound group of scattered tribes with very little power. A sense of these transitional times empowers the entire storyline of the events that transpired on Last Stand Hill.

These underlying historical transitions can also be found in many literary works. Both the novel and film versions of **Gone with the Wind** take place during one of the most turbulent transitional times in American history, when this country would become either two separate nations or one deeply divided nation with very different views of slavery. Arthur Miller's play, ***The Crucible***, is set in 1692, during a time when the Puritan theocracy has been steadily losing power. Sensing this loss of control over the inhabitants of New England, the Puritan theocrats exploit the fear of witches in Salem to attempt to halt this inevitable transition into a more secular mindset among the inhabitants of the colonies. In 1916, Susan Glaspell wrote a play, *Trifles*, which was based on a real-life murder case in Iowa. Minnie Wright, who is the main character in the play even though she does not appear on stage, was a farmwife who finally decided she could no longer tolerate abuse at the hands of her husband—and she killed him while he was asleep. At first she is regarded as a deranged killer, but as the events of the story unfold, she becomes a sympathetic figure to both the audience and the members of her rural community. The action in the play thus parallels the transitional views of a nation that was slowly coming to grips with the horrors of domestic violence and abuse.

Times of transition are also important in many films. The 1979 film, ***Norma Rae***, starring Sally Fields, reflects the changing views of a woman's role in the workplace. Norma Rae, who is at first a somewhat submissive housewife and loyal factory worker, gradually transitions into a leader of a worker rebellion against the male-dominated, corporate owners of the textile factory where she works. In this respect, she reflects a similar transition that is occurring throughout this country regarding the roles of women in our nation's workforce. Another film, ***Urban Cowboy***, starring John Travolta, takes place mostly in an urban bar and dance hall where the characters compete on a mechanical bull ride. These characters, who might have once been breaking real bulls or horses on the open range, are transitioning into a more modern world where these opportunities to prove their cowboy skills are less available. Another film, ***Mcfarland USA***, starring Kevin Costner, explores the events in a small California town that is going through another kind of transition. The people of this largely Hispanic community are gradually transitioning out of a fondness for more conventional sports, in spite of their school's losing records, and into a love for cross country running, a sport still somewhat in its infancy. The film thus captures a transitional time when minor sports like cross country running are growing in stature, especially among less gifted athletes and poorer high schools.

In some respects, all times are transitional times. In some places and times, however, the transitional events in the background of the story are more intrinsically embedded in the plot. Those times of transition often yield the richest sources of characters and audience-grabbing storylines.

(See also Chapter 3, the section titled "Character Growth." When choosing and developing a story, personal transitions are as important as historical and cultural transitions.)

Stories from Film and Literary Genres

Other rich sources of screenwriting stories are films themselves. Westerns, science fiction, detective stories, love stories, and the other film genres all have their own unique histories. Most screenwriters who specialize in any of these genres understand their plots and character types.

One of the advantages of writing in an established film genre is that there is often instant audience identification with the characters and plots. Knowing this, the screenwriter can easily develop nuances and subtleties to create characters who deviate slightly or dramatically from their types. The screenwriter also knows what the members of this particular film audience expect in terms of plots and subplots, so it is relatively easy to set them up for unexpected surprises.

The trick, of course, is not to become tediously predictable by merely imitating previous films in a particular genre. The writer of every western, science fiction, detective, or love story knows the history of the genre, and then seeks to expand it in new and innovative ways. (Many of the films discussed earlier in this chapter accomplish precisely this creative miracle, which is why they are considered classics.)

There is also a very practical advantage to writing in an established film genre. Film producers, like book publishers, know that every film genre has its own specific, dedicated audience. Hence, there is less financial risk.

Having said that, I must confess I have mixed feelings about the generic treatment of stories in films and literature. Usually, the great breakthroughs in storytelling come not from writers who adhere to strict generic expectations, but rather from writers who are willing to challenge generic stereotypes. The most obvious example in our literary canon is Herman Melville's *Moby Dick* (1850). Melville had developed a respectable audience with his early South Seas adventure stories like *Typee* (1846) and *Omoo* (1847). However, after the publication of Moby Dick—an intellectually sophisticated novel that challenged our national values, the foibles of the entire human race, and the very powers that control the universe we live in—Melville lost much of his reading audience. Today, however, Moby Dick is regarded by many literary critics as the greatest novel ever written by an American writer.

The film equivalent of this story would have to be Orson Welles, who challenged everything about Hollywood when he created his great film, *Citizen Kane*. In the process, he created numerous technical innovations involving dialogue, camera angles, shifting narrative devices, and other such modern ways of storytelling. He also created many powerful enemies because the character of Charles Foster Kane in the film was so obviously based on wealthy newspaper and business tycoons William Randolph Hearst and Howard Hunt. The film was well received, and today it is often ranked as the greatest motion picture ever made. Yet, Orson Welles made so many enemies during his groundbreaking attempts to breathe new storytelling life into motion pictures that he struggled throughout the rest of his career against the powerful forces that were aligned against him.

To achieve their reputations as two of the greatest storytellers of all time, both Melville and Welles had to challenge existing generic stereotypes of fiction. But they paid a dear price for breaking with these generic expectations and developing innovative approaches to storytelling.[10]

---

10   The stories of both Herman Melville's and Orson Welles's falls from grace in the film and literary communities are well-documented in numerous anthologies and film histories.

The Place is the Story

Eudora Welty, the great southern writer, argued that all great stories evolve from a strong sense of place. She believed characters, symbols, scenes, plots, and subplots are all deeply connected to the setting of the story. To Welty, the place is the story.[11]

Welty attributed the entire southern literary movement in the early part of the twentieth century to the strong sense of place writers like William Faulkner, Robert Penn Warren, and others developed in their fiction. Her ideas regarding the importance of place also apply to other American literary classics. When we think of Willa Cather's *O Pioneers!* and *My Antonia,* we inevitably think of the Nebraska prairie. *The Adventures of Huckleberry Finn* evokes memories of a wooden raft sailing serenely down the Mississippi River. James Fenimore Cooper's *Leatherstocking Tales* are synonymous with the early American frontier. F. Scott Fitzgerald's *The Great Gatsby* transformed New York City and Long Island into the living embodiment of the American dream earlier immigrants brought to the New World.

It would be difficult to think of a great work of literature that is not identified with a specific locale that often becomes deeply symbolic. The same is true for screenplays. When we think of the great films we have watched, we almost always associate them with some tangible, visible setting. *Sunset Boulevard* is indistinguishable from its Hollywood setting. *A Streetcar Named Desire* would probably never have achieved its emotional power in any city other than New Orleans. *Fargo* needed the frozen North Dakota prairie to succeed as a film. Every scene in *Serpico* is grounded in the sights and sounds of New York City.

---

11 George McMichael and James Leonard, eds., *Anthology of American Literature*, vol. II, 9th ed. (Upper Saddle River, NJ: Pearson Prentice Hall, 2007) 1633.

The list is virtually endless. We would be hard pressed to find a great movie or novel that could be placed in a different location and still achieve its full emotional and dramatic impact. *A sense of place is as important as a sense of purpose in writing any story.* An editor once told me, "Without a sense of place, the reader is in limbo. The story will never have the same emotional impact as it would if the reader literally felt that he or she was standing in the story, experiencing the events as they happen." The writer achieves this by shrewdly manipulating the reader to identify with the main character and by creating a tangible sense of place. The task of finding a story for a screenplay is indistinguishable from identifying the sights and sounds of the place where the story occurs—even if it is fiction. Novelists and screenwriters need to feel a deep, subliminal attachment to the very place where the characters walk, live, and sometimes die. Otherwise, readers and film audiences will not feel them either.

    I have been reminded of Welty's and that editor's advice with everything I have published. In *Prairie Son*, my father's story of how he was adopted by a farm family and treated more like a worker than a son, I had the stories he had told me, the notes he left behind, and many memories before he died. However, I didn't really understand his story until I visited the old abandoned farm sites where he had labored as a boy and teenager for the family that had adopted him to be their worker. As I gazed out over that forlorn, isolated section of West Central Minnesota, I visualized what it must have been like for him when he trudged across those same fields to another farm miles away to ask that family if he could live with them because he was treated so badly in his adoptive home. That's when the place became his story.

    Similarly, I had walked among the homeless on the streets of San Diego while I was writing *The Accountant's Apprentice*, a novel that addresses the homelessness issue in our country. I had

Storytelling as Art and Craftsmanship

even spoken to some of the area's homeless. However, it wasn't until I learned of the Evergreen Cemetery, San Diego's version of a "potter's field," that I really understood what it was like to live and die on the streets. As I gazed out over the brush- and weed-covered field where four thousand people in unmarked graves are buried on ten acres of unirrigated land, I felt for the first time the agony of the lost souls who lived and died homeless without any loved ones to gather around their deathbeds or their graves. That's when the place became their story.

The One-Sentence Summary or Logline

During my early experiments with screenplay form, I submitted a screenplay to my agent, and two weeks later she called to set up an appointment. I was both excited and apprehensive, not quite knowing what to expect from her. When I showed up at her office, we made small talk for a time, and then she informed me she wanted to ask me a question about the screenplay I had submitted. She said, "Can you summarize what you are doing in this screenplay in one sentence?" I struggled to articulate what she had requested, but finally gave up. I could not summarize the story in one sentence.

"I thought that might be difficult for you to do," she responded warmly, but firmly. "I have all my writers try to summarize their stories in one sentence. I have learned that writers who can do it have a firm grasp and control of their storylines, and they know precisely what they are trying to do with their screenplays or novels. Writers who have less control of their storylines usually struggle with a one-sentence summary."

She went on to explain that she liked much of what she had read in my screenplay, but she felt I needed a stronger sense of direction and purpose. She added that she knew I would struggle with the one-sentence summary (also known as a "logline"), and I did. *That day I learned the importance of being able to summarize any writing project in one sentence.* I do it to this day, even in the freelance newspaper column I wrote. With my one-sentence summary, I feel much more in control and I have a clearer sense of purpose.

I have also incorporated the one-sentence summary into my screenwriting classes. As soon as students decide on their stories, I have them submit a one-sentence summary to me. I keep returning those one-sentence summaries to them until I am convinced they have established a stronger sense of control and purpose in their scripts. By the time they have submitted several one-sentence summaries, they have memorized and can repeat verbatim every word of it. I also encourage them to change a word or two of their one-sentence summaries as they get deeper into their scripts and their sense of purpose becomes even more clear and refined.

I recommend the one-sentence summary requirement for every screenwriting or creative writing class. Nothing I have learned has been so simple or so effective in improving my own writing and my students' writing. As soon as screenwriters decide on the stories they will develop, they should reduce their plots to one-sentence statements that will guide them from the opening scenes to the final scenes of their scripts.

Final Thoughts on Choosing a Story

Choosing a story for a screenplay is a bit like choosing a career. Young people who choose a career for superficial reasons—it pays well, it is prestigious, it is what their parents told them they should do for a living, and so on—are seldom successful. They usually lack the drive and motivation to succeed. On the other hand, young people who choose the career that is right for them often succeed regardless of the obstacles that are thrown in their paths. They succeed because they are deeply and passionately committed to their career choices.

The same is true for all storytellers. Some of the least successful stories students have written in my classes are based on stories they chose for superficial reasons. Some decided, "It is the kind of story Hollywood seems to be looking for." Others decided, "Violence seems to sell screenplays, so that's what I want to emphasize in my screenplay." Still others have only a vague sense of where their story is going or why they are writing it, but they "think it would make a good screenplay."

Usually, I try to convince these students to write about something else, something that grabs them at some deeper level of emotional commitment. I have learned through experience that these superficial reasons for writing a story usually result in screenplays that never capture the readers' interest.

The best screenplays I have read are the ones in which the screenwriters felt a deep and passionate emotional commitment to their stories. In one of my classes, an Iraq war veteran wrote a disturbing, hauntingly memorable screenplay about another veteran who struggled to distinguish between reality and his nightmares when he returned to civilian life. A young woman in another class created a screenplay about a hopelessly dysfunctional, abusive parent, whom she confided was based on a close relative. Another student chose to write a mystery story about a missing person in a small town, not because she wanted to write a detective story, but rather because a similar event had occurred in her own hometown.

The range of stories that can be turned into screenplays or novels is immense. Almost nothing is off limits. Still, the best stories come from the same deeply felt impulses that have created literary classics in all genres for centuries. It seldom comes from a superficial emotional commitment to the story.

EXERCISES

1. Many newspapers have an entire page that is devoted to unusual, quirky stories that do not make the front pages. Select two or three of these stories and try to determine which would make the best screenplay. Why might the other stories not work as well? What does the comparison teach us about stories that are more or less suitable for screenplays? Does a sense of place strengthen any of these stories?
2. Search your memory for a story about a distant relative who did something unusual or interesting. Write a brief paragraph that describes the story as you remember it. Then write another paragraph describing the changes you might make in the story to transform it into a screenplay. Why did you make these changes?
3. Is there someone in your immediate family who has a story that might be developed into a screenplay? What is that story and how might you refine and change the story to make it work in screenplay form?
4. Do you have a story in your own personal life that could be developed into a screenplay? As you think about this question, remember that each of us is a somewhat different person at different times in our lives. Age, experience, circumstances, and other factors all contribute to our identities (and the ways we view ourselves) at different stages in our lives. As you review your own life, is there some stage that is more interesting than others? Why?
5. The questions above were arranged in a specific order, the first encouraging you to address stories about people you do not know, but have only read about in the newspapers, and the others about people with whom you have an increasingly

Storytelling as Art and Craftsmanship

close personal relationship. What are the advantages and disadvantages of basing a screenplay on each of the stories you have identified in questions 1-4?

CHAPTER 3

DEVELOPING CHARACTERS IN SCREENPLAYS AND NOVELS

Screenplays and Novels are Character-Driven Stories

There is no such thing as a great film or novel without great characters—especially the main character. The same is true for all forms of literature. When we think of our favorite novels, plays, or films, we almost always have a strong visual image of the main character at the center of the story.

There are differences, however, in the ways characters are developed in screenplays and other forms of literature. The most obvious difference is that the novelist has much more time and space to develop physical descriptions and personalities. The novelist can also take a long, stream of consciousness journey inside the main character's mind to reveal a rich inner world of values, conflicts, ambitions—just about everything that makes individual human beings unique.

Screenwriters are much more limited in how they can develop characters. They must select some well-chosen details that bring their characters' physical appearances and personalities to life vividly and with a minimum of words. The line, "Brevity is the soul of wit, and tediousness the limbs and outward flourishes," albeit used ironically in Shakespeare's *Hamlet* because the speaker Polonius is anything but brief, should be inscribed on every screenwriter's desk. Brevity *is* the soul of screenwriting. The rest is up to the actors and the director. They will flesh out the words on the printed page and develop fully recognizable human beings.

The differences between character development in screenplays and novels can be easily demonstrated. The first description of Hester Prynne in Hawthorne's *The Scarlet Letter* is very long and detailed. It is rich and compelling, and it certainly works within the novel format. A screenwriter, however, does not have the luxury of such an extensive description of the main character. A screenplay must keep moving, and long, belabored descriptions often bring the story to a complete halt.

In Hawthorne's novel, here is how Hester is described as she exits from the jail and walks across the courtyard to the scaffold. The bold italicized sections, because they are mostly exposition and not descriptions of visual details, would be problematic in a screenplay description of the same character:

> The young woman was tall, with a figure of perfect elegance, on a large scale. She had dark and abundant hair, so glossy that it threw off the sunshine with a gleam, and a face which, besides being beautiful from regularity of feature and richness of complexion, had the impressiveness belonging to a marked brow and deep black eyes. She was lady-like, too, after the manner of the feminine gentility of those days; characterized by a certain state and dignity, **rather than by the delicate,**

evanescent, and indescribable grace: which is now recognized as its indication. And never had Hester Prynne appeared more lady-like, in the antique interpretation of the term, than as she issued from the prison. Those who had before known her, and had expected to behold her dimmed and obscured by a disastrous cloud, were astonished and even startled, to *perceive how* her beauty shone out, and made a halo of the misfortune and ignominy in which she was enveloped. *It may be true, that, to a sensitive observer, there was something exquisitely painful in it.* Her attire, *which, indeed she had wrought for the occasion, in prison, and had modeled much after her own fancy,* seemed to express the attitude of her spirit, the desperate recklessness of her mood, by its wild and picturesque peculiarity. But the point which drew all eyes, and, as it were, transfigured the wearer, —so that both men and women, who had been familiarly acquainted with Hester Prynne, were now impressed as if they beheld her for the first time,—was that SCARLET LETTER, so fantastically embroidered and illuminated upon her bosom. It had the effect of a spell, taking her out of the ordinary relations with humanity, and inclosing her in a sphere by herself.[12]

A screenwriter who was developing the character of Hester Prynne would have to delete most of the subjective information in italics or reveal it instead through dialogue or action descriptions. Using what is left of Hawthorne's description of Hester, the screenwriter would build the character's physical appearance and personality with some short, concise descriptions written in the present verb tense.

---

12 Nathaniel Hawthorne, *The Scarlet Letter* (The Project Gutenberg Etext of *The Scarlet Letter*) 44. <www.gutenberg.org/wiki/Main_Page>

The following description trims the description to a few essential details that would work in screenplay format. In subsequent rewrites, the screenwriter might condense the description even more to keep the story moving:

> HESTER PRYNNE is tall and elegant, with dark eyes and full, dark hair that shimmers in the sunlight. She wears the Scarlet Letter, fantastically embroidered and illuminated upon her bosom. Hester is alone and isolated, an object of scorn to the crowd that surrounds her. She radiates an inner beauty and a rebellious spirit as she carries PEARL, her illegitimate child, toward the scaffold.

Screenwriters have much in common with the Imagist poets who, early in the twentieth century, sought to remove subjective language from poetry. They created short, concise poems like William Carlos Williams's "The Red Wheelbarrow." The entire poem consists of sixteen well-chosen words that describe the visual details of two objects found in any farmyard.[13] Hemingway, also a product of the Imagist movement, is another writer who favored economy of style in physical descriptions and character development. For example, in his short story, "The Killers," he introduces the main character Nick Adams with a few short, terse sentences that could easily have appeared in a screenplay:

> Outside it was getting dark. The street-light came on outside the window. The two men at the counter read the menu. From the other end of the counter Nick Adams watched them. He had been talking to George when they came in.[14]

---

13 William Carlos Williams, *Selected Poems* (New York: New Directions Books, 1985) 56.
14 Ernest Hemingway, *The Short Stories* (New York: Scribner, 2003) 279.

Screenwriters can learn much by studying the writing styles of novelists and poets who were influenced by the Imagist movement. Their economy of statement and attention to physical details, especially visual details, can work very well for screenwriters who are describing actions or characters.

Classic Film Characters

The shooting scripts quoted below use some subjective information to develop characters, but they concentrate primarily on vivid physical details and short, terse descriptions to quickly establish the main character's physical appearance and personality:

> *Titanic:* Jack Dawson (Leonardo DiCaprio)
> JACK DAWSON and FABRIZIO DE ROSSI, both about 20, exchange a glance as the other two players argue in Swedish. Jack is American, a lanky drifter with his hair a little long for the standards of the times. He is also unshaven, and his clothes are rumpled from sleeping in them. He is an artist, and has adopted the bohemian style of the art scene in Paris. He is also very self-possessed and sure-footed for 20, having lived on his own since 15.[15]

The details that are provided in this short description create a strong visual image of Jack Dawson. We know that he is lanky, unshaven, has long hair and his clothes are rumpled. We also know that he is self-possessed, exudes an air of confidence, and is somewhat of a bohemian rebel. In a few carefully chosen words and details, the screenwriter provides a strong foundation for the director and actor to develop this character.

---

15 James Cameron and Randall Frakes, *Titanic James Cameron's Illustrated Screenplay* (New York: Harper Collins, 1998) 20.

Here are some other classic film characters as they are first described in their respective shooting scripts:

- *Butch Cassidy and the Sundance Kid:* Butch Cassidy (Paul Newman)
  A MAN idly walking around the building. He is BUTCH CASSIDY and hard to pin down. Thirty-five and bright, he has brown hair; but most people, if asked to describe him, would remember him as blond. He speaks well and quickly, and has been all his life a leader of men, but if you asked him, he would be damned to tell you why.[16]

- *Misery:* Annie Wilkes (Kathy Bates)
  A BUNDLED-UP FIGURE gently beginning to pull PAUL and the case from the car: For a moment, it's hard to tell if it's a man or a woman—not to let the cat out of the bag or anything, but it is very much, a woman. Her name is ANNIE WILKES and she is close to Paul's age. She is in many ways a remarkable creature. Strong, self-sufficient, passionate in her likes and dislikes, loves and hates.[17]

- *Casablanca:* Ilsa Lund (Ingrid Bergman)
  At the entrance of the cafe, a couple is just coming in. They are VICTOR LASZLO and his companion, known as MISS ILSA LUND. She wears a simple white gown. Her beauty is such that people turn to stare. The head-waiter comes up to them.[18]

---

16 William Goldman, *Four Screenplays* (New York: Applause Books, 1995) 10.
17 Goldman 400.
18 Howard Koch, *Casablanca Script and Legend* (New York: The Overlook Press, 1992) 79.

The advantage of these short, concise descriptions is that they provide just enough essential information to provide a foundation for the actors and director to build the characters, while not interrupting the forward movement of the story.

One-Sentence Character Descriptions

Screenwriters should be able to describe each character in a script with a concise, succinct, one-sentence description. *Little Miss Sunshine* is a marvelous film in this respect. Each member of the dysfunctional Hoover family can easily be summarized in a one-sentence description that is often rich with irony:

- *The father,* who is trying to sell his motivational success program, does not deal well with his own failure.
- *The mother,* who insists on honesty from others in her family, is not always honest with herself.
- *The gay brother-in-law,* a mental patient who is depressed and suicidal after being jilted by his lover, is often the clearest thinking member of the family.
- *The daughter* is a not-so-pretty contestant in a beauty pageant.
- *The grandfather* is a foulmouthed, cocaine-snorting, frequenter of strip clubs who nonetheless provides emotional support for his granddaughter in her quest to win the beauty contest.
- *The brother* quotes Nietzsche and does not talk for much of the film because he has taken a vow of silence.

In a well-written screenplay, the screenwriter should be able to summarize each of the characters in a short, concise sentence, often using irony to provide rich, compelling insights into their personalities. If not, the characters are probably vague and amorphous, and the screenwriter needs to rethink them so they become more real to a film audience.

Using Clothing and Objects to Build Characters

Since screenplay characters are developed with only a few details, it is important to select those details with great care. Often, we associate a character in a story with an object or something that he or she wears. This is true for all forms of literature. When we think of the characters below, we inevitably associate them with an object or something unique that they are wearing. Furthermore, those objects or articles of clothing usually symbolize something very significant about each character's values, state of mind, and/or function in the story. Sometimes an article of clothing or object is sufficient to memorialize a literary or film character for all time.

- *The Wizard of Oz:* Dorothy's ruby red slippers (Glinda's protective shield, but also a symbol of Dorothy's own inner magic she must find and unleash).
- *The Scarlet Letter:* Hester Prynne's scarlet letter (her sin and guilt, but also her redemption).
- *One Flew Over the Cuckoo's Nest:* R. P. McMurphy's leather jacket and black motorcycle cap (his masculine ethic).
- *The Adventures of Huckleberry Finn:* Huck's tattered clothing, which he refers to as his "old rags" (his leisurely, nonconformist lifestyle).
- *The Great Gatsby:* Jay Gatsby's pink shirts (his refined, elegant lifestyle).
- *Butch Cassidy and the Sundance Kid:* Butch's slightly modern sport coat (the modern world encroaching on the Old West).

- *Hamlet:* Hamlet's black clothing (his state of depression and the darkness that covers Denmark).
- *Gone with the Wind:* Scarlett O'Hara's elegant gowns (her need to cling to the Old South even as the Confederacy is being systematically destroyed).
- *Titanic.* Jack Dawson's rumpled clothing (his independent, nonconformist life-style).
- *Mary Poppins:* Mary Poppins's magical umbrella (her ability to fly and encourage others to elevate their lives).
- *The Caine Mutiny:* the steel balls Captain Queeg obsessively rolls in the palm of his hand (his underlying paranoia and mental instability).

Distinguishing Physical Characteristics

Many literary and film characters have some unique physical characteristic or handicap that develops their identity and makes them unforgettable. Actors generally love to play these roles because they provide unique acting challenges:

- *Moby Dick:* Captain Ahab's whalebone leg after his encounter with Moby Dick.
- *One Flew Over the Cuckoo's Nest:* R. P. McMurphy's many scars and tattoos; Nurse Ratched's suppressed femininity and cold, unemotional countenance.
- *Pink Panther movies:* Chief Dreyfuss' nervously twitching eyes.
- *What's Eating Gilbert Grape:* Mama's obesity; the mentally challenged younger brother who struggles to communicate.
- *The Scarlet Letter:* Arthur Dimmesdale's obsessive stroking of his chest; Roger Chillingworth's bent, misshapen body.

- *The Fall of the House of Usher:* Roderick Usher's acute sensitivity to sound.
- *Of Mice and Men:* Lennie's mentally challenged personality and superhuman strength.
- *Rear Window:* L. B. Jefferies' broken leg that confines him to a wheelchair.
- *The Miracle Worker:* the blind, deaf, and mute Helen Keller.

Names of Characters

One of the questions my students frequently ask in my screenwriting and creative writing courses is, "How should I choose a character's name?" This is a common question because most students have taken literature courses that dwell on the meanings of characters' names to identify larger thematic concerns. Indeed, most of us have been trained since we took our first literature courses to look for the meanings to literary works in the characters' names. So when we are engaged in creative writing projects, it is understandable that we would devote much time to naming our own characters.

Some authors have put considerable thought into their characters' names. In Ken Kesey's **One Flew Over the Cuckoo's Nest,** R. P. McMurphy's name is appropriate because he is the very symbol of revolutions per minute (rpm), and Nurse Ratched is the wrench that fixes the broken patients so they will fit into the Combine. In F. Scott Fitzgerald's **The Great Gatsby,** Jay Gatsby is a beautiful predator, like the bird he is named after. Ishmael, the narrator of **Moby Dick,** is a wanderer like the biblical Ishmael. Pearl, Hester Prynne's daughter in **The Scarlet Letter,** is her mother's most precious possession, but also an unemotional child who lacks human warmth and the capacity for love.

Many authors enjoy the allegorical "name game," and their efforts provide the foundations for some interesting and informative classroom discussions. When creative writing students choose names for their own characters, however, they should probably make their decisions rather quickly. In the early stages of writing a screenplay or novel, there are more important concerns. Students should choose names that seem appropriate. As characters develop, they will probably fit their names, rather than the other way around. If not, the names can always be changed to something more appropriate.

To simplify these decisions, some writers choose names not by what they mean in an allegorical sense, but rather by how they sound. A name with a harder sound can often reinforce the personality of a cruel, calculating villain. If the character is gentle and loving, a name with a softer sound might be more evocative. If all else fails, writers can page through the telephone book until they find a name that seems or sounds appropriate.

Some of the world's greatest authors have made time-consuming, conscious decisions regarding the names of their characters, and readers are often the beneficiaries of their efforts. However, even Hawthorne eventually admitted that his efforts to choose precisely the right names with the right allegorical meanings for his characters were probably counterproductive and even annoying to some of his readers.

Rather than belabor the decision, creative writers should choose a name for a character rather quickly. Unless the name is woefully inappropriate, the character should grow into it. If not, once the screenwriter knows the character better, a more appropriate name will probably evolve out of the organic process of writing and rewriting. Hemingway's advice to all writers—that they should not force symbolism, but rather allow it to evolve naturally and instinctively during the writing process—should be the guiding principle for selecting characters' names.[19]

Exploring a Character's Weaknesses

The strongest film and literary characters are often defined not so much by their virtues, although they are important, but rather by their weaknesses. Weaknesses make characters living, breathing human beings. They enable actors and directors to turn a screenwriter's words into more fully developed and believable characters.

Some creative writers are unwilling to delve into the darker side of human nature to create characters who are less than virtuous. Conversely, sometimes when they explore the darker side of their characters, they start to see only the negative—and those characters also become one-dimensional. A little balance generally creates the best characters.

Heroes have weaknesses, and villains are stronger if they have some redeeming qualities. For example, Hester Prynne became the moral center of Hawthorne's *The Scarlet Letter*, but she was originally a petulant and headstrong adulterer. Jay Gatsby, the symbol of the American dream in Fitzgerald's ***The Great Gatsby***, was also a bootlegger who seemed indifferent to the human lives he destroyed while amassing a fortune and achieving the social status he so desired. In the film ***Casablanca***, Rich Blaine (Humphrey Bogart) is a cynical, self-serving former soldier of fortune who cares only for himself. Yet he forgoes the opportunity to destroy Victor Laszlo (Paul Henreid), his rival for the affections of Ilsa Laszlo (Ingrid Bergman). Instead, he helps them escape from Nazi tyranny and certain death. Even Claudius in Shakespeare's ***Hamlet***, one of the most cunning and treacherous of all villains in

---

19 Earl Rovit and Gerry Brenner, eds. *Ernest Hemingway Revised Edition* (Boston: Twayne Publishers, 1986) 68-69.

world literature, had some redeeming features: he was a good king, and he felt remorse for assassinating his brother, King Hamlet.

Our weaknesses make us human. Any actor would rather play a deeply flawed human being than a superficially virtuous one. Screenwriters should explore their characters' weaknesses as well as their strengths. This will make for much stronger film and literary characters.

When Characters Do the Unexpected

Another question I am often asked in my creative writing courses is, "My characters seem to be doing things that I would not expect from them. What do I do now?"

My answer is, "Go along for the ride." When characters start to do unexpected and unpredictable things, it means they are coming alive inside the writer's mind. If so, they will also be more alive on the printed page of a screenplay or novel. No character will be alive for the reader unless it is first alive in the writer's imagination. These unruly characters often lead the story in new and unexpected directions that create a richer plot.

The reason students express concern about unruly, uncontrollable characters is because they feel like they are losing control of their stories if their characters start acting in unexpected ways. This is why it is so important to establish a tentative structure and ending to the screenplay early in the process. (See Chapter 4, "Structuring the Story.") With these temporary controls in place, the writer can allow the characters more freedom to find their own paths in the story. This is possible because the writer knows where all the plots and subplots come together again. It is often possible to be more creative and spontaneous in a structured environment than an unstructured one.

I get excited when my students express concerns about characters they have created who suddenly demand different roles in their stories. These students are experiencing one of the greatest joys of creative writing: when individual words bring characters to life that will eventually come alive in the reader's, as well as the writer's, imagination.

Character Relationships

Most of us are raised to try to get along with one another. It would be a terrible world it we were taught to fight, squabble, and engage in endless feuds with everyone we meet. In screenplays and novels, however, the latter would be preferable to the former. Too much compatibility between characters will destroy any story. (As they flee from the law, even Butch and Sundance disagree about many things, albeit Sundance eventually yields to Butch, whom he considers to be much smarter than him.) Dramatic tension between characters is essential if a writer is to pull the reader into a story.

The classic example of this in American literature is Mark Twain's ***The Adventures of Huckleberry Finn.*** Twain has been criticized for over one-hundred years for shaping his story around a young adolescent boy who comes out of a racist background and is convinced he is the runaway slave Jim's intellectual superior. Many of Twain's critics would have preferred that he had selected a nice boy from an abolitionist background who recognized that Jim was his equal.

Twain was too much the artist to fall into that trap. He understood that Huck and Jim had to air their differences frequently as they journeyed down the Mississippi River, or the story would lose its dramatic tension. In the process, he created a novel that motivated Ernest Hemingway to proclaim, "All modern

American literature comes from one book by Mark Twain called Huckleberry Finn."[20]

Although he was writing a novel and not a screenplay, Twain instinctively understood what every good storyteller knows: Too much compatibility between characters will destroy a story, whereas dramatic tension and disagreements between characters will keep the story alive and moving.

Fast forward seventy years to the 1958 film, *The Defiant Ones,* starring Tony Curtis as John "Joker" Jackson and Sidney Poitier as Noah Cullen. Jackson and Cullen, both chain gang convicts, escape after a bus accident and attempt to gain their freedom even as they remain chained to one another. Both men are deeply prejudiced against white and black Americans respectively, and the dramatic tension of the film is created almost as much by their antagonistic relationship as by their attempts to flee from the law. They refuse to ignore their prejudices even when their very survival depends on their ability to work together. Director Stanley Kramer, like Mark Twain, understood that he would have a much stronger story if the screenwriters created two deeply prejudiced men of different races, than he would if Noah Cullen was an affable black man or Joker Jackson was a northern liberal rather than a southern racist.

Even romantic comedies like the 1989 film, *When Harry Met Sally,* depend on personal and philosophical differences between the two main characters. Harry and Sally disagree on just about everything. Only after disagreeing for many years do they finally realize that perhaps they agree on enough things to build a marriage together.

---

20 George McMichael and James Leonard, eds. *Anthology of American Literature*, vol. II, 9th ed. (Upper Saddle River, NJ: Pearson Prentice Hall, 2007) 222.

Too much compatibility between characters ruins screenplays. Differences and hostilities sustain the dramatic tension that will keep the reader or viewer involved in the story.

Building Strong Antagonists

An editor once told me that one of the biggest weaknesses she experienced in beginning storytellers is their failure to create strong, convincing antagonists. A strong antagonist—the character, characters, or force that is opposed to the main character—is essential in any effective story. If the antagonist is weak, the main character has nothing to overcome, and the story loses its power and appeal.

The antagonist must be at least as strong as, if not stronger than the main character. Ideally, the antagonist should be capable of destroying the main character. Weak antagonists are certain to bring a screenplay or novel crashing to the ground. Strong antagonists keep the reader or viewer involved in the storyline.

The following are some of the main characters and their antagonists in film and literary classics that were discussed earlier in this chapter. Notice the immense strength and power of each of these antagonists:

- *Hester Prynne:* the entire Puritan community that considers her to be the worst sinner in the New World.
- *R. P. McMurphy:* Nurse Ratched and the forces of civilized conformity that seek to crush and destroy independent spirits.
- *Huckleberry Finn:* southern racism and all of civilized society.
- *Jay Gatsby:* eastern established wealth.

- *Butch Cassidy:* the law and the forces of civilization that are overwhelming the Old West.
- *Hamlet:* King Claudius, the most powerful man in all of Denmark.
- *Scarlett O'Hara:* the invading Union Army.
- *Jack Dawson:* privileged upper-class society and the freezing waters of the Northern Atlantic Ocean.
- *Dorothy:* the wicked witch of the west, the symbol of pure evil.
- *George and Lennie:* the Great Depression and unscrupulous landowners who dominate and suppress the working class.
- *L. B. Jefferies:* a cold, calculating psychopath who has killed and dismembered his wife.
- *Helen Keller:* her struggles with being blind, mute, and deaf—and a society that sees little hope for such people.

Screenplays and novels seldom fail because the character, characters, or force that opposes the main character is too strong. Many screenplays and novels have failed because the antagonist that opposed the main character is too weak to sustain the audience's interest.

A Character's Internal Conflicts

Characters should not only be challenged by external antagonists. They should also struggle with their own internal conflicts and demons. Otherwise, these characters can become flat and one-dimensional. Main characters in any story, regardless of literary or film genre, need to struggle with internal conflicts as they grow and evolve.

Storytelling as Art and Craftsmanship

Examples of deeply troubled characters are everywhere in literature. Indeed, it would be hard to imagine a play, short story, or novel without a character who is struggling with internal conflicts. Many of the strongest characters become living, breathing paradoxes. In Tennessee Williams's *The Glass Menagerie,* Tom Wingfield is deeply devoted to his younger sister even as he struggles with an overpowering wanderlust that will eventually motivate him to leave his family. In Mark Twain's *The Adventures of Huckleberry Finn,* Huck is simultaneously convinced that slavery is both legally justifiable and morally repugnant. Hence, he battles with his conscience throughout the journey down the Mississippi River. In William Shakespeare's *Hamlet,* Hamlet's deep hatred for Claudius is balanced by his deep love for his country and his own suicidal tendencies. He is also aware that he could destroy Denmark if he allows his desire for revenge against Claudius to overwhelm his love for his country. In F. Scott Fitzgerald's *The Great Gatsby,* narrator Nick Carraway is simultaneously attracted to, and repulsed by Jay Gatsby's romantic dream and ostentatious wealth. In Edith Wharton's *The Age of Innocence,* Newland Archer is simultaneously committed to the rigid social mores of upper-class New York society and the unrestricted, bohemian lifestyle of the Countess Ellen Olenska, the woman he loves more than his own wife. The question throughout the story is which of these two lifestyles will he choose in the end?

Internal conflicts are equally important in film characters, albeit the screenwriter generally does not use stream of consciousness and other forms of internal ruminations to depict these conflicts. Except for voice over narrative commentaries (screenwriting's equivalent of first person narrators), the screenwriter is usually limited to portraying these internal conflicts through plot, dialogue, and action descriptions.

The following are the internal conflicts some classic film characters must struggle to overcome:

- *High Noon:* Marshall Will Kane (Gary Cooper) must battle his own fears and insecurities as he struggles with the question of whether to flee or confront the gang of revenge-seeking criminals who are arriving by train at high noon to kill him.
- *Hoosiers:* Coach Norman Dale (Gene Hackman) must deal with his own troubled, checkered past while he simultaneously tries to earn the respect of his team and the townspeople, many of whom do not trust him.
- *Citizen Kane:* Charles Foster Kane (Orson Welles) is one of the wealthiest, most famous, and successful men of his time, but he is also a tortured soul who secretly cherishes a simpler time in his life when his most meaningful possession was a child's sled.
- *Vertigo:* Scottie Ferguson (Jimmy Stewart) must struggle with his debilitating fear of heights at the same time that he tries to solve a bewildering mystery involving the apparent death of a friend's wife.
- *JFK:* District Attorney Jim Garrison (Kevin Costner) must reconcile his faith in his government with the growing awareness that elements in that same government may have been responsible for the death of President John F. Kennedy.
- *Apocalypse Now:* Captain Willard (Martin Sheen) is both repulsed and fascinated by the cannibalistic Kurtz whom he has been sent to assassinate.
- *The Good Shepherd:* Edward Wilson (Matt Damon) is torn between love for country and love for family. Eventually, he chooses his country's security, even if it means he

is possibly complicit in the death of his son's fiancée and unborn child—who is also his own grandchild.

Characters who have internal demons tearing away at their hearts and souls are much more likely to capture a film audience's attention than characters who see their paths in life too clearly and with little internal tension or conflict.

Irony in Character Building

There is nothing more powerful in storytelling than a character who is caught in a web of irony from which there is apparently no escape or to which they are blind. That is even truer if the irony is of the character's own making. As mentioned in Chapter One in this book, Shakespeare is the master of irony. **Hamlet**, often cited as one of the greatest characters in all of literature, is strengthened and made more complex by the fact that he eventually commits the same crime he is seeking to avenge. Once he realizes his Uncle Claudius has most likely murdered his father, Hamlet proceeds to commit the same horrendous crime when he kills Polonius, the father of Laertes. Laertes then proceeds to plot his revenge against Hamlet with the same obsessive cunning Hamlet had used in pursuing Claudius. The ironies build in this greatest of all stories until Hamlet and Laertes are both destroyed by the same web of irony they have helped to construct.

Similarly, the ironies in Willa Cather's **My Antonia** resonate throughout the novel. Antonia Shimerda, a "Bohemian" immigrant, is often viewed with scorn and distrust by many of the residents in the Nebraska community where she lives. The townspeople look down on her because she is an immigrant who speaks with an accent and has different cultural values. She loves dancing and music, which the townspeople see as a sign of moral weakness. When Antonia becomes an unwed mother, the rumors about her moral character become even more vicious. The example she sets by having a child out of wedlock and displaying her young daughter to the community with pride is viewed as dangerous for other young women. However, Antonia becomes the best wife and mother in the community. Her children are healthy, morally strong, and well cared for, while some other children in the area suffer from indifferent and even abusive parenting. Throughout the story, author Willa Cather shrewdly manipulates the reader's response to highlight the hypocrisy of those in a small prairie town who consider an immigrant farm girl the least moral person living among them—when Antonia is far more moral and caring than her critics.

There is no great story without great irony. One powerful example of this truism is Peter Shaffer's stage and film versions of **Amadeus**, the story of Wolfgang Amadeus Mozart as seen through the eyes of Antonio Salieri, his rival and admirer. The entire story is based on one overwhelmingly powerful irony, supported by an accumulation of lesser, but equally effective ironies. The great irony is that Salieri is a devout, God-fearing, chaste man who is a competent, but not a great musician. Mozart, on the other hand, is a foul-mouthed, womanizing, sacrilegious, sex-obsessed narcissist with an annoying laugh; yet he has been gifted with musical genius. The question and irony that grates on Salieri's every thought until he is driven to a jealously bordering on madness is, "How could God gift such an impure, immoral man like Mozart with true musical genius, while I, Salieri, who worshipped and prayed to God every day, am reduced to mediocrity and humiliated in the presence of Mozart's divinely inspired musical compositions?"

The other ironies pile up around Salieri as he becomes as devious and cunning as Hamlet. In the opening scene, Salieri is an old man who tries to commit suicide to relieve the guilt and humiliation he feels as a musician who outlived his time and has been forgotten. After the suicide attempt, Salieri is committed to a mental institution, and a young priest is brought in to try to help him recover from his psychological collapse. The relationship between Salieri and the young priest frames the story, and the ironies gather force like a runaway train racing down the tracks toward an inevitable catastrophic accident. By the end of the story, the many ironies dominate the plot:

- **Mozart, who is depicted in the story as a gift from God,** is dumped like disposable garbage in a pauper's grave.
- **Salieri, who at first believed he was victorious in his self-proclaimed competition with Mozart** because he outlived the musical genius, has really lost because he lived long enough to see his own music forgotten. Meanwhile, Mozart's music grows in popularity and Mozart, whom Salieri despised and envied, is acknowledged to be the greatest musician of all time.
- **Salieri, who earlier in his life saw himself as God's musical emissary,** becomes a diabolical, devilish force that destroys Mozart, God's gift to the world.
- **The young priest, who came to the mental institution to help Salieri restore his faith in God,** has seen his own faith rocked to the core as he tries to comprehend how God could have allowed a monster like Salieri to destroy a musical genius like Mozart.
- **Salieri, who once played for adoring audiences and royal families,** has as his last audience the inmates in an insane asylum as he is wheeled down the hallway back to his room.
- **Even that final humiliation and irony is not enough.** As Salieri slips into self-delusional fantasies and believes he

is surrounded by adoring fans, he hears Mozart's mocking laughter somewhere in the packed corridor of mentally ill patients who surround him.

Great storytellers, regardless of genre, see life as inherently ironic. They understand that many of us on this small planet will inevitably become the very things we dislike, or do the things we once condemned in others. This irony is wired in the human psyche. Bringing these contradictions and ironies to the surface, and exploring them in stories that transcend time, is the very definition of superior storytelling. Whereas most of us will never create characters as strong and unforgettable as Shakespeare's **Hamlet**, Cather's **My Antonia** or Peter Shaffer's stage and film version of **Amadeus**, we can certainly learn from these masters of storytelling that life itself is not simple. It is complex and deeply ironic.

Character Growth

Characters must also grow if they are to be believable. If characters are the same at the end of the story as they were at the beginning, the audience will not be able to identify with their struggles.

Here are some examples of the different growth trajectories of characters in films mentioned elsewhere in this book:

- *Titanic*: Rose (Kate Winslet) is a privileged, upper-class young woman who is trapped in a lifestyle and pending marriage that are emotionally suffocating. She sees no way out except suicide and is preparing to jump over the side of the ship, when Jack Dawson (Leonardo DiCaprio) persuades her otherwise. He teaches Rose, who is going through life with a kind of robotic stiffness and emotional detachment, that life is really a grand adventure and should be savored as a gift. Dawson dies when the Titanic sinks, but the message is not lost on Rose. She heeds his advice and lives to be 101 years old. From photographs that surround her deathbed, we realize she lived her life to the fullest, something she was incapable of doing at the beginning of the film.

- *The Good Shepherd*: Edward Wilson (Matt Damon) reflects a similar growth trajectory, except in the opposite direction. As a young college student at Yale in 1939, he did not seem all that different from others in his classes. There were some family secrets, but he was capable of love and deep feelings for others, as is reflected in his relationship with Laura (Tammy Blanchard), a deaf girl. As his life progresses, however, he becomes colder, less emotional, and seems to lose all human capacity for love, as is evident when he has his future pregnant daughter-in-law, whom he believes to be a Russian spy, thrown out of an airplane. By the end of the film, he is portrayed as a government agent incapable of human emotions who will sacrifice anyone to what he believes are national security interests.
- *Chinatown*: Los Angeles Private Detective Jake Gittes (Jack Nicholson) is certainly no stranger to human frailties and tawdry behavior. He makes his living mostly by investigating the spouses of clients who believe their husbands or wives are having affairs. Through the course of the story, however, Gittes is pulled into an even more sordid world than the one he already inhabits. He is exposed to political treachery, murder, and incestuous relationships between powerful people and their children. By the end of the film, he is virtually speechless when he watches a grandfather (John Huston) with powerful political connections gain custody of his granddaughter,

who was conceived during an incestuous relationship with the girl's mother, who is also his own daughter. The full horror of that revelation shows on Gittes' face as he realizes this despicable old man is now in a position to do to his granddaughter what he already did to his daughter. It is growth, to be sure, but of a type that takes Gittes to the very depths of human depravity.

We might prefer a different kind of growth for some of these characters, but part of the intrigue in these films is watching characters ascend to higher plateaus in life than they ever thought possible, or yield to the darker side of their own personal demons. Either way it is their growth, for better or worse, that keeps film audiences involved in their stories.

Some Books on Character Building

Joseph Campbell's 1949 book, *The Hero with a Thousand Faces*, provides some fascinating insights into character development. Campbell's book has provided the foundation for an entire screenplay paradigm that has been used by George Lucas and others. (See Chapter 4, "Screenplay Structure.") The title of Campbell's book is informative. It suggests that at the core many heroes throughout world literature are really the same hero. Only the faces have changed.

Campbell describes the attributes of this hero in great detail in his book. According to Campbell, many heroes (main characters in screenplays) are capable of moving between the ordinary world and the supernatural world; they encounter many challenges and threats to their very existence; they eventually win a decisive victory; and they return to share their insights with other human beings.[21]

Another book, Linda N. Edelstein's ***Writer's Guide to Character Traits*** (2006), includes numerous profiles of various human behaviors and personality types. Screenwriters who are struggling to flesh out major or minor characters can flip through the pages of this book and find many different character types, or combinations of different character types, for their stories.[22]

Writer's Digest <writersdigest.com> also has several informative books on its list of "How to Books for Writers." Some of these books explore the challenges of developing stronger characters for novels and short stories. Many of the techniques are also applicable to creating stronger screenplay characters.

---

21 Joseph Campbell, *The Hero with a Thousand Faces* 1st. ed. 1949, 2nd ed. 1968 (Princeton: Princeton University Press, 1973) 30.
22 Linda Edelstein, *Writer's Guide to Character Traits*, 2nd ed. (Cincinnati: Writer's Digest Books, 2006) 3-5.

EXERCISES

1. Identify several easily identifiable, even stereotypical film characters, especially those who appear in various film genres. How might you change one or two things about these characters to create original, less stereotypical characters who would be fresh and more interesting to film audiences?
2. Identify a movie in which the characters are strong and well developed. What makes these characters stronger than similar characters in other films?
3. Go for a walk in the mall, the park, or any place where there are lots of people. Keep a small notebook and jot down key words and short descriptions, like an artist using a sketch pad. As you study these people, what physical characteristics stand out vividly and clearly? Why would some make better screenplay characters than others? Are there some things that make certain people more memorable and, therefore, more visually and emotionally accessible than others?
4. List some seemingly insurmountable obstacles that people might encounter in life. Then cite movies in which the main characters confront similar challenges. Next, list some lesser obstacles people might encounter in life. Can you cite movie plots based on these antagonists? If the antagonists in these films are weak, how does the screenwriter develop challenges for the main character to overcome?
5. Describe the most interesting character you have ever met. Would others find this character to be equally interesting? Why? Does this character have weaknesses? What are those weaknesses, and how do they help create a more interesting character? Describe the same character in one sentence. Does

Storytelling as Art and Craftsmanship

a one-sentence description enable you to develop a richer, fuller sense of this character's physical appearance and values?

6. If you are writing a screenplay, do one-sentence descriptions of your characters. Does the main character have weaknesses and internal conflicts? Is the antagonist sufficiently powerful to provide a meaningful challenge to your main character? What physical idiosyncrasies or personality traits make the other characters vivid and less generic?

CHAPTER 4

STRUCTURING SCREENPLAYS AND NOVELS

If You Build It, He Will Come

Everyone who loves movies knows that the line, "If you build it, he will come," is from the film, *Field of Dreams*, starring Kevin Costner as Iowa farmer Ray Kinsella. The film, which is based on the novella, *Shoeless Joe,* written by W. P. Kinsella, has a most improbable plot. The film character played by Costner believes he hears a voice whispering these words to him as he walks through his cornfield one day. Eventually, he believes he is being told to build a baseball field on the edge of his cornfield. If he does, he is convinced the ghosts of long-departed baseball player Shoeless Joe Jackson and some of the other players involved in the 1919 Black Sox Scandal will come out of the cornfield and play a game on it.

How about pitching that plot to a film producer? An impossible sale, right? It only proves that the movie business is a crazy business with no guarantees whatsoever. In this case, a novel with a farfetched and noncommercial plot, one that seemed to have no chance of succeeding on the silver screen, was adapted into a classic film. Yes, they built it, and they did come. Film audiences, that is. They came in droves to watch this strange tale unfold on the edge of an Iowa cornfield.

It might be stretching it a bit, but perhaps there is an analogy here that could be useful to screenwriters. The voice speaking to Kinsella in the cornfield didn't tell him, "Come out to the cow pasture someday, and we'll play a game of baseball with you." No, the voice said clearly and distinctly, "If you build it, he will come." So Kinsella built a baseball field complete with four bases ninety feet apart and a pitcher's mound in the middle. That is the structure that was requested by the voice in the cornfield, and that is how Kinsella built what he was told to build.

In some ways screenwriters are faced with a similar challenge. Screenplays are not just built on some random foundation. They are built using techniques and structural devices that have been honed and perfected ever since films were first invented. They even have antecedents in classical literature. There is, of course, room for innovation and creativity in screenwriting. But screenwriters also have their own version of a structured "baseball field," and often (not always) if they succeed in laying a solid story over the top of that playing field, it has a better chance of becoming a successful film.

Structural issues are paramount concerns for every screenwriter. As pointed out in the "Preface" of this book, the remarkably successful novelist and former screenwriter Sue Grafton said, "There's nothing like a film script to teach you structure."[23] Indeed, many screenwriters insist that the three most important elements in a screenplay are STRUCTURE, STRUCTURE, and

---

23 Macdonald, Moira. ""With 'Y' is for Yesterday,' Sue Grafton prepares for the alphabet series' end." The Seattle Times 10 September 2017.

STRUCTURE. However, when many writers are first introduced to screenplay form, they think structure stifles creativity because they have been conditioned to believe that creativity must always be spontaneous. It can never thrive in a structured format. They need to be convinced that structure and creativity are kindred spirits, not adversaries. Nonetheless, many writers still see screenplay structure as too formulaic. The idea that a screenplay should have a setup, plot point, confrontation, another plot point, and a resolution smacks too much of a predictable formula, not tools to produce better and more creative scripts. (These are not mere checkpoints along the screenwriter's highway, as we shall see later.)

Another analogy might be helpful. Screenplay structure has much in common with those old-fashioned looms people once used to create exquisite rugs, tapestries, and other fabrics. Simple handlooms, table looms, and floor looms all have essentially the same features. Their primary function is to support and guide the weaving process so the individual threads that are creating the fabric do not unravel and become an unsightly mess. Yet, these same looms create artistically designed fabrics that are as different and varied as the many screenplays that have been made into superb films. No human weaver, no matter how talented, could have created such magnificent artistic fabrics without a loom.

The same is true of screenplay structure. It supports the screenwriter's story so it does not become an unraveled, unreadable mess that falls apart at the end of the story. It does not have to be formulaic. If practiced skillfully, screenplay structure should blend into and become as unrecognizable in the script as the loom is once the fabric is removed from its supporting structure.

Most people in a movie audience probably would not even recognize screenplay structure in the films they watch. But they would certainly recognize it if it was not there. Those stories, to paraphrase from Mark Twain's essay, "Fenimore Cooper's Literary

Offences," would start nowhere, accomplish nothing, and arrive in the air.[24]

The Classic Film Paradigm

In his book, **Screenplay: The Foundations of Screenwriting** (1979), Syd Field identified the underlying structure of virtually all screenplays. The paradigm is simple, which is what makes it such an attractive tool for writers. Like many stage plays, the screenplay has three acts (a beginning, middle, and end). According to Field, however, a 120-page screenplay (each page translating into one minute of film time) has a fivefold division:

Setup	Confrontation	Resolution
pp. 1-30	pp. 30-90	pp. 90-120

	Plot Point I		Plot Point II	
	pp. 25-27		pp. 85-90	

The purpose of the setup is to hook the viewer of the movie. Since film audiences are notoriously fickle, this usually occurs in the first three to five pages of the screenplay. The rest of the setup leads the audience to expect that the plot will move in a certain direction. Plot Point I, however, sends the plot off in an unexpected direction. The confrontation is divided into a series of sequences, each of which tells a smaller story within the larger story the film is developing. Plot Point II sends the plot off in yet another unexpected direction, and the resolution ties the

---

24 Mark Twain, "Fenimore Cooper's Literary Offences," *The Norton Anthology of American Literature*, short 5th ed. (New York: W. W. Norton & Company, 1999) 1457.

various plots and sub-plots together into what will hopefully be a satisfying and fulfilling conclusion to the film.[25]

Although this structural paradigm can be traced back to ancient storytelling techniques, many writers still believe it is too mechanical and contrived. They do not believe it can possibly support creative storytelling. The bard himself, William Shakespeare, should quickly put those assumptions to rest. Shakespeare's plays are virtually flawless examples of the structural devices Field identified, and they have provoked deeply subliminal responses from audiences for over four hundred years. One could even argue that Shakespeare invented, or at least popularized screenplay structure almost three centuries before films were invented.

In *Hamlet,* for example, Shakespeare introduces the ghost of King Hamlet in the opening scene. Together with the threat of an invasion from Norway, which is also introduced in the first scene, readers are hooked. This kind of supernatural intervention in human affairs is as much of an attention-grabber today as it was in Shakespeare's time. The rest of the action in the play is spread across the structural loom Shakespeare virtually created. The first plot point is when Hamlet decides to feign insanity to get to the truth about the death of his father, King Hamlet. The confrontation involves a series of scenes and sequences in which Hamlet and King Claudius engage in various intellectual duels as Hamlet struggles to learn how his father died, and who is responsible for his death. The second plot point occurs when Hamlet fails in a series of disastrous attempts to avenge his father's murder, and he decides instead to trust in providence to restore order to Denmark. The resolution is the dueling scene between Hamlet and Laertes at the very end of the play, when Claudius's treachery is exposed for all of Denmark to see, albeit

---

25 Syd Field, *Screenplay, The Foundations of Screenwriting*, 1st ed. 1979, 2nd ed. 1982 (New York: Dell Publishing, 1994) 9.

Storytelling as Art and Craftsmanship

the price of that cleansing ritual is the death of Hamlet and the entire royal family.

In what is one of the greatest (perhaps even *the* greatest) literary works of all time, Shakespeare has demonstrated the efficacy of developing stories in a structured environment, while still maintaining numerous opportunities to be creative. These creative elements are obvious in his plays in the powerful juxtaposition of scenes to maximize dramatic effect, complex and nuanced character relationships, some of the most effective dialogue ever written, and other elements of great storytelling. The structural paradigm simply holds the story in place so the more organic and spontaneous elements of storytelling can be explored and perfected. In Shakespeare's plays, the structural devices enhance, not suppress creativity.

This is a simple and highly effective paradigm, one that countless screenwriters have used to structure and develop their screenplays. Perhaps they do not have the skills of a William Shakespeare, but they have created some truly memorable stories in a structured format. Films as diverse as **Chinatown, Butch Cassidy and the Sundance Kid, Network,** and many others utilized this screenplay structure to provide unity and coherence in their respective plots.

Pulling the Reader into the Story

The most important challenge for any screenwriter is to pull the reader into the story in the opening scenes. One of my former students had an aunt who read scripts for a major Hollywood film studio. She told him the thing she looked for was whether or not the first pages of the script enabled her to "feel the main character's story at some deeper emotional level." Without an effective hook and setup in the early pages of the screenplay, this is impossible.

All readers have read something that makes them feel like there is an invisible hand reaching out of the printed page to push them away from the story. That invisible hand keeps readers at a distance. It never allows them to find a place to stand in the story where they can share the protagonist's plight at some deep, subliminal level. Most readers have also experienced a story that immediately grabs their interest and moves them along, seemingly without effort, from the opening scene to the ending. Structure, that often maligned and ignored literary technique in college literature and creative writing courses, is what pulls readers out of their ordinary worlds and into the writer's fictional world.

(See Chapter 5, "Beginnings and Endings," for several examples of screenplays, films, and novels that pull the reader into the story in the opening pages.)

Plot Points

Plot points that send the action in a different direction than the audience might expect are some of the major structural devices that support a screenplay. Their primary function is to keep the story from becoming tediously predictable. A screenplay, like all stories, should delight and surprise. This was as true for Aristotle (384-322 B. C), whose **Poetics** helped shape western literature, as it is today. Plot points contribute significantly to the structures of all stories from ancient tragedies to contemporary films and novels.

The problem is that plots points, if they are not used skillfully, can make the unpredictable predictable. Usually, however, they contribute significantly to a movie's entertainment value because their very purpose is to delight and surprise film audiences.

Plot points are usually not readily apparent on the surface of the story. Once we go looking for them, however, we can generally find them. This is as true for novels and plays as it is for screenplays. The most important plot points generally occur about one-quarter of the way into the story, and again three-quarters of the way into the story.

The examples below are some of the major plot points in several classic novels, plays, and films. The titles are followed by the first major plot point and then the second major plot point. There are certainly other unexpected and unpredictable actions that occur in each of these stories, but the plot points listed below significantly redirect the plots.

Plot Points in Plays and Novels

- *Death of a Salesman:* Biff tries to appease his father by promising he will go to see Bill Oliver about a job/ Biff does not meet with Oliver, but instead hooks up with his brother Hap and leaves his father Willie stranded in a downtown bar.
- *The Adventures of Huckleberry Finn:* Huck and Jim flee from Jackson's Island and head down the Mississippi River/ Their adventures on the Mississippi River end, and Huck arrives at the Phelps's plantation.
- *The Scarlet Letter:* Hester is released from prison and must learn to live with a moral code she has violated/ Dimmesdale decides to publicly acknowledge that he is Pearl's father.
- *Moby Dick:* Captain Ahab reveals his insane desire to find and kill Moby Dick/ Ahab refuses to join the Rachel in the search for a member of its crew who has fallen overboard, thus dooming the Pequod and its crew to a watery grave.

- *My Antonia*: Antonia's father commits suicide, leaving her in charge of the farm/ Jim leaves for Harvard and a new life.

Plot Points in Films

- *Butch Cassidy and the Sundance Kid*: The superposse arrives and relentlessly hunts for Butch and Sundance/ Butch and Sundance flee for Bolivia.
- *Little Miss Sunshine*: The Hoovers set out down the road in a van without a clutch to get Olive to the beauty pageant/ Grandpa dies just prior to the contest.
- *One Flew Over the Cuckoo's Nest*: R. P. McMurphy decides to acquiesce to Nurse Ratched when he learns that most of the other mental patients are not committed, but he is/ The fishing trip and farewell party for McMurphy trigger a series of tragic events that lead to Billy Bibbit's suicide and the final confrontation between McMurphy and Nurse Ratched.
- *Titanic*: Jack and Rose meet and their antagonistic relationship gradually turns to love/ Jack realizes he might be able to save Rose, but he will probably not be able to save himself.

Some may disagree that these are the major plot points in these novels and films, and a case could be made that there are undoubtedly other unexpected moments in these stories. Few would disagree that these plot points also send the action spinning off in unexpected directions.

A word of caution: Beginning screenwriters should remember that just because something is unpredictable does not mean that it will always enhance the plot. There are other things that must be taken into consideration. The best plot points are those that are unpredictable; yet, upon closer examination, the audience or reader eventually recognizes that they are logical, even deftly foreshadowed in earlier events in the story. Such is the case with each of the plot points in the films, plays, and novels cited above. Once the reader or viewer moves beyond the plot points and casts a backwards glance, the unpredictable becomes the logical in the larger context of the story.

The Hero's Journey

Other ways of defining screenplay structure have become popular since Syd Field's seminal study of the form. One of these paradigm, often referred to as "the hero's journey," evolved out of the scholarly works of Joseph Campbell, and especially his book, **The Hero with a Thousand Faces** (1949).

After a lifetime of studying ancient and modern myths and stories, Campbell identified the "monomyth" or unifying structure that organizes most stories. Campbell describes this structure as follows: "A hero ventures forth from the world of common day into a region of supernatural wonder: fabulous forces are there encountered and a decisive victory is won: the hero comes back from this mysterious adventure with the power to bestow boons [insights or wisdom] on his fellow man."[26]

Writers like Christopher Vogler, in his book **The Writer's Journey** (1998), have further defined "The Stages of the Hero's Journey" as a structural paradigm that takes the protagonist of a story through the following sequence of adventures, obstacles, and other challenges:

---

26 Joseph Campbell, *The Hero with a Thousand Faces*, 1st ed. 1949, 2nd ed. 1968 (Princeton: Princeton University Press, 1973) 30.

1. Ordinary World
2. Call to Adventure
3. Refusal of the Call
4. Meeting with the Mentor
5. Crossing the First Threshold
6. Tests, Allies, Enemies
7. Approach to the Inmost Cave
8. Ordeal
9. Reward (Seizing the Sword)
10. The Road Back
11. Resurrection
12. Return with the Elixir[27]

This may seem somewhat complicated, but the key stages in this paradigm can be summarized rather simply. The hero, who exists in the ordinary world, experiences a call to adventure, which he refuses until an older, more experienced mentor encourages him to cross over to the special world of adventure. In this world, the hero confronts numerous tests and enemies, including a death-defying final confrontation with an overpowering, often supernatural force or character. The victorious hero then returns to the ordinary world with wisdom and insights that he seeks to bestow on his fellow human beings.

George Lucas popularized this film paradigm in the *Star Wars* series, but he certainly did not invent it. One can see this structure in the Greek and Roman epics, many of Shakespeare's plays, *The Wizard of Oz, Peter Pan,* and a host of other literary classics. The reason it works so well, as Joseph Campbell explains in *The Hero with a Thousand Faces,* is because it has been around so long, and has become such an integral part of storytelling

---

27 Christopher Vogler, *The Writer's Journey: Mythic Structure for Writers,* 2nd ed. (Studio City, CA: Michael Wiese Productions, 1998) 26.

Storytelling as Art and Craftsmanship

and cultural traditions worldwide, that it speaks to some deeper, subliminal side of human nature.

To illustrate how this structural paradigm works in a single film, here are the various stages from Oliver Stone's epic film, **JFK**, which explores New Orleans' District Attorney Jim Garrison's (played by Kevin Costner) attempts to expose a possible conspiracy behind the assassination of President John F. Kennedy on November 22, 1963. There is an opening montage of the events that led up to the assassination. The heightened intrigue and suspense culminate with the few seconds during which gunshots were heard in Dallas's Dealey Plaza. Through District Attorney Jim Garrison's point of view, the rest of the film will try to answer the seemingly unanswerable questions: "What exactly happened during those few seconds when gunfire rained down on the President of the United States, and who was responsible for this heinous, unpatriotic act?"

1. **Ordinary World**: Garrison is working in his New Orleans' office when an associate enters and tells him the president has been assassinated.
2. **Call to Adventure**: Garrison learns from television coverage that David Ferrie, who lives in his jurisdiction, might be involved in the assassination.
3. **Refusal of the Call**: After interviewing a very nervous David Ferrie, Garrison decides to look into the assassination. However, a government spokesman appears on television and says the FBI has confirmed that "there was no conspiracy in the death of President Kennedy." Garrison then calls off his investigation and returns to his work as a district attorney.
4. **Meeting with the Mentor**: Three years later, Garrison has an accidental meeting with Louisiana Senator Huey

Long, who expresses significant doubts about the official version of the assassination. After that encounter, Garrison decides to review his earlier decision to shut down his office's investigation into David Ferrie and other suspicious characters in his jurisdiction.

5. **Crossing the First Threshold**: Garrison reads the entire Warren Commission Report on the assassination of President Kennedy, and he concludes the commissioners were engaged in a cover-up more than a conscientious attempt to expose the facts behind the Kennedy assassination.
6. **Tests, Allies, Enemies**: As his investigation proceeds, Garrison receives death threats to himself and his family from unknown sources. His allies are his loyal and dedicated legal associates who support him and his investigation.
7. **Approach to the Inmost Cave**: Garrison realizes his investigation is challenging the most powerful institutions in the federal government.
8. **Ordeal**: Garrison continues to be threatened, David Ferrie dies under mysterious circumstances, and other important witnesses die or are murdered, weakening Garrison's case.
9. **Reward (Seizing the Sword)**: A meeting with a mysterious Mr. X (played by Donald Sutherland), a former intelligence officer, convinces Garrison he is on the right track regarding a conspiracy in the death of President Kennedy. For the sake of the nation, he decides he must not give up on his investigation.
10. **The Road Back**: Garrison continues to receive hate mail and death threats, his office is bugged, the IRS threatens him with an audit, and the National Guard disavows any relationship with him. He is also humiliated on national television when he is not allowed to discuss the evidence he has compiled that proves a conspiracy took place. Most

Storytelling as Art and Craftsmanship

importantly, one of his associates is threatened, quits working for Garrison, and turns everything the investigation has produced over to the government. Nonetheless, Garrison meets with his remaining associates and tells them they will proceed to the trial against Clay Shaw, one of the alleged conspirators, even though his case has been virtually destroyed by the deaths of his witnesses and the betrayal of one of his associates. Garrison explains that they must get the evidence into the public record through the trial so the American people do not unwittingly accept a falsified record (the Warren Commission Report) of how and why President Kennedy was assassinated.

11. **Resurrection**: After an impassioned closing speech to the jury in which he insists the American people have a right to know what happened to their President, Garrison loses the trial, as he expected. However, some of the jury members express significant doubts about the government's versions of the assassination. Garrison has lost the trial, but he has succeeded in presenting his case to the American people.

12. **Return with the Elixir**: Garrison expresses his determination to continue his investigation. Then he walks back down the hallway and returns to his "Ordinary World" as the New Orleans District Attorney. However, he does not give up on seeking justice for his "fallen leader."

Closing Credits and Commentaries: As Garrison exits the courthouse, closing commentaries reveal that Shaw *was* a government agent, Garrison was reelected as the District Attorney of New Orleans, and the escalation of the Vietnam War was the most probable motive behind the assassination of President Kennedy. Under oath, a former CIA agent also had to admit that Kennedy was the victim of a "probable conspiracy." Garrison has succeeded in bringing his case to the American people.

Use and Misuse of the Paradigms

The important thing to remember about the paradigms—as they have been defined by Syd Field, Joseph Campbell, Christopher Vogler, and others—is that they are not some convenient formula or checklist that can be pulled out and scrupulously followed to produce a brilliant screenplay. Nor are they recipes that will produce magnificent screenplays simply because they always contain the same elements.

Perhaps a better analogy for these paradigms can be found in human anatomy. Every human being shares the same skeletal structure without which none of us could stand, walk, or even exist. Yet, this same skeletal structure supports human beings who are extraordinarily varied and diverse.

So, too, a screenplay is merely a skeletal structure that can support some extraordinarily different stories. Some of those stories are brilliant; some are mediocre; and some are tediously boring. One thing is certain. Since a screenplay is a skeletal structure the director will flesh out and develop into a film, it ceases to serve any useful purpose if it is structurally weak.

The Rule of Threes

There are other storytelling techniques writers use to organize stories and maximize their dramatic effect. During my studies of literature and early attempts at creative writing, I discovered what I call "the rule of threes." I am certainly not the first person to discover it. Many writers understood it, or at least practiced it. (I

Storytelling as Art and Craftsmanship

have been told the number "three" is also structurally significant to painters and other artists.)

The idea is fairly simple. When a scene or incident is repeated a minimum of three times in a story, usually with a slightly different twist or context, it builds a powerful subliminal foundation for the ending. In American literature, one of the most obvious examples of the rule of threes is the way Nathaniel Hawthorne manipulates the scaffold scenes in **The Scarlet letter.**

- **The first scaffold scene** occurs early in the story, when Hester Prynne is forced to stand on the scaffold where others have been hung. The scaffold in this scene is primarily a stage prop that is used to show how isolated and humiliated Hester has become now that she has been exposed as a common adulterer. The scaffold is also the symbol of the Puritan theocracy's power, for they could have executed Hester for her sexual transgression. They chose not to because they believed she had been recently widowed, and she had just given birth to her daughter Pearl. However, the scaffold at the center of the town square reminds everyone in the Massachusetts Bay Colony that the Puritan theocracy holds the power of life and death in their hands.
- **The second scaffold scene** occurs in the very middle of the story, when Hester, Pearl, and Dimmesdale (Pearl's father) stand on the scaffold late at night. The scaffold in this scene starts to take on even richer symbolic meanings and deeper subliminal overtones. The scaffold becomes the very symbol of sin and redemption, albeit the irony is that Dimmesdale can only confess to his own participation in the adulterous affair under the cover of darkness, when

no one else in Boston is aware of his confession that he is the father of Hester's child.
- **In the third and final scaffold scene**, Dimmesdale climbs the scaffold again, this time to publicly confess to his adulterous relationship with Hester Prynne. When Hester and Pearl join Dimmesdale on the scaffold to lend their strength to the dying, guilt-ridden minister, this scene becomes one of the most poignant in all of American literature. Had it existed in isolation, without the two earlier scaffold scenes, it would never have achieved this kind of emotional impact. It achieves its strength and dramatic power from the earlier scenes that have helped shape the audience's emotional response to the symbolic meanings of the scaffold.

Another example of the rule of threes is evident in the film version of Ken *Kesey's* novel, **One Flew Over the Cuckoo's Nest.** Screenwriters Lawrence Hauben and Bo Goldman, and director Milos Forman, clearly understood the significance of the control panel in the tub room, one of the essential stage props in Kesey's novel. In the early scenes in the shower room, the control panel is merely another of the many props the viewing audience sees on the mental ward. Later, R. P. McMurphy, played by Jack Nicholson, turns the control panel into a powerful symbol when he wagers with the other patients that he can pull it out of the floor.

Although McMurphy fails, he turns the control panel into a symbol of rebellion against the "Combine," the mechanical, authoritarian society that forces eccentric, independent souls into mental institutions. The control panel also symbolizes the importance of trying, even if one fails, to regain some sense of independence from the Combine. As McMurphy says, "But I tried, though ... Goddammit, I sure as hell did that much, now, didn't I?"[28]

Fueled by these early scenes, the control panel achieves its ultimate power in the final scene when Chief Bromden suffocates the lobotomized McMurphy so Big Nurse cannot use him as an example of what happens to all those who challenge her authority. Bromden then wrenches the control panel out of the floor and throws it out the barred window to gain his freedom. It is one of the most powerful scenes in all of film history, and it is achieved by the screenwriters' (and Kesey's) utilization of the rule of threes to maximize the dramatic impact of the control panel in the final scene in the film.

Structure and Voice in Literary Classics

In American Literature the debate regarding *voice* versus *structure* has been playing out for well over a century, probably ever since Mark Twain liberated our national literature from its reliance on both plot and the more proper English language we inherited from Great Britain. Huckleberry Finn's semi-literate utterances and point of view created a whole new way of looking at our national literature and the voices that created it.

The dominance of voice over structure prevailed, even though Twain's novels themselves were often structurally weak. This is especially true of the ending to *The Adventures of Huckleberry Finn*, which Twain delayed writing for several years because he did not know how to complete the story. The ending he finally decided on, which reunited Huck Finn and Tom Sawyer on the Phelps' plantation where they went through the charade of freeing Jim when he was already a free man, was to many readers and

---

28 Ken Kesey, *One Flew Over the Cuckoo's Nest* (New York: Penquin Press, 1976) 120-21.

critics very unsatisfying. It seemed to them to be "tacked on," and not an organic part of the story. However, Twain is often forgiven for this lapse of judgment because the voice of the story is so strong and innovative.

This debate regarding voice and structure continued long after Twain departed from the literary scene. In the early decades of the last century, Edith Wharton, author of *The Age of Innocence*, was often regarded as a lesser Henry James because he experimented with voice and point of view, whereas she clung to an outdated reliance on structure and plot. Or did she? More recent scholarship has been kinder to her, as a new breed of scholars have sensed in her writings a distinctively satirical feminine voice, one that is the equal of Jane Austen, her British counterpart. In essence these scholars argue that Wharton's novel is a fully satisfying and complete literary experience because it does not discard structure for voice, but rather coordinates the two literary techniques rather deftly and subtly.

If readers of this book are still not convinced that structure is a major element in all forms of storytelling—whether it be screenplays, novels, or plays—I strongly recommend an article in *Daily Mail.com* with the long title, "Notes and diagrams show how famous authors including J. K. Rowling and Sylvia Plath planned out their novels."[29] The article provides copious examples from archival materials when authors wrote or typed their texts. The list is quite long. In addition to Rowling and Plath, it also includes James Salter, Joseph Heller, Jennifer Egan, Norman Mailer, Gay Talese, Henry Miller, and William Faulkner. To be sure, none of them used a screenplay as an outline for a novel. Their individual outlining styles were highly idiosyncratic and exquisitely detailed.

---

29 Daily Mail.com, "Notes and diagrams show how famous authors including J. K. Rowling and Sylvia Plath planned out their novels," 18 May 2013, updated 19 May 2013.

Storytelling as Art and Craftsmanship

However, within each of their outlines these authors addressed many of the same concerns writers of screenplays must address: character relationships, scene juxtapositions, overall structure of scenes and chapters, and other such technical issues.

This might not prove that screenwriting is the preferred outline for all writers—nor should it be. But it certainly demonstrates that many of the greatest writers the world has ever created valued structure as well as voice in their respective literary works.

EXERCISES

1. Watch some of your favorite movies again and try to determine how long it took for you to be pulled into the story. What specifically provided the "hook" that enabled you to identify with the protagonist and gave you a place to stand in the story? Conversely, can you identify some movies that failed to pull you into the story? Why didn't the hook work in these films?
2. Watch a film or stage version of any of Shakespeare's great tragedies. Can you identify the major structural devices (setup, plot points, confrontation, and resolution) we have already discussed in *Hamlet*? Can Shakespeare still teach modern screenwriters and novelists something about structuring a story?
3. Screenplay structure (or lack thereof) is often most apparent in stories that seem to fall apart somewhere in the middle of the film. Identify one such film and describe precisely where the structure implodes and the plot unravels. How might the structure be strengthened to create a more compelling plot?
4. Cite some turning points in your own life and the lives of others you know. What did these events do for the people involved? Did they make their lives more or less interesting? What can the turning points in the lives of real people teach us about plot points in movies?
5. Using your favorite novels or movies, try to identify the major plot points. Why did the authors or screenwriters decide to send the action spinning off in different directions at these specific stages in their storylines? What would have happened to these stories if the plot had proceeded along anticipated lines, rather than moved off in unpredictable directions?

6. Many novellas and short stories like Ambrose Bierce's "**The Occurrence at Owl Creek Bridge**," John Steinbeck's *Of Mice and Men*, and Willa Cather's "**Paul's Case**" have been made into films. Read the original stories and try to identify the major structural devices. Do these same structural devices appear in the film versions? Why or why not? What did the screenwriters gain or lose by changing the structural devices?
7. Novellas like Herman Melville's *Bartleby the, Scrivener* and Joseph Conrad's *The Heart of Darkness* have been adapted and made into films like Francis Ford Coppola's *Apocalypse Now* that are set in a different time and place than the original story. What similarities and differences do you see between the structural devices in the novella and film versions of these and other stories? Why did the screenwriters make these changes?

CHAPTER 5

BEGINNINGS AND ENDINGS

The End is the Beginning

In his book, *Screenplay: The Foundations of Screenwriting* (1979), Syd Field is adamant that if screenwriters do not have an ending, they also do not have a beginning. He argues instead that *"The ending comes out of the beginning."*[30] This symbiotic relationship between endings and beginnings is one of the most important points he makes in his book. In his view, professional screenwriters know instinctively that endings and beginnings have to be tied together into a structural whole very early in the writing process. He acknowledges that amateur screenwriters and many novelists are often less committed to that relationship. They prefer to allow the story to find its own ending. Since Field's view is based on the thousands of screenplays he evaluated during his

---

30 Syd Field, *Screenplay, The Foundations of Screenwriting*, 1st ed. 1979, 2nd ed. 1982) New York: Dell Publishing, 1994), 104

Storytelling as Art and Craftsmanship

career as a script reader for major film production companies, all storytellers would be wise to consider his advice.

Field was certainly not the first person to recognize the relationship between beginnings and endings in storytelling. Structure and unity have been important concepts ever since the human race first created literature. Early Greek plays that were produced long before Shakespeare came on the scene rigidly adhered to three unities: unity of place, time, and action. Unity of place confined the play to one location. Unity of time confined the play to a single 24-hour day. And unity of action confined the play to those events that were essential to the story. Nothing was to be included that was extraneous or loosely connected to the plot.

Literary history reflects a gradual loosening of each of these classical unities, primarily because new genres did not have the obvious spatial and temporal restrictions of early stage plays. Novelists, especially, developed techniques that transcended the three unities of classical drama. In the twentieth century, the technologies that made films possible rendered the three unities obsolete. Or did they?

The best screenplays still contain tightly woven plots and a strong sense of place. That has not changed. Nor has the need for an audience to feel a strong connection between the opening and final scenes of the screenplay. Many screenwriters continue to practice unity of place by creating opening and closing scenes that are like bookends at opposite ends of the story. This is not essential, but it often works to create a richer and more compelling plot.

(**Spoiler alert!** The following pages in this chapter contain discussions of the beginnings and endings in a number of different films and literary works. If you have not read some of these novels or seen some of these films, and plan to do so someday, you might want to skip the discussions of these titles. If you have already read these literary works or seen these films, hopefully the discussions in this chapter will enable you to appreciate them even more.)

Beginnings and Endings as Bookends

In *Citizen Kane*, the lengthy opening montage ends with the dying Charles Foster Kane mouthing the single word, "Rosebud," before his hand falls limply to the side of the bed. The rest of the movie provides mountains of speculation as to what this word might mean. The film audience does not learn the significance of "Rosebud" until the final scene in the warehouse where Kane has stored his vast art collection and other treasures. As flames flicker around a child's sled a worker has tossed into a huge furnace, we see the single word "Rosebud" painted on the wood. In his dying moments, Charles Foster Kane, who had every possible material possession any human being could ever want, remembered only a sled that appeared briefly in one of the earlier scenes and reminded him of a happier, more innocent time in his life. The search for the meaning of "Rosebud," the elusive sled that is burned before its secrets are revealed to any of the characters in the film, provided much of the intrigue that unites the rest of the story into a fully unified whole.

In *Primal Fear,* Chicago attorney Martin Vail (Richard Gere) wins a case by practicing legal skills that skirt the edge of ethical respectability. After his victory, Vail emerges from the courtroom somewhat arrogant and overly confident. Shortly thereafter, he becomes involved in a murder case to defend a seemingly unworldly teenage altar boy (Ed Norton) who is accused of murdering the local archbishop. As the story unfolds, we learn that the altar boy probably did murder the archbishop, but he has no recollection of his actions because he is apparently suffering from a split personality. Furthermore, the archbishop is exposed as a man who sexually abused the altar boy and others. When Vail proves to the court that the altar boy is mentally incapable of understanding what he has done, he succeeds in getting the young teenager confined to a mental institution for a few years rather than a state prison for life. Only at the end of the film does Vail learn that the altar boy is no mentally challenged, unworldly teenager. He is, instead, a dangerous psychopath who slaughtered the archbishop simply because he enjoyed the carnage. This time, when Vail walks out of the courthouse, he has lost all of his bluster and arrogance. He knows that he has unleashed a psychopathic killer on society—and there is nothing he can do to stop the bloodbath that is sure to follow.

In Oliver Stone's *JFK*, the opening montage ends with a fade to black, the sound of a single gunshot echoing in the darkness, and some frightened pigeons flying off the Texas School Book Depository in Dallas's Dealey Plaza, where President John F. Kennedy was assassinated in November of 1963. This scene raises the two questions the film will explore and try to answer: what happened during those few seconds when gunfire rained down on Kennedy's motorcade, and who was responsible for the assassination? Those questions are answered at the end of the film, when Oliver Stone recreates from New Orleans District Attorney Jim Garrison's point of view what might have really happened in Dealey Plaza that day. The ending then returns to the Texas School Book Depository through a series of flashbacks as Garrison speculates about the events before and after the gunfire erupted in Dealey Plaza and the pigeons flew off the roof of the Texas School Book Depository.

The 1975 film, **One Flew Over the Cuckoo's Nest**, also utilizes this structural technique very effectively. The film opens with a view of an Oregon mountain range silhouetted against the early morning sunrise. It is still dark in the valley. All is quiet. Then we hear the natural sounds of the wind blowing through the brush and weeds, some birds in the distance, and the muted sounds of other wildlife. These sounds fade and are followed by the mournful music of a Native American flute-like instrument. The higher pitched tones of the flute are soon accompanied by a steady, haunting drumbeat. Together, they sound like a Native American funeral dirge for a lost way of life that is occurring somewhere in the distant mountain range. Suddenly an automobile's headlights appear and slowly travel across the screen, followed by a cut to some mental patients lying listlessly in their beds. The scene has shifted quickly from the wild openness of the Oregon mountain range to the claustrophobic, prisonlike atmosphere of a mental ward.

Except for a brief fishing trip, the action in the rest of the film takes place in the mental hospital. We do not hear an extended replay of the drumbeat and flute again until Bromden mercifully kills the lobotomized McMurphy and strides over to the shower room to retrieve the control panel. Nor do we see the mountain range again until Bromden throws the control panel out the window and leaps out after it. At that point, the drumbeat builds to a crescendo as Bromden runs across the hospital lawn and disappears into the shadows of the mountain range, symbolizing his return to the Native American culture he left behind many years earlier.

Hence, the beginning and ending of this film perfectly parallel one another. They are virtual bookends. The drumbeat, flute, and darkened mountain range are all there at both ends of the film. The only real difference is that the music is louder and there is more action as Bromden escapes from his paranoid-schizophrenic stupor to "fly over the cuckoo's nest" that has been his psychological prison.

Storytelling as Art and Craftsmanship

Sometimes a writer can open and close a story with an extension of the same scene, albeit it takes on a more powerful meaning by the end of the film. An example of this is the 1992 film version of Norman Maclean's memoir, *A River Runs Through It*. Robert Redford, the director of the film, understood the spirit of Maclean's original story, and he utilized his own considerable artistic skills to do justice to the memoir. The film opens with a close-up view of rippling water flowing across some submerged rocks in a shallow stream. We do not see the wider view of where the stream is located or anything else about the setting. Then we see the wrinkled hands of an old man tying a fly to a fishing line. We do not see his face or anything else—only his hands. The voice-over narrator provides just a little commentary when he says, "Long ago when I was a young man, my father said to me, Norman, you like to write stories, and I said, 'Yes, I do.' Then he said, someday when you're ready, you might tell our family story. Only then will you understand what happened and why." We know nothing else about the old man, only that his name is "Norman," he enjoys fly fishing, and there is apparently an important story somewhere in his family history.

The scene is very short, approximately half-a-minute. Then the action shifts to a photograph of two brothers, followed by another photograph of the same boys with their mother and father. Simultaneously, the voice-over narrator comments that in his family "there was no clear line between religion and fly fishing." We do not learn the significance of the short opening scene or that cryptic statement until the very end of the film when the action shifts back to the old man who, we now see in a wider view, is standing in the middle of a mountain stream, casting his line expertly out over the water. We see his heavily wrinkled face, and we watch him deftly, skillfully cast the line repeatedly out over the rippling waters.

Then the voice-over narrator explains what fly fishing means to the elderly man. We learn that he is alone, his younger brother having been murdered, his mother and father long deceased. He has even outlived his wife. The voice-over narrative, more poetry than dialogue, explains in exceedingly lyrical language how the elderly man perceives the relationship between fly fishing and religion. It is both a form of art and a religion that enables him to deal with the tragedies and losses he has sustained throughout his long life. Fly fishing is what kept him alive. In this way the beginning and ending of the film are tied together as expertly and skillfully as the older Norman tied his fly to the fishing line in the opening scene, or how he cast his line out over the water in the final scene.

The endings in each of these films complete the cycle, connecting beginnings and endings in much the same way the earlier Greek playwrights used the three unities—and especially unity of place—to connect the opening and final scenes of their plays. Film audiences may not consciously remember the relationship between opening and closing scenes. But they will remember those connections at some deeper level that only great stories can reach.

The Endings Behind the Ending

Something very interesting often happens when writers write their endings early. Frequently, the anticipated ending turns out to be only part of the ending. There may be other endings lurking behind that ending. This is one of the great advantages of having an early sense of how the story might end. It frees the writer to explore more nuanced and subtle possibilities behind the anticipated final ending.

Literary classics often have multiple endings. For example, in Herman Melville's **Moby Dick,** the anticipated ending is the final confrontation between the Pequod and the white whale that destroys the ship and its crew. The ending behind the ending occurs shortly thereafter in the "Epilogue," when the crew of another ship, the *Rachel*, spots Ishmael floating on a coffin that he has used as a life buoy. Ishmael, the one survivor of the tragedy, is rescued and lives to tell his story and share its moral with anyone who will listen to him. That moral, a repudiation of selfish individualism and a plea for all human beings to accept their shared responsibilities to one another, is the "Epilogue" and final ending of the story.

William Shakespeare's **Hamlet** provides another example of prolonging the anticipated ending with multiple endings. In some respects, the action in the play ends with the death of Hamlet. He has gained his revenge against Claudius, and he has appointed Horatio to be his successor. Then he dies. That should be the end of the play. Right? Well, actually, Shakespeare connected his beginning and endings in a much more sophisticated and effective manner to enhance the dramatic impact of his storyline. Young Fortinbras of Norway, whom the guards at Elsinore fear in the opening scenes of the play, finally arrives with his army just after the dueling scene has ended and Hamlet is dead. Fortinbras's presence not only connects the opening and closing scenes of the play; he also provides a commentary on Hamlet's courage and noble ancestry. Fortinbras insists that Hamlet be carried off the stage in a manner commensurate with his royal heritage. The final ending behind the ending is thus the slow, funeral-like procession of the characters who witnessed the carnage and are now carrying their young prince to the grave he had commented on so frequently throughout the play.

In screenplays, endings behind the ending are probably the norm rather than the exception. Horror films like **Nightmare on Elm Street, Psycho,** and many others inevitably resurrect the monster or psychopathic killer for one last attempt on the hero's life, or to imply that the threat has not been completely eliminated. Romantic comedies like **When Harry Met Sally** usually do not end with the final kiss; that scene is often followed by another scene that places the reunited couple in a future domestic setting. Courtroom dramas like **Witness for the Prosecution, To Kill a Mockingbird,** and **Primal Fear** do not end with the final verdict; they usually have another twist, or series of twists, that provide a different view of the verdict. Detective stories like **Chinatown** do not end with the final confrontation between the detective and the killer; there is generally another scene or two that focus on how the resolution has affected the main character or characters.

As discussed briefly in the previous chapter, Oliver Stone also utilizes several endings behind the ending in his film, **JFK**. District Attorney Jim Garrison makes a final impassioned speech to the jury, but the verdict goes against him. Clay Shaw, one of the men Garrison believes conspired to kill President John F. Kennedy, was found not guilty. This ending is followed by several other endings: a jury member interviewed in the hallway states that there was most likely a conspiracy involved in the death of Kennedy, but the jury was not convinced that Clay Shaw was involved; Garrison, as he makes his final, dramatic exit from the courthouse, tells reporters that he will devote the rest of his life to finding all those who conspired to assassinate President John F. Kennedy; and a brief epilogue provides evidence that Garrison, although he lost in court, was much closer to the truth than were his critics.

The endings behind the ending can be powerful tools in all forms of storytelling. Here are some more examples of writers who deftly integrated the technique of multiple endings to enrichen their storylines.

The Scarlet Letter

There are many great films and literary works that lure the reader or viewer into thinking the story is over when the last climactic confrontation between the protagonist and antagonist occurs, only to find that there are more surprises and twists to follow. One of those stories is the 1979 PBS film adaptation of Nathaniel Hawthorne's *The Scarlet Letter.* The director of this film remained true to Hawthorne's plot and guided the story skillfully toward what appeared to be the final climactic scaffold scene when Arthur Dimmesdale finally admits that he is the father of the illegitimate child, Pearl. Dimmesdale makes his anguished confession to the townspeople, revealing the dark secret that has tormented his soul for so many years. When he takes his last breath while lying on the scaffold and clinging to Hester and Pearl, their only time together as a family, we are fairly certain this is the end of the story. What more is there to tell about this tragic tale of love, betrayal, and adultery in an early Puritan community? It is a very poignant, deeply dramatic scene, and PBS might have been forgiven if it had ended the film on that note.

There was, however, much more to come—and each new revelation after the climactic final scaffold scene added another level of richness and depth to an already emotionally compelling tale:

- **Roger Chillingworth, the twisted and depraved monomaniac, bequeaths much of his property to Pearl**, the daughter born out of his wife's adulterous relationship with a minister. In the process, Chillingworth finds a path to redemption and forgiveness for himself.
- **Pearl becomes "the richest heiress" of the New World in both spirit and property** with the wealth she has inherited from Chillingworth and Dimmesdale's acknowledgement that he is her father.

- **Hester and Pearl escape to a foreign country** to start a new life for themselves.
- **Hester eventually returns to Boston**, places the scarlet letter A on her bosom, and wears it for the rest of her life as the symbol of a moral universe from which there is ultimately no escape.
- **Pearl does not come back to America**, but stays in some anonymous foreign country where she is rumored to be alive and happily married.
- **Hester becomes the trusted counselor** and pillar of emotional support for other women who committed sins or crimes, including infanticide when they abandoned their illegitimate babies in the wilderness rather than raise them and face the cruel accusations of the townspeople.
- **Hester eventually dies and is buried near Dimmesdale.** They share a single marker, as would befit a married couple. However, there is a space between their two graves so the dust of their mortal remains will never intermix, leaving just a touch of ambiguity in the final ending.

Had the PBS film version of *The Scarlet Letter* ended the story at the final scaffold scene, it would still have been a very powerful story. The endings behind the ending, however, expose a hidden substratum of irony and paradoxes that elevate the tale to a whole new dimension of rich classical storytelling.

K-PAX

The 2001 film *K-PAX*, an adaptation of Gene Brewer's science fiction novel by the same name, also leads the reader through a string of endings behind the ending, each one adding more richness and emotional intensity to the story. The plot involves a mysterious other worldly character by the name of prot (uncapitalized and played by Kevin Spacey), who arrives in New York's Grand Central Station seemingly from out of nowhere. Convinced that he is mentally ill, the authorities place prot in a mental hospital, the Psychiatric Institute of Manhattan, where he is introduced to psychiatrist Mark Powell (Jeff Bridges). Like others at the mental hospital, Powell is convinced that prot is a delusional schizophrenic, and at first he does not take prot's story seriously that he is from a planet called "K-PAX." Later, Powell is not so sure what to make of his mysterious patient. The other mental patients, however, are united in their belief that prot is what he claims to be: an extraterrestrial visitor from the planet K-PAX.

We soon learn that Powell has his own personal problems to contend with, including an estranged son from a previous marriage. When prot learns of this, he tells Powell how important it is to make amends with those we have hurt in this world because any mistake that is unresolved will repeat itself in some future dimension of time and space.

As the plot progresses, prot reveals extraordinary intellectual gifts and knowledge of planetary systems that far exceed anything even the most brilliant human scientist can envision. Through the course of the story, however, Powell learns that prot is really "Robert Porter," a married man whose wife and daughter were violently murderer by a drifter. Powell then concludes that Porter's assumed identity as "prot" was his way of coping with this horrible tragedy. There are many more twists and turns to the plot until prot finally announces that he will be leaving Earth soon, and he will be taking one of the other mental patients with him. He even announces the day and time when he will be leaving.

Powell still believes prot's story is the delusions of a seriously mentally ill Robert Porter trying to cope with the loss of his wife and daughter, and so he oversleeps on the day prot has told him he will be returning to K-PAX. When Powell finally awakens, he rushes up to prot's room—only to find no one there, or so he thinks. Then he glances under the bed and sees prot/ Porter huddled in the fetal position, fully catatonic.

This is the end of the story! Right? Robert Porter has been revealed to be a man who created an alter ego to help him cope with the murder of his wife and daughter. Or is there more to the story? Well, actually there is a whole lot more, as film audiences realized as the following endings behind the ending gradually unfolded *after* the climactic scene in prot's hospital room:

- **A frantic search of the mental hospital reveals that one patient, Bess, is indeed missing.** She also happens to be the loneliest and most isolated of all the patients on the ward because she has no home and no friends or relatives who ever come to visit her.
- **Back in his office, Powell listens to a tape recording of his own conclusions regarding the strange case of Robert Porter.** Then prot cuts in with a voice-over narrative that reminds Powell what he told the doctor earlier: that the mistakes we make in this life, and the people we hurt, will follow us into another dimension of space and time unless we rectify them before we leave this world.
- **Dr. Powell becomes prot/Porter's caretaker, and he speaks openly and candidly to the catatonic mental patient** as he wheels him around the hospital grounds. Powell is still not sure what to make of his patient, although some of his comments seem to suggest that he believes Porter may be faking his catatonic condition.
- **Following prot's advice, Powell reunites with his estranged son at the airport.** They exchange small talk

as they walk away, and the scene dissolves to black as the credits roll.

We are finally at the end of the story—right? Well, not really, although many viewers of the film might be forgiven if they missed the final ending behind the ending. After the credits have rolled for a full four minutes, and most members of the audience have left the theater, there is one final scene where Dr. Powell is standing in his backyard, looking through a telescope at the night sky. He steps away from the telescope and gazes directly at the stars, then turns and walks back to his house. He pauses again and stares once more at the night sky—then he turns and disappears into his house.

Probably not too many people hung around long enough to endure four full minutes of credits scrolling across the screen before the final scene in the film. Too bad! If they had stayed, they would have realized that there was yet another ending behind the ending. They would have realized that Dr. Powell, in spite of his many doubts and misgivings, became somewhat of a believer in prot's extraterrestrial origins on the planet K-PAX.

Cast Away

The 2000 Tom Hanks' film, *Cast Away*, also skillfully integrates multiple endings behind the ending to create a more compelling storyline. The film opens on a desolate, windswept prairie as a FedEx truck approaches a rural crossroads and turns onto a narrow dirt road. As the FedEx truck drives up to a farmhouse, we can see a pair of angel wings in the middle of the name "Dick Bettina" at the top of a wood and wrought-iron entranceway.

The truck pulls up to a barnlike structure and a woman identified as "Mrs. Peterson," whose face is hidden behind a welding mask, greets the driver. An Elvis Presley song is playing loudly in the background as she gives him a large mailing box with the same angel wings stenciled on the front. The next scene is in Russia, as another FedEx driver extracts a box with the same angel wings from the back of his truck and walks up to the front door of a large house. A man in a cowboy hat, also with the last name "Peterson," steps out of the front door to accept the package. An attractive, scantily dressed Russian woman joins him at the doorway. We quickly realize the woman behind the welding mask was probably his wife, and the woman standing by him in the doorway is most likely his mistress.

The action soon shifts to a FedEx warehouse in Russia, where Chuck Noland (Tom Hanks) is chastising his employees for their slovenly work habits. Noland is clearly a time-obsessed corporate executive who demands that his employees make the maximum effort to get FedEx packages to their destinations without any delays. Eventually, we also learn that he is engaged to Kelly Frears (Helen Hunt), a woman he loves very much. They plan to marry, but fate intervenes and strands him on an uninhabited remote island after his plane flies off course and crashes in the ocean. He thinks of Kelly constantly when he is on the island and is desperate to reunite with her.

Noland survives on the island for four years, utilizing the items in the FedEx boxes that wash up on shore. One of the boxes contains a "Wilson" soccer ball that Noland turns into an imaginary companion when he realizes that his own bloody palm print on the ball faintly resembles a human face. He proceeds to converse with Wilson as though the soccer ball were a real human companion. Another box that washes up on the shore is similar to the box with the angel wings the woman behind the welding mask gave to the FedEx driver in the opening scene. Noland never opens that box. He apparently wants something to look forward to, something to sustain him during his long hours of loneliness on the island. For the rest of the film, the angel wings on the box are a constant presence during Noland's long ordeal. He is so attached to it that he takes the box with him when he manages to escape from the island on a raft and is picked up by a passing ship.

Once he is back in civilization, he learns that Kelly, the fiancé he had loved so deeply and thought about constantly while he was on the island, is married and has a family. The most important thing that had sustained him during those long, difficult years has been taken away from him. Devastated, he tries to find a reason to go on living. Eventually he drives over to Kelly's house to meet with her. They get into his car and fantasize about leaving together, but they both soon realize that is impossible. Although they are still very much in love, Noland drives Kelly back to her house and leaves alone.

In some ways this is the final scene in the film, but there is much more that follows as the endings behind the ending create a richer and more compelling narrative:

- **After his meeting with Kelly, Noland has a deeply emotional, soul-searching conversation with a male friend.** In this conversation, Noland pours out his heart regarding how very much he loves Kelly—and what that loss meant to him.
- **Then he goes on a long journey, apparently living out of his car as he drives across the country** to the address on the FedEx package with the angel wings stencil he had saved during his ordeal on the island.
- **When he approaches a rural crossroads, we see it is the same setting as the opening scene in the movie.** At the farmhouse, he realizes no one is home, so he writes a

message on the package, explaining its history and what it meant to him, and he leaves it by the front door.

- **He drives back to the crossroads, steps out of his car, and places an open map on the hood.** He looks up and down the crossroads, apparently trying to determine which direction he should travel.
- **In the distance he sees a pickup truck approaching the area where he is standing.** When an attractive young woman steps out of the pickup to assist him, we realize she is the "Mrs. Peterson" from the opening scene in the film. As she drives away, he sees the angel wing stencil on the back of her truck, and he looks puzzled, trying to contemplate what it all might mean.
- **He looks up and down the crossroads, seemingly trying to decide which direction to go.** He also glances down the dirt road where the young woman's pickup truck had disappeared. He seems to be pondering whether or not fate had a different plan for him than a marriage to Kelly when he was stranded on the remote island. He seems instead to be questioning whether, through a very circuitous route, he had been directed to this isolated prairie crossroads, and perhaps to the young woman he had just met.

The plot thus illustrates several essential storytelling techniques. However, it is the endings behind the ending that take the story to a whole new level of storytelling intensity. In the final scene, Noland does not decide which road he will take. Nor should he. The ambiguity of which direction he will eventually take works beautifully as he stands in the middle of the crossroads, pondering his choices. We can only speculate on what is going

Storytelling as Art and Craftsmanship

through his mind. Perhaps he is questioning whether the vagaries of life are such that none of us knows what our final destination will be. Still, the audience undoubtedly hopes he will take the road back to the farmhouse, the one he is looking down when the film ends, and tell the young woman in the pickup truck his story in greater detail.

Maybe he is thinking that she, not Kelly, was the real angel in his life. Maybe through the angel wings stenciled on the box, she was the one who gave him the strength to survive during his long ordeal on the uninhabited island. Maybe their paths were destined to cross, and perhaps evolve into a permanent relationship, after the most circuitous sequence of events imaginable.

Those are some of the rich, philosophically tantalizing thoughts that might be going through Noland's mind in the final ending behind the ending. They are probably also also going through the audience's minds in this tantalizing, superbly written script.

The Hidden Story Behind the Story

Screenwriting, like all storytelling, is the art of knowing how much to reveal to the audience at any point in the plot, and when to reveal it. If a storyteller reveals too much too early, the ending frequently becomes predictable. If a storyteller reveals too little, the audience will probably not be pulled into the story. The key is to reveal just enough to sustain audience interest in the story, but not so much as to give away the ending prematurely.

This is true of all film and literary genres with very few exceptions. Often by the end of the story, readers and viewers realize there is another story, often with more universal implications, hidden below the surface and waiting to be revealed in the last scene or scenes.

Dennis M. Clausen

Apocalypse Now

Francis Ford Coppola's *Apocalypse Now* (1979), set in Vietnam and Cambodia in 1967, gradually strips away the fraudulent veils of patriotism and phony heroism that justify most wars. Instead, it reveals the brutality, murder, and barbarism that are often inflicted on native populations where these wars occur. In telling this tale, Coppola is beholden to another master storyteller, Joseph Conrad, who wrote the novella, *The Heart of Darkness* (1899). Conrad virtually invented the technique of keeping the main character, in this case Kurtz, off stage until later in the story. Instead, Kurtz's true self is revealed gradually through intriguing, but often contradictory accounts by those who knew him or claim they knew him. The real mystery the reader must participate in is to peel away these superficial insights and myths regarding this mysterious figure to answer the question, "Who is Kurtz, and what does he ultimately represent?" The answer to that question doesn't come until the very end of the story.

Coppola does something very similar in his film based on Conrad's novella. Captain Benjamin Willard (Martin Sheen) is sent on a mission into the Vietnam and Cambodian jungles to kill Colonel Walter E. Kurtz (Marlon Brando). Kurtz, an Army Special Forces officer who is rumored to have gone slightly insane, has apparently created his own army of misfits and other unstable personalities in Cambodia. The audience learns the intimate details of Kurtz's life at the same time as Willard, mostly through the dossier of information he carries with him as he journeys upriver with a small crew of soldiers. Willard often opens and reads the materials in this dossier, or studies the photographs of Kurtz at different times in the officer's life. The film audience participates in this gradual revelation of Kurtz's true character through Willard's voice-over narrative.

Storytelling as Art and Craftsmanship

We learn that Kurtz was a heroic, highly decorated Special Forces Officer, which begs the question, "Why, then, was Willard sent to kill him?" The reasons are parceled out slowly, each new bit of information creating a more complicated, often contradictory view of Kurtz. Some of the characters they meet during their journey upriver view Kurtz favorably; others are convinced he has gone native and is no longer mentally stable. Only near the end of the film, when Willard finally arrives at Kurtz's outpost, do we learn of the true depravity of this former war hero. Kurtz has tortured and killed members of the native population, become maniacal in his depraved desires, and is clearly insane. It is even implied that he may have engaged in cannibalistic rituals.

Willard eventually kills Kurtz, but only after these revelations reveal a more and more demented picture of this Special Forces Officer's true character. There are hints of his madness earlier in the story, but Coppola is too gifted a storyteller to allow the full impact of Kurtz's almost satanic capitulation to the forces of evil to be revealed prematurely. He only gives the film audience the same hints and clues that Willard must decipher as he journeys deeper into the Cambodian jungle. Ironically and fittingly, it is not Willard who pronounces the final judgement on Kurtz's demented character. It is Kurtz himself, who proclaims in his dying breath, "The horror! The Horror," words that come right out of Conrad's novella.

In Conrad's novella, Kurtz's final words were not only a judgment on his own depraved soul. They were also a final judgment on western imperialism in Africa, and what it had done to the native populations. In Coppola's film, Kurtz's final words were likewise a judgment on his own demented soul, but they were also a judgment on war and the awful horrors it unleashes on the human race. Kurtz becomes the very symbol of the atrocities committed against the people of Southeast Asia during the Vietnam

War. That is the hidden story. In this way Conrad and Coppola, both expert storytellers, very deftly conceal the final revelation regarding Kurtz and what he ultimately represents until the very end of their respective stories.

The Great Gatsby

Another story that utilizes a similar technique is F. Scott Fitzgerald's 1925 novel, *The Great Gatsby*, and the 1974 and 2012 film versions of the same story. Like Francis Ford Coppola, Fitzgerald learned from Joseph Conrad how to build a character by having others comment on him/ her in a variety of ways long before the character actually enters the story. In Fitzgerald's novel, we don't meet Jay Gatsby until the middle of chapter three, fully one-fourth of the way into the story. By that time, readers have been introduced to several contradictory accounts from characters who claim to have met Gatsby or have learned about him from various sources. They claim he is many things: a kindly wealthy donor, murderer, war hero, cousin of the Kaiser, German spy, bootlegger—and much more.

Both film versions of the story utilize a similar technique of releasing a flood of disinformation the reader must try to decipher to get to the truth about Gatsby. They keep much of Gatsby's real life and background hidden until later in the story, when we learn he does not come from the wealthy family he claims. Rather, he is the son of a poor North Dakota farmer, and he only escaped from that poverty through the assistance of a wealthy benefactor, Dan Cody, and later an organized crime figure, Meyer Wolfsheim. The entire story is designed to lure the reader or viewer deeper into Gatsby' world, each clue about his real identity subtly intermixed with many false clues. Some of Nick Carraway's voice-over narratives provide hints into Gatsby's true character. But who Gatsby really is remains elusive. It is only at the very end of the story, when Nick returns to Gatsby's mansion for the last time, that he is able to put everything altogether into a more coherent picture of a very complicated character, Jay Gatsby.

We have early hints that Gatsby is, in addition to his other personality traits, a romantic dreamer. We also learn that Daisy is more than just a former love interest who continues to fuel Gatsby's romantic obsessions. Gatsby and Daisy symbolize something much greater than what they appear to be earlier in their affair. Fitzgerald, at the very end of the story, connects Gatsby to the whole of American history. Gatsby has much in common with many earlier historical figures: the "Dutch sailors" who arrived in the new world in the 1620s; Ben Franklin whose ideas on how to achieve success and the American dream are reflected in some handwritten comments a young Jay Gatsby made in a comic book; and the pioneers who participated in the nineteenth century westward movement as symbolized by Dan Cody (Buffalo Bill Cody). Gatsby is thus the symbol of every person who ever came to America with a dream of reinventing himself or herself and starting all over again. He is the symbol of every person who set off across the continent to pursue an elusive dream during the frontier phase in American history. The early speculation regarding who he is was merely false foreshadowing that concealed his larger symbolic role. He is not just the Jay Gatsby who tried to relive a lost, irretrievable love in the 1920s. He is the very epitome of the American dreamer who has existed throughout our history.

Daisy is the object of that dream, a 1920s symbol of the green continent of the New World that lured the early settlers to these shores. She is the green light in the distance that lured pioneers across the continent during the era of westward expansion. She is the symbol of the very thing the Dutch Sailors in 1620 gazed at while they leaned against the guardrails of their ships and contemplated the continent they had dreamed about for so many years and would soon touch. So they savored that moment as much as Gatsby savored the moment when he gazed at Daisy from a distance, knowing that he would soon be able to touch the person who had brought so many heightened romantic fantasies and expectations into his life.

But the writer must not allow those connections to be made prematurely. They can only be hinted at earlier in the plot, along with considerable false foreshadowing. The hidden story must not be fully exposed until the very last scene when Nick Carraway, the narrator, returns to Gatsby's mansion. He walks down to the beach, looks across the bay, and realizes that Jay Gatsby symbolized something that transcended all of the earlier speculation about his life and background.

The Parallax View

The Parallax View (1974) also keeps its secrets very well hidden until the end, at which point it becomes an allegory of several earlier events in American history. Probably no one saw the ending coming unless they had read Loren Singer's novel, *The Parallax View* (1970). Even then, there were undoubtedly a few surprises they had not anticipated.

In the film adaptation of the novel, Joe Frady (Warren Beatty) is an ordinary newspaper reporter who is slowly pulled into a world of political intrigues and assassinations after his girlfriend, Lee Carter (Paula Prentiss), tells him that six of the witnesses to the assassination of a presidential candidate three years earlier have themselves been killed. Although a congressional special committee ruled that the political assassination was the work of a "lone assassin" who died immediately afterwards, Carter is convinced the story is a cover-up for more sinister motives. She is also concerned

Storytelling as Art and Craftsmanship

that she might be on the list of those to be eliminated, a prophecy that turns out to be true when shortly after her meeting with Frady she is found dead of a suspicious drug overdose. After her death, Frady feels morally obligated to investigate her suspicions regarding a possible string of murders and cover-ups in the aftermath of an assassination of a presidential candidate.

Almost immediately, Frady finds his own life threatened as he gets closer to what he believes is the truth about the assassination and the subsequent mysterious deaths connected to it. He soon learns of a business that recruits political assassins, and he tries to penetrate that organization by posing as an applicant. Surprisingly, they accept him, and he goes through an extensive training program. Afterwards, he finds himself in situations where his own life is once again threatened, albeit he manages to extricate himself from each of them.

The final scene in the film is probably the one most viewers remember. Frady learns of yet another plan to assassinate a political candidate at a rally in a large auditorium. Determined to thwart the assassination attempt, Frady gains access to the building and makes his way to the catwalk near the ceiling. From that vantage point, he watches as Senator George Hammond (Jim Davis) enters the auditorium floor in a golf cart. When a shot rings out and Senator Hammond is mortally wounded, Frady senses what is really going on. He realizes he has been lured into the political assassination business because he has a vital role to play: *he is the patsy who will provide the cover up for the assassination of yet another political candidate.*

Recognizing that his life is once again in great danger, Frady turns and starts running down the catwalk, only to be greeted by a gunman who steps out of the shadows and kills him. Six months later the same congressional special committee that ruled the first political assassination to be the work of a "lone gunman" renders its verdict on the assassination of Senator Hammond. Frady is portrayed by the committee as another lone, deranged gunman whose mental instability and political extremism motivated him to commit the heinous act. The committee also urged the media and the public to end all talk of a possible conspiracy behind these murders.

Until the very end of the film, the audience probably thinks this is just another clever "Who done it?" The final revelation of what is really happening is so cleverly concealed that we do not suspect that Frady is anything other than an investigative reporter, and the organization he is investigating is just another radical fringe group. Most viewers probably do not realize that this film would ultimately be an indictment of our own government's apparent participation in political assassinations and cover ups in the previous decade.

In retrospect, *The Parallax View* is an allegory of the many political assassinations that occurred in the 1960s and the supposedly "lone deranged gunmen" who committed these violent acts. Instead, the film suggests that many of these gunmen were probably what they said they were: patsies set up to take the fall by powerful political forces that were behind the assassinations. The genius of the film, however, is that the larger, almost allegorical significance of the plot was a surprise to most members of the audience until Frady was shot and killed on the catwalk. In retrospect, the foreshadowing was always there. It was just so subtly integrated into the plot that it was easy to miss until the very last scene when viewers heard almost word for word the disclaimers they had heard previously after the assassinations of John F. Kennedy, Robert Kennedy, and Martin Luther King.

One of the signs of great storytelling skills is when a final unexpected plot twist catches the audience by complete surprise, and yet in retrospect the signs were there all along. They were just cleverly concealed. Novelist Loren Singer—and screenwriters David Giler, Lorenzo Semple Jr, and Robert Towne who adapted *The Parallax View*—used a writer's version of the old magician's trick of fixating the audience's attention on one part of the stage, while the real action is occurring elsewhere. It is the art of subtle deception, and it works equally well for magicians and storytellers.

The Sixth Sense (1999)

Not every story has to have a national or universal significance. Some films and novels are good stories simply because they are well crafted. *The Sixth Sense* is one such story.

Many film viewers, myself included, like to brag about how they figured out the ending of a movie long before it actually ended. There is something inside of all of us that takes pride in being more clever than the storytellers. In bad writing, it *is* often possible to figure out the ending early. In *The Sixth Sense*, however, most viewers did not see the ending coming—even though the signs were certainly there throughout the film.

There are many reasons why this film successfully tricked audiences into accepting one reality, when another reality was actually occurring right in front of their eyes. Perhaps the most important reason is that the screenplay was so well designed that there *were* two stories going on simultaneously. Furthermore, the story was written with such precision that each scene had to serve a dual purpose. It had to be plausible in the context of what the audience thought was happening. But it also had to be plausible in retrospect, when the audience had to look back and reevaluate what they had seen earlier in the film from a completely different perspective. Writing such a screenplay is no small challenge, but screenwriter M. Night Shyamalan managed to accomplish this Herculean task with considerable skill.

The plot involves a child psychologist, Dr. Malcolm Crowe (Bruce Willis), who is shot in the opening scenes by a former patient who harbors a grudge against him because he believes Crowe did not heal him of his debilitating hallucinations. The young man then kills himself. Later that year, after he recovered, Crowe begins working with another young boy, Cole Sears (Haley Joel Osment), who appears to suffer from some of the same psychological disorders as his former patient who tried to kill him. Determined not to fail again, Crowe devotes most of his time to his young patient, often ignoring his wife in the process. Indeed, Crowe becomes so obsessed with Sears that he and his wife seem to exist in different worlds. He appears to have almost no time for her.

When young Sears reveals that he often "sees dead people" walking among the living, the plot takes a series of twists and turns as Crowe probes deeper into his young patient's fantasies. We do not learn until the end of the film that the boy's perceptions are accurate, and Crowe, who is one of the "dead people" walking among the living, was actually killed when he was shot in the opening scenes of the story. We also learn that Crowe, like the other dead people Sears sees, has unfinished business that needs to be taken care of before he can leave this world. Realizing this, Crowe returns home and finds his grieving wife asleep. After communicating to his wife that he really did love her in spite of his inattentiveness, Crowe is finally free and is able to leave the world of the living.

The genius of the film is that at the end the audience has to change perspectives and review the entire plot from beginning to end through the eyes of young Sears, who turns out to be the more reliable point of view in the story. However, the events as they unfold through the perspective of Crowe must be equally plausible, or viewers will figure out rather quickly that the entire film is an elaborate trick. Anyone who has viewed the movie a second time, just to determine if there was a slip up or two when Sears's perspective would not fit the events as they unfolded from Crowe's perspective, would be greatly disappointed. The storyline is like an elaborate puzzle that could be put together two different ways, and yet both would make sense.

It is a challenge to put the final piece of any plot in its place and find that all the previous pieces fit the storyline. That challenge increases exponentially when the writer puts the final piece in place, and it tells a different story than the one the audience imagined, while still being plausible in the context of the original story. Such was the challenge in *The Sixth Sense*. The final piece not only completed the first puzzle (Crowe's perspective), but the second one as well (Sears's perspective). Screenwriter and director Shyamalan understood the importance of keeping many things hidden from the audience and only revealing them gradually, and he succeeded brilliantly.

What we can learn from Shyamalan's film can be summarized in one sentence: *Keep the ending plausible, but also try to provide a richer, more compelling perspective on everything that happened previously.*

Write the Ending Early

Syd Fields' advice that screenwriters should know their endings as soon as they begin writing their screenplays is good advice. I would take it one step further and add that it is often helpful for writers to write their endings as soon as they are far enough into their scripts to know where their stories might end. That does not mean the first ending has to be the final ending. It is a moving target, but nonetheless one that provides significant focus and direction for the earlier elements in the story.

Perhaps another analogy will help to demonstrate the importance of writing, or at least anticipating an ending early. If we lay a thick piece of rope on the floor in a large room and unravel and spread out the individual strands, we will have a mess of individual fibers that crisscross in every conceivable direction and never come together. However, if we tie a knot at one end of the rope and then unravel the individual strands, we can separate them any way we want—and we will still know where they all come together again.

So it is with the ending to a screenplay, or any story for that matter. As an undergraduate, I often marveled at how Shakespeare was able to pull everything together in the final scenes of his plays. My first reaction was, "He sure did get lucky." Later, I realized he was most likely practicing what contemporary screenwriters learned from earlier literary masters, including Shakespeare himself. Shakespeare probably wrote his endings early and then deftly channeled the individual strands of his stories into the final scene. There is too much intricate detail that comes together at the end of Shakespeare's plays to think otherwise.

John Steinbeck utilized a similar methodology in ***Of Mice and Men.*** The ending, when George shoots Lennie on the riverbank, is deftly foreshadowed in the opening scene when George tells Lennie if he is ever in trouble he is to return to this same riverbank. Later, Carlson foreshadows Lennie's death when he shoots Candy's dog after convincing the old swamper that the dog is too old to go on living. Steinbeck absolutely knew what he was doing in these earlier scenes because he had anticipated his ending in the earliest stages of writing his story.

The same is true in the film ***Butch Cassidy and the Sundance Kid.*** The final scene, when Butch and Sundance step out of a small building into the courtyard to encounter the overpowering firepower of the Bolivian Army, is deftly set up several times earlier in the film when they have close escapes from the Pinkerton posse that is tracking them down. They have escaped so often that the film audience probably expects them to escape again, only to learn that this time escape is impossible. There are many other examples of films with cleverly crafted endings that were obviously written early, or at least anticipated in great detail in earlier scenes.

Many writers have learned the importance of anticipating their endings in the early stages of the writing process. This simple trick has enabled them to make the transition from unpublished to published writers. Editors can usually tell immediately if writers have control of their stories, and whether or not they know where their stories will end. Once writers know their endings, it is helpful to write the scene before the ending, and the scene before that scene, and so on. Writing several of the scenes that lead into the ending fortifies in the writer's mind a clear sense of how the earlier attempts to unravel the individual strands in the story will come together in the final scene. When writers return to writing the earlier scenes of the screenplay, they can do so with a much greater sense of confidence that their story is moving toward some workable resolution.

EXERCISES

1. View any two films that are based on the same story like the Battle of the Alamo or the sinking of the Titanic. Try to differentiate between the various ways screenwriters use the same plot, but structure it differently. If one version of the story is more effective than the other, how important were the beginnings and endings? Why didn't the beginnings and endings work as well in the other film?
2. Play the first ten or fifteen minutes of any film you have enjoyed watching. Then play the last ten or fifteen minutes. What parallels do you see between the beginning and ending of the film? Do these parallels between the opening and closing scenes add depth and power to the plot? Why?
3. Chart the endings behind the ending in some of your favorite movies. What might have been your reaction to the film if it had ended on one of the earlier endings?

CHAPTER 6

SCREENPLAY ADAPTATIONS OF NOVELS

Know the Inner Spirit of the Literary Work

Writing a screenplay adaptation of a novel is one of the most challenging of all writing assignments. For that reason, studying these adaptations and the films they created can teach us much about writing in all genres. There are, of course, many differences between a screenplay and novel treatment of the same story—and we will explore those differences in this chapter. There are, however, also some important similarities that unite all forms of storytelling. The great novels and screenplays we have discussed in this book were written by storytellers who searched for and found the inner spirit of their stories. Once they found that inner spirit, they used it to inform every decision they made during the writing of their stories. Foreshadowing, character development, character interactions, and all the other elements of screenwriting and novel writing are guided by the inner spirit of the story. This is especially true for writers who are adapting literary works for films.

Are there any guaranteed techniques to guide screenwriters through the challenges of writing film adaptations of literary works? Probably not. Yet, adaptations constitute up to sixty-five percent of all the stories that appear on the silver screen as feature films.[31] How then do we account for the mixed receptions of the film adaptations of many literary classics, some of which were huge hits and others colossal failures?

Perhaps the answer to this question can be found in another art form: sculpture. Michelangelo, the great Italian artist and sculptor, did not believe he was *creating* art when he produced his version of *David*, the *Pieta*, and other sculptures. He believed they were already inside the stone, and he was merely *releasing* them for everyone to see. Some Native American artists had a similar theory. They believed they too were merely releasing whatever was trapped inside the wood they were carving. Screenwriters who adapt literary works for film would be wise to remember this theory of how art is created. Rather than take a chainsaw to their literary sources, as some adapters have unfortunately done, it would be wise to think of themselves as releasing the inner spirit of the story even as they make the cuts and other necessary changes for a film.

The 1979 PBS television version of *The Scarlet Letter* is arguably among the best adaptations of a literary classic ever created. It remains true to Nathaniel Hawthorne's novel, *The Scarlet Letter*, which has been adapted over the years by many different screenwriters. This one succeeded in ways that made both critics and film audiences nod in agreement that it was a superior adaptation. However, the more recent 1995 adaptation of

---

31 This figure varies from year to year, and from genre to genre. What is clear is that adaptions provide over half of the stories for feature-length films.

the same novel with Demi Moore as Hester Prynne is considered by many critics and film audiences to be one of the least successful film adaptations of a literary classic. They argue that this film version of the story abandoned Hawthorne's plot and invented a whole new story.

They are right to a large extent. Hester Prynne is not the romantic rebel as she is portrayed in this 1995 movie. In Hawthorne's novel, after a brief early rebellion, Hester submits to the Puritan moral code and tries to assert her humanity and the strength of her femininity within these cultural and religious constraints. This creates a much richer sense of internal and external conflicts than the simplistic and superficial forms of Hester's rebellion in the 1995 movie. Other liberties in the 1995 film were also so over the top, including the Native American attack during the final scaffold scene, that viewers often laughed openly at scenes that were intended to be taken seriously. The film's failure, then, in the eyes of these viewers is due to the fact that the screenwriters did not "find the inner spirit" of a literary classic involving some deeply complex and conflicted characters.

Conversely, the 1965 film version of Boris Pasternak's novel, **Doctor Zhivago**, is an adaptation that succeeded by recognizing the power and strength of its original source and remaining true to its plot and inner spirit. Both the novel and the film are stunning recreations of the events surrounding the Russian Revolution and the story of the two doomed lovers intertwined throughout those turbulent events. Doctor Zhivago and Lara are separated and reunited repeatedly throughout the story until the very end, when Zhivago dies of a heart attack moments after he believes he has seen her walk past the tram where he is a passenger. Bad screenwriting would have reconciled the two doomed lovers at the end of the film. Fortunately, that did not happen. They must remain the symbols of the unrequited loves and hopes of a nation torn apart by political turmoil and war. The film, which honored this ending, is every bit as powerful as the novel, and it is often held up as an example of an adaptation that succeeds by remaining true to its original source in both spirit and content.

The 1992 film, *The Last of the Mohicans,* had a very different history. It is a very good film, one that captures the hopes, brutality, and wild openness of the early American frontier. It has another distinction as well: *it is much better than James Fenimore Cooper's novel by the same name.* Like all of Cooper's five novels under the title, *The Leatherstocking Tales,* the original story of *The Last of the Mohicans* is cluttered with weak and overwritten dialogue, poorly structured scenes and sequences, unbelievable plot shifts, and characters that are usually dull and stereotypical. Take my word for it, as one of the few people who has read all five of the stories in the Leatherstocking series, *The Last of the Mohicans* as a film is infinitely superior to the original story from which it was adapted. So how did this miracle occur? I guess the only answer is that Hollywood can occasionally improve on a poorly written work of literature. It does not happen often, but when it does, it shifts the vagaries of artistic integrity out of the literary establishment and places it in the film community. The screenwriters who adapted **The Last of the Mohicans** to film treatment understood the inner spirit of the American frontier better than Cooper, who knew it only from stories he had heard from previous generations. In the process, these screenwriters actually improved on a poorly written literary classic.

Other literary classics illustrate an even wider range of relationships between film adaptations and their sources. F. Scott Fitzgerald's novel, *The Great Gatsby* (1925), is a universally acknowledged classic, a novel that critics and readers alike often place at the top of the very best novels ever written by an American writer. It has also been the source of several film adaptations, the most famous being the 1974 film version starring Robert Redford and Mia Farrow, and the 2012 version starring Leonardo DiCaprio and Carey Mulligan. For the purists, the 1974 version is generally cited as the superior adaptation. For the more adventuresome, the 2012 version—which remains generally true to the spirit and plot of the original story, but colors the screen with a wild assortment of film techniques and visual effects to capture the greed and debauchery of the Roaring Twenties—is the superior adaptation. So who is right about this one? Older viewers tend to favor the 1974 version, while younger viewers often favor the over-the-top treatment of the novel in the 2012 version. They tend to enjoy the fact that the technical wizardry often overpowers the literary text. Perhaps we can only conclude that certain film adaptations will succeed in the eyes of some film audiences, but not other audiences.

Then there are writers like Mark Twain, of whom another great writer Ernest Hemingway famously said: "All modern American literature comes from one book by Mark Twain called Huckleberry Finn."[32] Yet, film historians would be hard pressed to identify even one of Twain's novels that was adapted into a great film. Virtually all of the film versions of Twain's stories are embarrassingly weak and poorly written. Why, then, would a writer as prolific and versatile as Twain produce story after story that could not be adapted successfully to film? Probably the most obvious reason is that the strength of Twain's fiction is in his manipulation of the voice of the story, and voice is arguably not as important as structure and other elements in film adaptations. Another reason might be that perhaps Twain's tall tale humor does not translate well into film, albeit *Blazing Saddles* and *Cat Ballou* utilized the same over-the-top tall tale humor and were very good

---

32   www.forbes.com/quotes/2772/

films. There may be other more profound answers, including the fact that bad novels can often become very good films in the hands of skilled screenwriters, and yet the very best literary works often resist all efforts to adapt them to films. Twain's novels may be examples of the latter.

Ken Kesey's novel, **One Flew Over the Cuckoo's Nest** (1962), provides yet another insight into the challenges of adapting novels into films. Shortly after the publication of the novel, it was adapted into a stage play that failed, although it would eventually become extremely successful after some careful rewriting and rethinking of the original story. The play preserved Chief Bromden as the first person narrator, the same role he had in the novel. The novel was not adapted into a movie until 1975. Kesey wrote the first screenplay for the film version, and he included Bromden as the narrator. However, his screenplay was rejected by the film's producers, who wanted Bromden to play a less significant role in the story. Kesey was extremely distraught that the film version of the novel did not include Chief Bromden as the first person narrator. He insisted the story was Bromden's story, but his objections were overruled, and he left the project. Bromden is still a major character in the movie version, but he plays a subordinate role to R. P. McMurphy (Jack Nicholson). To the more literary minded members of the audiences who are devoted to the original story, this is often considered a flaw in the film because to them it is a story about a Native American's efforts to escape from the madness of modern-day American conformity. To others who had not read the novel, or only knew the plot on a very superficial level, the decision to remove Bromden as the narrator probably went unnoticed.[33]

---

33 The story of Kesey's disputes with the film producers of his novel is well documented. One account is *"One Flew Over the Cuckoo's Nest*: 10 things you didn't know about the film." <www.telegraph.co.uk>

It is certainly difficult to argue with the success of the film adaptation of Kesey's novel. It garnered nine academy award nominations and was the recipient of seven Oscars, including best picture (Michael Douglas and Saul Zaentz), best actor (Jack Nicholson), best actress (Louise Fletcher), best director (Milos Forman) and best writing and screenplay adaptation (Lawrence Hauben and Bo Goldman). It also inspired a number of other films, including *Girl, Interrupted* and *The Longest Yard*. Perhaps all one can conclude from this example is that literary purists will prefer the stage play, and film buffs will probably prefer the movie version of the same novel.

The range of successes and failures is so widespread that it is almost impossible to argue for or against absolute rules to guide screenwriters when they are adapting works of literature into films. Still, there are a few things that are as close to truisms as we are likely to get on this topic. If a literary work has *not* had a widespread readership, the challenge of writing the film adaptation is usually somewhat easier because there will be less people with a fixed view of what the movie version of the story should be. If the novel is hugely successful, screenwriters should remember that its readers have established a personal relationship with the story, and they will want to see elements that hold true in the film version. When screenwriters are working with literary classics with widespread readerships, their success will be measured by how well they understand the inner spirit, plot, and characterizations of the original stories.

Film adaptations of literary classics are crapshoots. They can be huge successes or colossal failures, and the line between these distinctions can be very thin. If there is one cardinal rule that should guide screenwriters when they write a film adaptation of a literary work, it probably should be: *Don't write over the top of the original literary work as though it did not exist or was the screenwriter's own story. Find the inner spirit of the story and use that insight to guide decisions regarding cuts, additions, and other necessary changes for a film adaptation.*

Know the Dramatic Conflict in Each Scene

The examples of film adaptations used in this chapter and subsequent chapters are primarily from literary works. They will be used to explore film adaptation strategies and review the basic formatting issues in all screenplays. Once screenwriters have made the necessary cuts and selected the essential materials for their adaptations, the formatting issues are the same as screenplays based on original stories.

Screenplays for silent films read more like plot summaries of individually numbered scenes. However, as film technology evolved to incorporate dialogue into movies, screenplays developed a very different look on the printed page. They became less wordy and descriptive, and more lean and sparse with considerable white space on the printed page.

The modern screenplay is a story that is told primarily through dialogue and concise, vivid descriptions of actions. Screenwriters must learn to *think in pictures*. Long expository descriptions and stream of consciousness ruminations usually do not translate well to film.

The examples below are original scenes from Nathaniel Hawthorne's *The Scarlet Letter,* Stephen Crane's *The Red Badge of Courage,* and Willa Cather's *My Antonia.* They are followed by examples of the way a screenwriter might rewrite these same scenes for a film adaptation. Screenplay abbreviations and technical terms are used sparingly in these scenes. (These terms will be discussed in greater detail in Chapter 7, "Reading Scripts & Shooting Scripts.") The emphasis in the following examples is on what might be cut or preserved in the original storyline. A subsequent commentary for each scene discusses how the inner spirit of the original story, and the dramatic conflict in each scene, helped guide these decisions to cut or preserve original materials.

The Scarlet Letter: Original First Scaffold Scene in the Novel

The Reverend Mr. Dimmesdale bent his head, in silent prayer, as it seemed, and then came forward.

"Hester Prynne," said he, leaning over the balcony, and looking down steadfastly into her eyes, "thou hearest what this good man says, and seest the accountability under which I labor. If thou feelest it to be for thy soul's peace, and that thy earthly punishment will thereby be made more effectual to salvation, I charge thee to speak out the name of thy fellow-sinner and fellow-sufferer! Be not silent from any mistaken pity and tenderness for him; for, believe me, Hester, though he were to step down from a high place, and stand there beside thee, on thy pedestal of shame, yet better were it so, than to hide a guilty heart through life. What can thy silence do for him, except it tempt him,—yea, compel him, as it were—to add hypocrisy to sin? Heaven hath granted thee an open ignominy, that thereby thou mayest work out an open triumph over the evil within thee, and the sorrow without. Take heed how thou deniest to him—who, perchance, hath not the courage to grasp it for himself—the bitter, but wholesome, cup that is now presented to thy lips!"

The young pastor's voice was tremulously sweet, rich, deep, and broken. The feeling that it so evidently manifested, rather than the direct purport of the words, caused it to vibrate within all hearts, and brought the listeners into one accord of sympathy. Even the poor baby, at Hester's bosom, was affected by the same influence; for it directed its hitherto vacant gaze towards Mr.

Dimmesdale, and held up its little arms, with a half pleased, half plaintive murmur. So powerful seemed the minister's appeal that the people could not believe but that Hester Prynne would speak out the guilty name; or else that the guilty one himself, in whatever high or lowly place he stood, would be drawn forth by an inward and inevitable necessity, and compelled to ascend the scaffold.

Hester shook her head.

"Woman, transgress not beyond the limits of Heaven's mercy!" cried the Reverend Mr. Wilson, more harshly than before. "That little babe hath been gifted with a voice, to second and confirm the counsel which thou hast heard. Speak out the name! That, and thy repentance, may avail to take the scarlet letter off thy breast."

"Never!" replied Hester Prynne, looking, not at Mr. Wilson, but into the deep and troubled eyes of the younger clergyman. "It is too deeply branded. Ye cannot take it off. And would that I might endure his agony, as well as mine!"

"Speak, woman!" said another voice, coldly, and sternly, proceeding from the crowd about the scaffold. "Speak; and give your child a father!"

"I will not speak!" answered Hester, turning pale as death, but responding to this voice, which she too surely recognized. "And my child must seek a heavenly Father; she shall never know an earthly one!"

"She will not speak!" murmured Dimmesdale, who, leaning over the balcony, with his hand upon his heart, had awaited the result of his appeal. He now drew back, with a long respiration. "Wondrous strength and generosity of a woman's heart! She will not speak!"

Discerning the impracticable state of the poor culprit's mind, the elder clergyman who had carefully prepared himself for the occasion, addressed to the multitude a discourse on sin, in all its branches, but with continual reference to the ignominious letter. So forcibly did he dwell upon this symbol, for the hour or more during which his periods were rolling over the people's heads, that it assumed new terrors in their imagination, and seemed to derive its scarlet hue from the flames of the infernal pit. Hester Prynne, meanwhile, kept her place upon the pedestal of shame, with glazed eyes, and an air of weary indifference. She had borne, that morning, all that nature could endure; and as her temperament was not of the order that escapes from too intense suffering by a swoon, her spirit could only shelter itself beneath a stony crust of insensibility, while the faculties of animal life remained entire. In this state, the voice of the preacher thundered remorselessly, but unavailingly, upon her ears. The infant, during the latter portion of her ordeal, pierced the air with its wailings and screams; she strove to hush it, mechanically, but seemed scarcely to sympathize with its trouble. With the same hard demeanour, she was led back to prison, and vanished from the public gaze within its iron-clamped portal. It was whispered, by those who peered after her, that the scarlet letter threw a lurid gleam along the dark passage-way of the interior.[34]

Scaffold Scene: Screenplay Form

EXT. BOSTON MARKET PLACE – DAY

A GROUP OF PURITANS are gathered in the market place next to the church and a scaffold.
HESTER PRYNNE stands alone on the scaffold, holding her baby daughter PEARL.

---

34   Nathaniel Hawthorne, *The Scarlet Letter* (The Project Gutenberg Etext of *The Scarlet Letter*) 40-41. <www.gutenberg.org/wiki/Main_Page>

REVEREND DIMMESDALE bends his head in SILENT prayer on the church balcony, steps forward and approaches the scaffold. He leans on the balcony as he stares steadfastly into Hester Prynne's eyes.

DIMMESDALE

Hester Prynne. Thou hearest what this good man says, and seest the accountability under which I labor. If thou feelest it to be for thy soul's peace, and that thy earthly punishment will thereby be made more effectual to salvation, I charge thee to speak out the name of thy fellow-sinner and fellow-sufferer! Be not silent from any mistaken pity and tenderness for him; for, believe me, Hester, though he were to step down from a high place, and stand there beside thee, on thy pedestal of shame, yet better were it so, than to hide a guilty heart through life. What can thy silence do for him, except it tempt him—yea, compel him, as it were to add hypocrisy to sin? Heaven hath granted thee an open ignominy, that thereby thou mayest work out an open triumph over the evil within thee, and the sorrow without. Take heed how thou deniest to him—who, perchance, hath not the courage to grasp it for himself the bitter, but wholesome, cup that is now presented to thy lips.

Pearl raises her little arms with a half pleased, half plaintive MURMUR, but Hester remains SILENT and shakes her head. The PEOPLE gathered at the foot of the scaffold are incredulous, unable to comprehend why Hester would refuse to answer Dimmesdale's questions.
REVEREND WILSON, an elderly pastor, steps forward on the balcony and begins to harshly admonish Hester.

REVEREND WILSON

Woman, transgress not beyond the limits of Heaven's mercy! That little babe hath been gifted with a voice to second and confirm the counsel which thou hast heard. Speak out the name! That, and thy repentance, may avail to take the scarlet letter off thy breast.

HESTER

(looking at Dimmesdale)
Never! It is too deeply branded. Ye cannot take it off. And would that I might endure his agony, as well as mine!

VOICE IN THE CROWD

Speak, woman! Speak and give your child a father!

HESTER

I will not speak! And my child must seek a heavenly Father. She shall never know an earthly one!

Dimmesdale leans over the balcony with his hand upon his heart and then steps back with a long respiration.

DIMMESDALE

She will not speak! Wondrous strength and generosity of a woman's heart! She will not speak!

Hester continues to hold baby Pearl, while Reverend Wilson addresses the multitude with a THUNDEROUS DISCOURSE on sin, making continual reference to the ignominious letter A on Hester's breast. Her eyes are glazed, weary. She tries to hush Pearl when the baby pierces the air with its WAILINGS and SCREAMS.

Scaffold Scene: Novel versus Screenplay

- **The most obvious difference between the treatments of the same scene is that the screenplay is a greatly stripped down version** of the first scaffold scene. It is not a fully developed scene that describes all of the nuances and subtleties of what is happening in the marketplace as Hester stands alone on the scaffold. Instead, it concentrates on the essential elements in the scene and ignores many of the details.
- **Scene setting in the screenplay is reduced to "EXT. BOSTON MARKET PLACE – DAY."** This designates an exterior scene that takes place in a specific location during the day. If it were a scene that took place in the church at night, the opening header or slug line would be, "INT. CHURCH – NIGHT."
- **Much of the information in the third paragraph and the final paragraph from the novel has to be deleted** because it purports to know what people in the crowd are thinking or feeling without providing a viable visual or auditory means of communicating these insights to a film audience. Examples are, "the people could not believe but that Hester Prynne would speak out the guilty name," and Reverend Wilson's sermon made the letter A assume "new terrors in their imagination, and seemed to derive its scarlet hue from the flames of the infernal pit." These are internal ruminations that usually need to be

communicated through pictures, dialogue, or voice-over narration to work on film.

- **Action descriptions are kept to a minimum** because there isn't much physical action in this scene. The emotional intensity is conveyed mostly through dialogue.
- **In screenplays the unspoken is often as powerful as the spoken.** There is plenty of room in this scene for actors to communicate this emotional intensity through subtle nuanced gestures, especially between Dimmesdale and Hester. The screenwriter does not have to alert the director and actors to all of these possibilities. There is always room for collaborative interpretations in screenplays.
- **When writing action descriptions, the screenwriter is "thinking in pictures"** rather than vague, amorphous intellectual or emotional concepts.
- **When a character's name first appears in a scene, it is capitalized. Sounds are also capitalized.** Subsequent characters' names in the action descriptions in the same scene are not capitalized, but all sounds continue to be capitalized. This makes for an easier, quicker read, while simultaneously helping the script reader visualize and hear what the film experience will be for audiences in movie theaters.
- **When a character's name first appears in a new scene, it is also capitalized.** When a character's name is repeated in the same scene, it is not capitalized.
- **Characters' names are capitalized and aligned on the same left hand margin.** Dialogue appears directly under the characters' names. Quotation marks are not used for centered dialogue.
- **Parenthetical clarifications should be placed on the line below the character's name** and aligned five to seven spaces from the left dialogue margin. These clarifications should

be used sparingly because it is best to let the director and actors interpret the dialogue and how it should be delivered.
- **Long monologues like Dimmesdale's opening speech are risky in screenplays.** In this case, however, Dimmesdale's long, sermon-like comments are appropriate for the public occasion in which they appear. They are also laced with rich irony, since he is Pearl's father.
- **The screenwriter would probably replicate the actual words** to Reverend Wilson's "thunderous discourse on sin," even though they do not appear in the novel.

Dramatic Conflict and Intensity in *The Scarlet Letter* Scene

This scene is rich with irony, hypocrisy, and forbidden love. Reverend Wilson has placed Reverend Dimmesdale in the untenable position of having to lecture and chastise a woman for her adulterous behavior. Dimmesdale is thus forced to demand that Hester reveal the name of her fellow adulterer, when he is the man with whom she had the affair. When he comments on the "wondrous strength and generosity of a woman's heart," he is also commenting on Hester's decision to bear the burden of guilt and shame alone, while simultaneously protecting his name and status in the community. If that is not enough dramatic intensity and conflict, Dimmesdale also knows that the Puritan court that sentenced Hester Prynne to wear the letter A was being merciful in the eyes of their laws. The court could have executed her for sexual misconduct that produced a child. That is how seriously they viewed any kind of sexual activity outside of marriage. They spared her the ultimate punishment only because she had recently lost her husband, Roger Prynne, who was presumed to be dead. Yet, the gallows upon which she stands is undoubtedly a constant reminder to her that it could have been the very place where she was executed.

Both Dimmesdale and Hester know she could have been more severely punished. They also know that any admission on her part that Dimmesdale, a Man of God whom the Puritan community believed to be almost saint-like was instead a common adulterer, would probably have resulted in both of them being executed. An admission that she had seduced the most saintly member of their community would not have been tolerated. This is the dramatic intensity and irony that pervades this entire scene, for even as Dimmesdale exhorts Hester to reveal the name of her child's father, he knows such a revelation would be a death sentence for her and possibly for both of them. Yet, he is overwhelmed by her strength and determination to protect him even as she is subjected to cruel ridicule and humiliation. The screenwriter does not have to belabor this explanation, but feeling that intensity and irony can help to release the "inner spirit" of this scene even in the condensed form of a screenplay.

The Red Badge of Courage: Original Battlefield Scene in the Novel

There is, as stated earlier, very little physical action in the first scaffold scene in *The Scarlet Letter*. The dramatic tension is created primarily through dialogue. Some scenes, however, require more in the way of action descriptions to release the inner spirit and dramatic conflict. Screenwriters who write action scenes can make some minor modifications in screenplay form and style to create nervous, staccato rhythms that reinforce the actions they are describing.

The example below is one of the Civil War battlefield scenes Stephen Crane creates in his novel, *The Red Badge of Courage*. It is followed by a screenplay version of the same scene:

Someone cried, "Here they come!"

There was rustling and muttering among the men. They displayed a feverish desire to have every possible cartridge ready to their hands. The boxes were pulled around into various positions, and adjusted with great care. It was as if seven hundred new bonnets were being tried on.

The tall soldier, having prepared his rifle, produced a red handkerchief of some kind. He was engaged in knotting it about his throat with exquisite attention to its position, when the cry was repeated up and down the line in a muffled roar of sound.

"Here they come! Here they come!" Gun locks clicked.

Across the smoke-infested fields came a brown swarm of running men who were giving shrill yells. They came on, stooping and swinging their rifles at all angles. A flag, tilted forward, sped near the front.

As he caught sight of them the youth was momentarily startled by a thought that perhaps his gun was not loaded. He stood trying to rally his faltering intellect so that he might recollect the moment when he had loaded, but he could not.

A hatless general pulled his dripping horse to a stand near the colonel of the 304th. He shook his fist in the other's face. "You've got to hold 'em back!" he shouted, savagely; "you've got to hold 'em back!"

In his agitation the colonel began to stammer. "A-all r-right, General, all right, by Gawd! We-we'll do our—we we'll d-d-do—do our best, General." The general made a passionate gesture and galloped away. The colonel, perchance to relieve his feelings, began to scold like a wet parrot. The youth, turning swiftly to make sure that the rear was unmolested, saw the commander regarding his men in a highly resentful manner, as if he regretted above everything his association with them.

The man at the youth's elbow was mumbling, as if to himself: "Oh, we're in for it now! Oh, we're in for it now!"

The captain of the company had been pacing excitedly to and fro in the rear. He coaxed in schoolmistress fashion, as to a congregation of boys with primers. His talk was an endless repetition. "Reserve your fire, boys—don't shoot till I tell you—save your fire—wait till they get close up—don't be damned fools—"

Perspiration streamed down the youth's face, which was soiled like that of a weeping urchin. He frequently, with a nervous movement, wiped his eyes with his coat sleeve. His mouth was still a little ways open.

He got the one glance at the foe-swarming field in front of him, and instantly ceased to debate the question of his piece being loaded. Before he was ready to begin—before he had announced to himself that he was about to fight—he threw the obedient, well-balanced rifle into position and fired a first wild shot. Directly he was working at his weapon like an automatic affair.[35]

Battlefield Scene: Screenplay Form
EXT. CIVIL WAR BATTLEFIELD – DAY

                UNION SOLDIER
Here they come!

There is a RUSTLING and MUTTERING among the MEN.

Boxes of cartridges are pulled around into various positions.

Hands reach feverishly for every possible cartridge.

---

35 Stephen Crane, *The Red Badge of Courage* (The Project Gutenberg Etext of *The Red Badge of Courage*) 24-25. <www.gutenberg.org/wiki/Main_Pages>

A TALL SOLDIER knots a red handkerchief around his throat with exquisite attention to its position.

CRIES up and down the line become a MUFFLED ROAR of sound.

               UNION SOLDIERS
    Here they come! Here they come!

Gun locks CLICK.

Across the smoke-infested fields a brown swarm of RUNNING MEN give SHRILL YELLS. They come on, stooping and swinging their rifles at all angles. A flag, tilted forward, speeds near the front.

A YOUTH checks his rifle to see if it is loaded.

A HATLESS GENERAL pulls his dripping horse to a stand near the COLONEL of the 304th. He shakes his fist in the other's face.

                  GENERAL
    You've got to hold 'em back! You've got to hold 'em back!

                  COLONEL
       (stammering)
    A-all r-right, General, all right, by Gawd! We—we'll do our—we-we'll d-d-do—do our best, General.

The general makes a passionate gesture and gallops away.

The colonel begins to SCOLD the men around him.

The youth turns and looks apprehensively at the rear. He sees the general gesturing and speaking to OTHER MEN in a highly resentful manner.

>ANOTHER SOLDIER
>(mumbling to himself)
>Oh, we're in for it now! Oh, we're in for it now!

The CAPTAIN of the company paces excitedly to and fro in the rear.

>CAPTAIN
>Reserve your fire, boys. Don't shoot till I tell you. Save your fire. Wait till they get close up. Don't be damned fools—

Perspiration streams down the youth's face. He nervously wipes his eyes with his coat sleeve. His mouth is still a little ways open.

The youth glances at the FOE-SWARMING FIELD in front of him. He throws his obedient, well-balanced rifle into position and fires a first wild shot.

The youth is soon firing his weapon quickly, automatically.

Battlefield Scene: Novel versus Screenplay

- **The novelist's expository observations and stream of consciousness ruminations have been deleted** because they are not expressed in the dialogue exchanges. Nor do they create pictures or describe actions that can be reproduced on film.

- **The screenwriter uses many shorter descriptive sentences** to replicate the nervous excitement and fear the Union soldiers feel as they face the charging Confederate soldiers who are storming across the battlefield.
- **Stephen Crane's original language** gives the screenwriter much to work with because the dialogue is appropriately short, choppy and nervously fragmented to reinforce the battlefield action being described.
- **Crane's visual descriptions are clear, vivid, and already compatible with a screenplay format.** In writing this scene, Crane was "thinking in pictures" which convert easily to screenplay style and formatting.
- **The spaces between many of the sentences** further reinforce the disconnected, chaotic, frantic activity that surrounds the youth everywhere on the battlefield where nothing seems to be unified or carefully coordinated.

Dramatic Conflict and Intensity in *The Red Badge of Courage*

Stephen Crane, the author of *The Red Badge of Courage*, was deeply cynical about the motives behind most wars, the way they were conducted on battlefields, and the strategies (or lack thereof) that caused armies to win or lose. During the many military campaigns he covered as a newspaper correspondent, he concluded that most military battles are chaotic, unpredictable events where victory or defeat often turned on some unexpected quirk that no one, not even the highest ranking generals, saw coming. For these reasons, most of the battlefield scenes in *The Red Badge of Courage* are described as chaotic, unpredictable places of mass confusion where the outcome is due to luck rather than military strategies. Hence, his battlefield scenes are often depicted as places where military discipline breaks down and is replaced by an "every man for himself" mindset, as self-preservation, not victory or defeat, becomes the dominant motivating force.

The screenwriter who wrote this battlefield scene preserved many of these features in the film adaptation. A thinly disguised semblance of order still exists, but the nervous excitement Crane created in the novel treatment of the scene will soon increase significantly, and chaos and confusion will rule almost every action taken by the men on the battlefield. What we are witnessing are the last moments before military discipline will start to collapse. The higher ranking officers will try to restore some sense of military strategy because their overriding concern is to hold their positions. But the men actually fighting the advancing Confederate troops will be concerned with something quite different: personal survival.

This is the "inner spirit" of this battlefield scene, and the screenwriter has released it using several different storytelling techniques: the nervous, staccato rhythms of the prose style in the action descriptions; the short almost fragmented sentence structures; and the frenzied, deeply emotional rhythms of the dialogue exchanges.

My Antonia: Original Scene from the Novel

One of the scenes in Willa Cather's **My Antonia** that has always puzzled readers and scholars is when Jim, the first person narrator of the novel, returns home from New York City and learns that Antonia is unmarried and the mother of an illegitimate child. Jim, who has loved Antonia since he was a teenager, has the perfect opportunity to propose marriage, rescue her from her humiliating predicament, and fulfill his adolescent fantasies. Yet, he does not. Instead, they meet out on the Nebraska prairie and express their feelings for one another, but they do not take their relationship to the next logical step. Instead, Jim returns to New York and does not see Antonia again for twenty years. Here is how Willa Cather describes that meeting between two people who seem destined to someday marry, and yet they decide instead to take different paths in life.

(**Note**: The sections in bold are the ones I decided to cut before converting the scene into screenplay form. There were other cuts, condensing, and rearranging of what remained. Some of the dialogue exchanges were also shortened. The rationale for all of these cuts appear at the end of this excerpt from Cather's original novel.)

THE NEXT AFTERNOON I walked over to the Shimerdas'. **Yulka showed me the baby and told me that Antonia was shocking wheat on the southwest quarter. I went down across the fields, and Tony saw me from a long way off. She stood still by her shocks, leaning on her pitchfork, watching me as I came.** We met like the people in the old song, in silence, if not in tears. Her warm hand clasped mine.

"I thought you'd come, Jim. I heard you were at Mrs. Steavens's last night. I've been looking for you all day."

She was thinner than I had ever seen her, and looked as Mrs. Steavens said, "worked down," but there was a new kind of strength in the gravity of her face, and her colour still gave her that look of deep-seated health and ardour. Still? Why, it flashed across me that though so much had happened in her life and in mine, she was barely twenty-four years old.

Antonia stuck her fork in the ground, and instinctively we walked toward that unploughed patch at the crossing of the roads as the fittest place to talk to each other. We sat down outside the sagging wire fence that shut Mr. Shimerda's plot off from the rest of the world. **The tall red grass had never been cut there. It had died down in winter and come up again in the spring until it was as thick and shrubby as some tropical garden-grass. I found myself telling her everything: why I had decided to study law and** to go into the law office of one of my mother's relatives in New York City; **about Gaston Cleric's death from pneumonia last winter, and the difference it had made in my life. She wanted to know about my friends, and my way of living, and my dearest hopes.**

"Of course it means you are going away from us for good," she said with a sigh. "But that don't mean I'll lose you. Look at my papa here; he's been dead all these years, and yet he is more real to me than almost anybody else, he never goes out of my life, I talk to him and consult him all the time. **The older I grow, the better I know him and the more I understand him.**"

She asked me whether I had learned to like big cities. "I'd always be miserable in a city. I'd die of lonesomeness. I like to be where I know every stack and tree, and where all the ground is friendly. I want to live and die here. **Father Kelly says everybody's put into this world for something, and I know what I've got to do. I'm going to see that my little girl has a better chance than ever I had. I'm going to take care of that girl, Jim.**"

I told her I knew she would. "Do you know, Antonia, since I've been away, I think of you more often than of anyone else in this part of the world. I'd have liked to have you for a sweetheart, or a wife, or my mother or my sister—anything that a woman can be to a man. The idea of you is a part of my mind; you influence my likes and dislikes, all my tastes, hundreds of times when I don't realize it. You really are a part of me."

She turned her bright, believing eyes to me, and the tears came up in them slowly, "How can it be like that, when you know so many people, and when I've disappointed you so? Ain't it wonderful, Jim, how much people can mean to each other? I'm so glad we had each other when we were little. **I can't wait till my little girl's old enough to tell her about all the things we used to do.** You'll always remember me when you think about old times, won't you? And I guess everybody thinks about old times, even the happiest people."

As we walked homeward across the fields, the sun dropped and lay like a great golden globe in the low west. **While it hung there, the moon rose in the east, as big as a cart-wheel, pale silver and streaked with rose colour, thin as a bubble or a ghost-moon. For five, perhaps ten minutes, the two luminaries confronted each other across the level land, resting on opposite edges of the world.**

In that singular light every little tree and shock of wheat, every sunflower stalk **and clump of snow-on-the-mountain,** drew itself up high and pointed; **the very clods and furrows in the fields seemed to stand up sharply.** I felt the old pull of the earth, the solemn magic that comes out of those fields at nightfall. I wished I could be a little boy again, and that my way could end there.

We reached the edge of the field, where our ways parted. I took her hands and held them against my breast, feeling once more how strong and warm and good they were, those brown hands, and remembering how many kind things they had done for me. I held them now a long while, over my heart. About us it was growing darker and darker, and I had to look hard to see her face, **which I meant always to carry with me; the closest, realest face, under all the shadows of women's faces, at the very bottom of my memory.**

"I'll come back," **I said earnestly, through the soft, intrusive darkness.**

"Perhaps you will" —I felt rather than saw her smile. "But even if you don't, you're here, like my father. So I won't be lonesome."

As I went back alone over that familiar road, I could almost believe that a boy and girl ran along beside me, as our shadows used to do, laughing and whispering to each other in the grass.[36]

My Antonia: Screenplay Treatment of the Same Scene

After the items in bold are cut from the original source, the screenwriter might convert what remains into the following scene. I have placed some more sentences in bold that might still be cut to achieve a leaner, sparser style, albeit this is a deeply emotional final exchange between Jim and Antonia, and the longer, more impassioned dialogue is fully justified in this context.

EXT. NEBRASKA PRAIRIE – AFTERNOON

JIM walks toward a field where ANTONIA is shocking wheat.

> JIM (V. O.)
> The next afternoon I walked over to the Shimerdas'. I went down across the fields, and Tony saw me coming from a long way off. We met like people in the old song, in silence, if not in tears.

Antonia walks out to greet him and clasps his hand warmly.

> ANTONIA
> I thought you'd come, Jim. I heard you were at Mrs. Steavens's last night. I've been looking for you all day.

---

36 Willa Cather, *My Antonia* (The Project Gutenberg Etext of *My Antonia*) Book IV "The Pioneer Woman's Story," Part IV. <www.gutenberg.org>

They walk toward the crossing of the roads where Antonia's father is buried. They sit next to a sagging wire fence.

ANTONIA (CONT.)
I heard you are living in New York and are a lawyer.
Do you like living in a big city?

Jim nods, but seems unable to answer her question. Antonia smiles knowingly, sensing he has made a decision not to return to the prairie.

ANTONIA (CONT.)
Of course it means you are going away from us for good. But that don't mean I'll lose you. Look at my papa here. **He's been dead all these years, and yet he is more real to me than almost anybody else.** He never goes out of my life. I talk to him and consult him all the time (Pause) I would be miserable in a city. I'd die of lonesomeness. I like to be where I know every stack and tree, and where all the ground is friendly. I want to live and die here.

Jim has seemed at a loss for words, but he finally speaks.

JIM
Do you know, Antonia, since I've been away, I think of you more often than of anyone else in this part of the world. I'd have liked to have you for a sweetheart, or a wife, or my mother or my sister—anything that a woman can be to a man. The idea of you is a part of my mind; you influence my likes and dislikes, all my tastes, hundreds of times when I don't realize it. You really are a part of me.

ANTONIA
(tearfully)
How can it be like that, when you know so many people, and when I've disappointed you so? **Ain't it wonderful, Jim, how much people can mean to each other?** I'm so glad we had each other when we were little. You'll always remember me when you think about old times, won't you? **I guess everybody thinks about old times, even the happiest people.**

JIM (V.O.)
As we talked, I felt the old pull of the earth again, the solemn magic that comes out of those fields at nightfall. I wished I could be a little boy again, and that my way could end there.

They stand and walk together across the prairie for the last time.

JIM (V.O. / CONT.)
As we walked homeward across the fields, the sun dropped and lay like a great golden globe in the low west. **In that singular light every little tree and shock of wheat, every sunflower stalk drew itself up high.** We reached the edge of the field, where our ways parted. I took her hands and held them against my breast, feeling once more how strong and warm and good they were, those brown hands, and remembering how many kind things they had done for me. I held them now a long while, over my heart. About us it was growing darker and darker, and I had to look hard to see her face.

Antonia smiles warmly at him and lets go of his hand.

> JIM
>
> I'll come back.
>
> ANTONIA
>
> (gesturing at her own heart)
> Perhaps you will. But even if you don't, you're here, like my father. So I won't be lonesome.

They part and walk away in opposite directions. Jim looks down at some shadows mingling on the ground.

> JIM (V.O.)
>
> As I went back alone over that familiar road, I could almost believe that a boy and girl ran along beside me, as our shadows used to do, laughing and whispering to each other in the grass.

My Antonia: Novel versus Screenplay Treatment of the Scene

This screenplay adaptation is not that different from other adaptations discussed in this chapter, except for the fact that it uses voice over (V. O.) narrative form to simulate the first person point of view of the novel. The dialogue exchanges are also somewhat longer as both Antonia and Jim struggle to express their feelings for one another. Other than that, the screenplay formatting and other technical issues are very similar. The real issue is the "inner spirit" of the scene and how it affects the choices of what should or should not be cut. To accomplish this, the screenwriter must carefully examine the motives of both Antonia and Jim to determine why they choose to take separate paths through life, when they seem destined to go through life together.

Once again we see the strength of ambiguity in storytelling because we have several different motivational forces at work in this scene. Jim, who has always been torn between the prairie and the more artistically and culturally superior east, may realize that although Antonia may be content, even happy, to live on the prairie—he cannot. Another possibility is that Antonia is the one who really makes the final decision. She seems to know that Jim might make the sacrifice to live on the prairie with her, but she wants him to go on to bigger and better things in his life. Or perhaps they both know they are different people who need different things in life, and a marriage would not work for either of them. Or maybe, as Jim acknowledges in the final sentence of this scene, the closeness they shared as "a boy and girl…laughing and whispering to each other in the grass" would always remain in his memories, but that is where their closer, more intimate relationship should end.

Again, it is the inner spirit of the scene in the context of everything that has come before that should guide the screenwriter in determining what should or should not be cut, condensed, or emphasized in the adaptation. In this case, the emphasis probably needs to be on their reasons for feeling that although they love one another very much, it is best that their relationship be a warm childhood memory and not a marriage.

The Last Detail: Screenplay Scene

Scenes in a film script are often more stripped down and sparse than the examples illustrated above. Frequently, these scenes combine brief action descriptions and even briefer dialogue exchanges, illustrating the concept that in screenwriting "less is often more."

Examples of this sparse screenwriting style are evident throughout Robert Towne's script of *The Last Detail,* adapted from Darryl Ponicsan's novel by the same name. In the 1973 film, two Navy lifers decide to teach a young petty thief some lessons about life while they escort him to a military prison in Boston. At first the two Navy lifers, "Bad-Ass" Buddusky (Jack Nicholson) and "Mule" Mulhall (Otis Young), enjoy this last detail and treat it as a welcome reprieve from their normal duties. When they realize that Meadows (Randy Quaid) is facing eight years in prison for stealing forty dollars from the general's wife's charity, they begin to empathize with him. They start to treat him like a younger brother who needs to grow up and live a little before he enters prison. This fantasy sustains them until they near the end of their assignment, when they must turn Meadows over to military authorities.

The scene below—which describes Buddusky, Mule, and Meadows eating in a hamburger joint—is typical of the sparse style used to develop most of the scenes in this screenplay.

(Note: This is a scene from a "shooting script," so the header is somewhat different than the header for a "reading or speculative script" described more fully in Chapter 7.)

The Last Detail: Scene from the Shooting Script

31 Int. Hamburger Joint

They sit at the counter. The hamburgers are brought, along with shakes and fries. Buddusky looks at Meadows' cheeseburger suspiciously.

BUDDUSKY
Cheese melted enough?

MEADOWS
Sure.

Buddusky looks at it closely.

> BUDDUSKY
> Ain't melted at all. Send it back.

> MEADOWS
> No, it's okay, really.

> BUDDUSKY
> Send the goddam thing back. You're paying for it, aren't you?

> MEADOWS
> It's all right, really.

> BUDDUSKY
> Have it the way you want it. Waiter?

> MEADOWS
> No please—

> WAITER
> Yes, sir?

> BUDDUSKY
> Melt the cheese on this for the Chief here, will you?

> WAITER
> Certainly.

The waiter takes it away.

BUDDUSKY
See, kid, it's easy to have it the way you want it.[37]

Dramatic Conflict and Intensity in *The Last Detail*

Not much there, right? Or is there? On the surface, this appears to be a sparsely developed and relatively meaningless scene about a minor disagreement between two characters regarding whether or not the cheese on a cheeseburger has been melted sufficiently. It seems almost like a throwaway scene. However, Robert Towne, who received an Oscar nomination for *The Last Detail* and an Oscar for *Chinatown* in 1974, is too gifted a screenwriter to write a scene without any real dramatic purpose.

If we scratch a little beneath the lean style of this scene, we can see it reveals much about the two characters. Meadows's passive refusal to return the cheeseburger reflects a childlike, diffident temperament that will not bode well for him in prison. In fact he will probably not survive if he remains so unassertive. Recognizing this, Buddusky in an almost fatherly way teaches him how to stand up for himself and be more assertive. This is a relatively innocuous lesson in a hamburger joint, but in prison it might be the difference between surviving or perishing. Still, it is not the job of the screenwriter to fill in all these details and character motivations. The screenwriter suggests these possibilities beneath some well-chosen words and action descriptions. It is the role of the director and actors to probe the depths of these possibilities and bring them fully to life.

In many creative writing courses, this lean style would not be considered an example of stellar prose. The writing would be considered too general, not appealing enough to the five senses,

---

37 Robert Towne, *Chinatown The Last Detail* (New York: The Grove Press) 181-82.

lacking in stylistic flair and distinctive voice, and failing to get sufficiently inside the minds of these characters to bring them to life. In screenwriting, however, these are considered virtues. A screenplay, unlike a novel or short story, is not a finished product. A screenplay is a manual that describes in general terms how the director and actors are to create the finished product. Screenplays are often judged by a different set of criteria than most forms of creative writing. Screenplays should be evocative, but not overly detailed.

Conclusions about Screenplay Adaptations and Formatting

From our earliest days as students, most of us have been taught to expand on everything we write. We have been told we need to explore every nuance and complexity of a subject matter to demonstrate that we have assimilated it at some deeper, more profound intellectual level. English majors, especially, have had this training. Unless they have read many screenplays, they instinctively tend to default to the more verbose style of novel writing rather than the leaner style of screenwriting.

There is certainly nothing wrong with this writing pedagogy. It may even be an essential part of creative writing. In screenwriting, however, the tendency to view writing as a forum to generate more, and still more words to capture these nuances and complexities is counterproductive. A few well-chosen words of dialogue or concise, vivid action descriptions do more to create film effects on paper than pages and pages of prose.

This does not mean that a screenplay should be simple or superficial. It means that screenwriting requires somewhat different talents and skills than novel writing. A screenplay is most effective when everything—characters, scene settings, dialogue, and action descriptions—is developed with a lean, sparse style that is evocative, while respecting the fact that actors and directors also have significant roles in the collaborative effort to create a film.

Adaptation exercises can be invaluable in this process. Learning to cut, condense, and adapt existing sources is one way to master the leaner style of screenwriting, while simultaneously learning how to make cuts in all writing projects. Once a writer has learned how to make these cuts in someone else's writing, it is much easier to make cuts in stories or screenplays in which the writer has a personal investment.

The other great advantage of learning to write in screenplay form is that it teaches writers how to produce more authentic dialogue. Screenplay dialogue is not an end in itself. It is dialogue written to be performed, not read silently as is the case with novels. As a result, the best screenwriters are able to produce dialogue that sounds like real human talk conveying real emotions to real people.

(See Chapter 10, "Writing Dialogue," for a longer, more detailed discussion of how to write better dialogue for both novels and screenplays.)

Screenwriting Software

A few words about screenwriting software programs before we move on to explore the distinctions between *speculative scripts* and *shooting scripts*. There are many software programs that will automatically space and format screenplays so the writer can concentrate on structure, character development, dialogue and the other elements of a successful film script. Some of these software programs are free downloads; others are quite expensive. Some will help the screenwriter organize the story. Others will even critique and offer suggestions for possible revisions of the script.

There is no one software program that is appropriate for all screenwriters. In their first attempts to write a screenplay, many screenwriters prefer a software program that takes over the entire formatting process and offers critiques and editorial suggestions. As screenwriters become more comfortable with screenplay format, they often prefer a software program that is less intrusive.

The five most commonly recommended screenwriting software programs are *Final Draft, Movie Magic Screenwriter, Celtx, WriterDuet, and Fade In*. *Final Draft* has been the industry standard for years and is still preferred by many professional screenwriters. *Movie Magic Screenwriter* has made considerable inroads into the world of professional screenwriting and has been used to create a number of successful films. *Celtx* is not as popular with professional screenwriters, although amateur and independent screenwriters often use it rather than the more expensive industry standards.

There are numerous screenwriting software programs that have been extensively reviewed on the internet. Before choosing which software program to use, screenwriters should research those reviews and find the program that best serves their needs, goals, and experiences. A good place to start is to consult the website https://www.scriptreaderpro.com/screenwriting-software/. This resource compares the various screenwriting software programs to help screenwriters decide which one is the best choice for them. Often that decision is based on whether screenwriters are beginners, more advanced, or using a screenplay as an outline for a novel.

The important thing for all screenwriters to remember is to concentrate on developing their storylines, not worry about spacing and other formatting issues. Let the screenwriting software program take over those concerns so the more important issues of storytelling can be addressed creatively and professionally.

EXERCISES

1. Choose any one of your favorite short stories and identify precisely how you would label the individual scenes (INT. or EXT., LOCATION and TIME) if the story were adapted into a screenplay.
2. Project Gutenberg has the complete texts of *The Scarlet Letter, The Red Badge of Courage*, and *My Antonia*. Select a scene from any one of these novels and convert it into a new screenplay scene, using the appropriate formatting. http://www.gutenberg.org/wiki/Main_Page
3. Read Robert Frost's poem, "Home Burial," and designate the headers as the action shifts from the farmhouse, to the yard, to the upstairs bedroom, and the staircase. Why is it important that the headers be accurately labelled in each of these scene shifts? What problems does it create if the headers are not accurately labeled?
4. Using the screenplay versions of the scenes from *The Scarlet Letter, The Red Badge of Courage*, and *My Antonia* illustrated in this chapter, make further cuts to emulate the leaner style of *The Last Detail*. Is anything important lost when you make those cuts?
5. Cut and refine the action descriptions and dialogue in any scene from a novel or short story to create the sparser screenplay style of telling a story. Then describe the criteria you used to determine what was essential and what could be cut from the scene.
6. In your own screenplay, choose any scene and delete as many words as you can until it looks and reads like the leaner, sparser style of the scene from *The Last Detail*. When you

have stripped the scene down to the essentials, what happens to the dialogue and action descriptions that are left? Are they more or less powerful? Why?

CHAPTER 7

READING SCRIPTS AND SHOOTING SCRIPTS

Introduction

Unless a screenwriter is under contract to write a script for a film that will soon go into production, most screenplays are *reading* or *speculative scripts* and not *shooting scripts.* The differences between a novel and a screenplay are readily apparent. The distinctions between reading and shooting scripts are often less clear.

Reading scripts that are devoid of all technical terms can look like stage plays and lack the unique ability of the screenplay to manipulate time and space to tell a good story. Screenplays that have too many technical terms often appear to be presumptuous attempts to direct the film. The question is what constitutes a legitimate use of the technical terms that are commonly used in shooting scripts, but without appearing to be an amateurish and presumptuous attempt to usurp the director's role in the film?

Storytelling as Art and Craftsmanship

Usually, the reading script steps over this line when the screenwriter starts calling too many camera shots and making other decisions that are within the purview of the director. At other times, some screenwriters use far too much technical jargon in an attempt to impress the reader of the script with their knowledge of screenplay terminology. This is generally counterproductive because it only serves as an impediment to the development of the story—and the primary goal of all reading scripts should be to tell a good story.

(Note: It was once considered taboo for scenes to be numbered in reading or speculative scripts. Numbered scenes were reserved for shooting scripts. However, since many of the scriptwriting software programs now automatically number scenes, it has become more acceptable for scenes in reading or speculative scripts to also be numbered.)

The following examples, based on different treatments of the final scene in Henry James's novella, ***The Turn of the Screw***, illustrate some of the subtle and not so subtle differences between: 1) two legitimate reading scripts; 2) an overly technical reading script that poses as a shooting script; and 3) a possible shooting script of the same scene.

The plot of the novella involves a nameless Governess who has been hired to look after a man's orphaned nephew and niece after his brother (the children's father) dies. Shortly after arriving at Bly, where she is to care for Miles and Flora, the Governess becomes convinced that the children are possessed by the ghosts of Peter Quint and Miss Jessel, two dead servants. Eventually, some readers begin to suspect that perhaps it is the Governess who is mentally unstable, and the ghosts exist only in her own mind.

Henry James writes the final scene so ambiguously that the reader cannot determine if Miles dies because the ghost of Peter Quint is making one last determined attempt to possess the boy's soul, or if the Governess kills Miles during one of her hallucinations. In this scene, the Governess believes she sees the ghost of Peter Quint peering at them from outside the window, and she pulls Miles close to her in a protective act, or so it seems. It could also be that she smothers Miles, either intentionally or unintentionally.

Final Scene: *The Turn of the Screw*

My sternness was all for his judge, his executioner; yet it made him avert himself again, and that movement made me, with a single bound and a irrepressible cry, spring straight upon him. For there again, against the glass, as if to blight his confession and stay his answer, was the hideous author of our woe—the white face of damnation. I felt a sick swim at the drop of my victory and all the return of my battle, so that the wildness of my veritable leap only served as a great betrayal. I saw him, from the midst of my act, meet it with a divination, and on the perception that even now he only guessed, and that the window was still to his own eyes free, I let the impulse flame up to convert the climax of his dismay into the very proof of his liberation. "No more, no more, no more!" I shrieked to my visitant as I tried to press him against me.

"Is she here?" Miles panted as he caught with his sealed eyes the direction of my words. Then as his strange "she" staggered me and, with a gasp, I echoed it, "Miss Jessel, Miss Jessel!" he with sudden fury gave me back.

I seized, stupefied, his supposition—some sequel to what we had done to Flora, but this made me only want to show him that it was better still than that. "It's not Miss Jessel! But it's at the window-straight before us. It's here—the coward horror, there for the last time!"

At this, after a second in which his head made the movement of a baffled dog's on a scent and then gave a frantic little shake for air and light, he was at me in a white rage, bewildered, glaring vainly over the place and missing wholly, though it now, to my sense, filled the room like the taste of poison, the wide overwhelming presence. "It's *he*?"

I was so determined to have all my proof that I flashed into ice to challenge him. "Whom do you mean by 'he'?"

"Peter Quint—you devil!" His face gave again, round the room, its convulsed supplication. "Where?"

They are in my ears still, his supreme surrender of the name and his tribute to my devotion. "What does he matter now, my own?—what will he *ever m*atter? I have you," I launched at the beast, "but he has lost you forever!" Then for the demonstration of my work, "There, there!" I said to Miles.

But he had already jerked straight round, stared, glared again, and seen but the quiet day. With the stroke of the loss I was so proud of he uttered the cry of a creature hurled over an abyss, and the grasp with which I recovered him might have been that of catching him in his fall. I caught him, yes, I held him—it may be imagined with what a passion; but at the end of a minute I began to feel what it truly was that I held. We were alone with the quiet day, and his little heart, disposed had stopped.[38]

Final Scene: Reading Script

The following scene is well within the purview of what constitutes a reading script. The screenwriter has avoided all of the technical jargon and terminology that are commonly used in shooting scripts. Rather than demonstrating the screenwriter's knowledge of film and screenwriting techniques, the emphasis in this scene is on telling a good story, which is what a reading script should do.

---

38 Henry James, *The Turn of the Screw* (The Project Gutenberg Etext of *The Turn of the Screw*) 79-80. <www.gutenberg.org/wiki/Main_Page>

INT. BLY - DAY

The GOVERNESS leaps at MILES with a single bound and an irrepressible CRY.

Miles's eyes remained fixed on a nearby window as a vague, GHOSTLY IMAGE stares into the room.

The Governess grasps Miles and pulls him close to her breast.

                    GOVERNESS
           (shrieking at the image in the window)
        No more, no more, no more!

                         MILES
           (panting, eyes closed)
        Is she here?

                    GOVERNESS
She?

                         MILES
           (furiously)
        Miss Jessel, Miss Jessel!

                    GOVERNESS
        It's not Miss Jessel! But it's at the window—straight before us. It's here—the coward horror, there for the last time!

Miles shakes his head frantically, GASPING for air and light as he desperately fights with the Governess to free himself from her grasp. He glares wildly around the room and in the direction of the window.

> MILES
>
> It's he?

> GOVERNESS
>
> (coldly)
> Whom do you mean by 'he'?

Miles continues to glare wildly around the room.

> MILES
>
> Peter Quint—you devil!

> GOVERNESS
>
> Where? What does he matter now, my own? What will he *ever* matter? I have you.
> (to the window)
> But he has lost you forever!
> (to Miles, gently)
> There, there!

The Governess continues to clutch Miles tightly to her breast. Miles is not moving, his head is limp and he does not seem to be breathing. The Governess's gaze is fixed on the clear day outside the window.

Final Scene: Another Reading Script

The following screenplay treatment of the same scene uses some technical terms to give the script the feel of a film, but without usurping the director's role by identifying specific camera shots or making other decisions that only belong in a shooting script. Instead, the word "ANGLE" is used in various ways to subtly direct the reader's attention to something or someone in the scene. The forbidden word "CAMERA" is never used.

INT. BLY – DAY

The GOVERNESS leaps at MILES with a single bound and an irrepressible CRY.

CLOSER VIEW reveals that her eyes are fixed on a nearby window, not on Miles.

ANGLE ON the window reveals a vague, GHOSTLY IMAGE staring at them.

The Governess pulls Miles close to her breast.

> GOVERNESS
> (shrieking at the image in the window)
> No more, no more, no more!

> MILES
> (panting, eyes closed)
> Is she here?

> GOVERNESS
> *She?*

> MILES
> (furiously)
> Miss Jessel, Miss Jessel!

GOVERNESS

It's not Miss Jessel! But it's at the window—straight before us. It's here—the coward horror, there for the Last time!

ANGLE ON Miles, his head shaking frantically, GASPING for air and light. He fights with the Governess to free himself from her grasp. He glares wildly around the room and in the direction of the window.

MILES

It's he?

GOVERNESS

(coldly)
Whom do you mean by 'he'?

Miles continues to glare wildly around the room.

MILES

Peter Quint—you devil!

GOVERNESS

Where? What does he matter now, my own? What will he *ever* matter? I have you.
(to the window)
But he has lost you forever!
(to Miles, gently)
There, there!

WIDER ANGLE reveals the Governess clutching Miles tightly to her breast. Miles is not moving, his head is limp and he does not seem to be breathing. The Governess's gaze is fixed on the clear day outside the window.

Final Scene: Overly Technical Reading Script

The scene below is an overly technical reading script trying to pose as a shooting script. The screenwriter has called too many camera shots, used the forbidden word "CAMERA," and relied on too many technical terms that clutter up the printed page rather than advance the storyline. This screenwriter has usurped the role of the director.

176. INT. BLY – DAY

The GOVERNESS looks O. S. to her left.

Her POV as a GHOSTLY IMAGE appears in a window.

WIDER ANGLE as she leaps at MILES with a single bound and an irrepressible CRY.

She pulls Miles close to her breast.

CLOSER VIEW reveals that her eyes are fixed on the window, not on Miles.

CAMERA ANGLE ON the window reveals a vague, ghostly image that might be PETER QUINT staring at them.

ANOTHER CAMERA ANGLE of the Governess and Miles.

> GOVERNESS
> (shrieking at the image in the window)
> No more, no more, no more!

> MILES
> (panting, eyes closed)
> Is she here?

> GOVERNESS
> *She?*

> MILES
> (furiously)
> Miss Jessel, Miss Jessel!

QUICK PAN back to the window reveals the image of a man, not a woman.

Governess's POV as she looks down at Miles and then pulls him even more closely to her breast.

> GOVERNESS
> It's not Miss Jessel! But it's at the window—straight before us. It's here—the coward horror, there for the Last time!

CLOSE SHOT of Miles, his head shaking frantically, GASPING for air and light, desperately fighting with the Governess to free himself from her grasp, glaring wildly around the room and in the direction of the window.

ANOTHER CAMERA ANGLE of the Governess and Miles.

                    MILES

It's he?

                  GOVERNESS
    (coldly)
    Whom do you mean by 'he'?

Miles continues to resist the Governess's firm, unyielding embrace as he glares wildly around the room.

                    MILES
    Peter Quint—you devil!

                  GOVERNESS
    Where? What does he matter now, my own? What will he *ever* matter? I have you.
        (to the window)
    But he has lost you forever!
        (to Miles, gently)
    There, there!

FADE TO BLACK

                GOVERNESS (V.O.)
    But he had already jerked straight round, stared, glared again, and seen but the quiet day. With the stroke of the loss I was so proud of he uttered the cry of a creature hurled over an abyss, and the grasp with which I recovered him might have been that of catching him in his fall. I caught him, yes, I held him—it may be imagined with what a passion; but at the end of a minute I began to

feel what it truly was that I held. We were alone with the quiet day, and his little heart, disposed had stopped.

Final Scene: Shooting Script

A shooting script of Henry James's novella might read something like the scene below. In a shooting script, the screenwriter would be making considerable use of technical terms to designate camera shots to help the director heighten the dramatic tension and reinforce the actions in the scene. There would also be many more quick CUTS to direct camera angles and maximize the emotional intensity of the scene.

Remember, however, that this is the kind of *shooting script a screenwriter under contract to a studio would produce*. All other screenwriters are writing reading or speculative scripts. They should emulate the first or second examples in this chapter. The example below is provided to give students an idea of what a shooting script of this scene from Henry James's novella might look like on the printed page.

148. INT. BLY – DAY

The GOVERNESS leaps at MILES with a single bound and an irrepressible CRY.

                                            CUT TO

Miles's eyes remained fixed on a nearby window.

                                            CUT TO

A vague, GHOSTLY IMAGE is staring into the room.

                                                    CUT TO

The Governess grasps Miles and pulls him close to her breast.

                    GOVERNESS
     (shrieking at the image in the window)
   No more, no more, no more!

                                                    CUT TO

The ghostly image in the window is even more menacing.

                                                    CUT TO

Miles and the Governess are struggling.

                    MILES
     (panting, eyes closed)
   Is she here?

                    GOVERNESS
She?

                    MILES
     (furiously)
   Miss Jessel, Miss Jessel!

GOVERNESS

It's not Miss Jessel! But it's at the window—straight before us. It's here—the coward horror, there for the last time!

CUT TO

The ghostly figure is nodding at Miles.

CUT TO

Miles shakes his head frantically, GASPING for air and light as he desperately fights with the Governess to free himself from her grasp. He glares wildly around the room and in the direction of the window.

MILES

It's he?

GOVERNESS

(coldly)
Whom do you mean by 'he'?

CLOSE SHOT

Miles continues to glare wildly around the room.

WIDER ANGLE

MILES

Peter Quint—you devil!

GOVERNESS

Where? What does he matter now, my own? What will he *ever* matter? I have you.
  (to the window)
But he has lost you forever!
  (to Miles, gently)
There, there!

CLOSE SHOT

The Governess continues to clutch Miles tightly to her breast. Miles is not moving, his head is limp and he does not seem to be breathing. He is apparently dead.

GOVERNESS' POV

The Governess' gaze is fixed on the clear day outside the window.

(Note: The technical terms used in the previous three examples are defined and described more fully in Chapter 8, "Technical Terms and Techniques.")

Good Will Hunting: An Exemplary Reading Script

Many screenwriters would rank Matt Damon's and Ben Affleck's *Good Will Hunting* (1997) as one of the best reading or speculative screenplays ever written. The argument is not difficult to make. *Good Will Hunting* went on to win an Oscar for Best Original Screenplay.

A published version of the screenplay, with an introduction by Gus Van Sant who directed the film, is available through

Hyperion Books. Van Sant reminisces that his first impression of the screenplay was that it might be "a little wordy."[39] Van Sant acknowledges, however, that Damon and Affleck "put together this story with such flawless clarity of purpose in their characters" that it was impossible not to recognize it as a little masterpiece of storytelling.[40]

Damon and Affleck avoided the tendency of many aspiring screenwriters to emphasize their knowledge of screenwriting techniques and jargon in their speculative or reading scripts. Instead, the authors of *Good Will Hunting* told a compelling story with characters the audience could identify with emotionally.

Most of the scenes are splendid examples of the leaner, sparser style of screenwriting discussed throughout this book. In the following scene, Will Hunting (Matt Damon) and his girlfriend Skylar (Minnie Driver) are getting to know more about one another through some fairly common, sparse dialogue and not much in the way of screenwriting directions and techniques:

EXT. WONDERLAND RACETRACK – DAY

Will and Skylar sit in the stands watching the dogs run. They ad lib teasing one another about England, Ireland and America.

                    SKYLAR
So you grew up around here?

                    WILL
Not far from here, South Boston.

---

39 Gus Van Sant, "Introduction," Matt Damon and Ben Affleck, *Good Will Hunting* (New York: Hyperion Books, 1997) x.
40 Van Sant v.

SKYLAR

How was that?

WILL

Pretty boring, I guess.

She smiles

SKYLAR

I bet you have a great family.

WILL

You know, nothing special.

SKYLAR

You have a lot of brothers and sisters?

WILL

Do I have a lot of brothers and sisters?

SKYLAR

Yeah.

WILL

Well, Irish Catholic. What do you think?

SKYLAR

How many?

WILL

You wouldn't believe me if I told you?

                    SKYLAR

What, five?

Will shakes his head.

                    SKYLAR

Seven?

Will shakes his head, smiles.

                    SKYLAR

Come on.

                    WILL

I have twelve big brothers.

                    SKYLAR

Not a chance.

                    WILL

Yup, you're lookin' at lucky thirteen.

                    SKYLAR

Bullshit.

                    WILL

I swear to God.

                    SKYLAR

Your house must have been a zoo.

WILL
It was great. There was always someone to play with, give you advice.[41]

Note that the dialogue between these two characters is mostly short, fragmented exchanges. Very few dialogue exchanges are complete sentences, and only two are more than one sentence. Still, we learn a great deal about these two characters and their families. Will comes from a large Irish-Catholic family of all boys, and he is the youngest. He also has fond memories of his family life because there was always someone to play with and offer advice. We learn less about Skylar, except that she obviously did not come from a similar background and appears to be somewhat more privileged, although she does not flaunt whatever advantages she had in life. She seems, instead, to have a keen sense of humor and appears to be very down-to-earth and good-natured.

The action descriptions are equally sparse. After the opening two-sentence description of Will and Skylar sitting in the racetrack stands, there are only three more short action descriptions ranging from two to five words in length. The rest is left for the actors and director to interpret.

Other scenes throughout **Good Will Hunting** utilize the same sparse dialogue and brief action descriptions, avoid camera directions and other technical jargon, and focus almost exclusively on character development and storyline. For these and many other reasons, Matt Damon's and Ben Affleck's **Good Will Hunting** is an exemplary model for all aspiring screenwriters to study and emulate.

---

41 Matt Damon and Ben Affleck, *Good Will Hunting* (New York: Hyperion Books, 1997) 66-69.

EXERCISES

1. Make whatever changes are necessary in the "Final Scene: Reading Script" of *The Turn of the Screw* in this chapter to make it more clear that the Governess, not Peter Quint, killed Miles. Is this scene more or less powerful once the ambiguity is removed?
2. Similarly, make whatever changes are necessary in the same "Final Scene: Reading Script" to make it more clear that Peter Quint, not the Governess, killed Miles. Once again, is this scene more or less powerful once the ambiguity is removed?
3. John Steinbeck's novella, *Of Mice and Men*, is already written in a lean, sparse style because Steinbeck was trying to create a hybrid form of literature that combined the novel with stage drama. Select any short scene from Steinbeck's novella and rewrite it as a reading script with little or no technical terms.

CHAPTER 8

SCREENWRITING TERMS AND TECHNIQUES

Glossary of Screenwriting Terms

The problem for many beginning screenwriters is that the more they learn about screenwriting, the more they want to manipulate point of view, camera angles, and other technical devices to develop their stories. It is an understandable temptation, but it should usually be avoided. The emphasis in a reading or speculative script should always be on telling a good story, not impressing potential script readers with one's knowledge of film techniques and technical jargon.

The abbreviations and terms that designate techniques that are common in shooting scripts should be used sparingly. Some of these terms should never be used. Others that include the word "ANGLE" can be used strategically to give the reading script the *feel* of a film, but without usurping the director's role. None of the terms should be used if they impede the flow and development of the storyline. They should only be used to create a subtle cinematic effect, not impress the script reader.

The abbreviations and terms below illustrate various screenwriting techniques that are often found in reading scripts. Subsequent examples illustrate how the most common of these techniques might be used in reading scripts to create cinematic effects. Still, the dialogue, action descriptions, structure, and other elements of screenwriting should enable the story to stand alone—with or without many of these technical supports.

ANGLE ON – The subject of a shot.

ANOTHER ANGLE – Another angle on the same subject.

CLOSE SHOT – A closer shot, usually to heighten dramatic tension.

CUT TO – A quick cut to another scene. Used sparingly in reading scripts, usually when a scene shifts dramatically and unexpectedly to another location or time.

DISSOLVE TO – When one scene dissolves slowly into another scene.

EXT. – Abbreviation for exterior scene.

FADE IN – Designates the start of the screenplay.

FADE OUT – Designates the ending of the screenplay.

FLASHBACKS – Brief recreations of previous events.

INT. – Abbreviation for interior scene.

INSERT – A close shot, usually of something for the audience to read or view in detail.

MONTAGE – A series of scenes that appear in rapid succession to compress longer periods of time and events into a few seconds or minutes. It provides a quick backstory.

MOVING SHOT – Designates something that is moving.

OFF SCREEN (O.S.) – A character speaks who is in a scene, but not in a shot.

PAN – A camera shot that moves from left to right or right to left.

PAUSE OR BEAT – A brief pause in dialogue, often when a character is pondering what to say next or has a sudden shift in thoughts.

POV – The point of view of a character in a scene.

SLUG LINE OR SCENE HEADER – The capitalized LOCATION, PLACE, and TIME at the beginning of each scene.

SPLIT SCREEN – Two or more scenes viewed simultaneously.

WIDER ANGLE – The opposite of a close shot; it provides a wider view of a scene.

VOICE OVER (V. O.) – A character narrates who is usually not in the shot or the scene.

Examples of Technical Terms in a Screenplay

To illustrate the techniques listed in the "Glossary," I have excerpted some scenes from a screenplay I wrote titled, *The Sins of Rachel Sims*, which was used as an outline for a novel by the same title.[42] Thus, the action descriptions are somewhat overwritten to accommodate subsequent novel treatment. Each scene is followed by explanations for why certain screenplay terms and/or techniques were used. Although these scenes would be spread across the entire screenplay, I have designated them Scene 1-6 for easy reference. I have also bolded the technical terms in each scene for easy reference, but this is not necessary in the actual screenplay.

In this story, a young woman by the name of Laura has found evidence that she may not be the person she thinks she is. She believes she might have been kidnapped at a very young age and raised by two people she thought were her parents, but probably were not. Following a trail of clues, she traces what she believes is her true lineage back to a small town. The story opens as she is driving across some typical Midwestern farmlands.

THE SINS OF RACHEL SIMS (SCENE 1)

FADE IN

EXT. MIDWESTERN FARMLANDS – DAY

LAURA'S car moves steadily across a farming area, leaves a major highway and continues on a series of progressively narrower roads.

---

42 Dennis M. Clausen, *The Sins of Rachel Sims* (Mechanicsburg, PA: Sunbury Press, Inc.).

INT. THE CAR – CONT.

LAURA looks out the front and side windows at the passing scenery. She spots a sign indicating that she is crossing the "Archer County Line." Another sign indicates that she is about to cross the "Lonely Willow River."

EXT. A BRIDGE OUTSIDE OF TOWN – CONT.

The car approaches a bridge that is constructed out of iron beams and posts that are rusty with age. The road across the bridge is constructed out of thick wooden planks that GROAN and RUMBLE under the weight of the car.

INT. LAURA'S CAR – CONT.

LAURA studies the terrain as the car passes an area with large granite boulders protruding out of a pasture. A THIN HUMAN FIGURE in bib overalls walks out of the ditch and stands on the shoulder of the road. He seems oblivious to his surroundings.

Laura glances in her rear view mirror and sees the man cross the road and shuffle into a field.

EXT. GAS STATION – CONT.

The car pulls into a gas station on the edge of town, and LAURA steps out. The ATTENDANT, a bearded middle-aged man in grease-stained bib overalls, sits in a lawn chair, gazing into the distance. He makes no effort to acknowledge Laura's presence.

>   LAURA
> Do you work here?

                    ATTENDANT
　Ya.

                      LAURA
          (gesturing at the rusty pumps)
      Do you have any gas?

The attendant nods slowly but does not speak.

                   LAURA (CONT.)
      Can you fill it up?

The attendant stands slowly, almost reluctantly, and walks over to the gas pumps.

SHIFTING HEADERS (EXT. AND INT.)

Most screenwriters understand that if there is a scene shift from Chicago to New York City, they have to use a new header. The whole purpose of a header is to give the reader a quick visual impression of the setting as each scene in the story unfolds. If the header does not change when the action shifts to another location, the visuals become very confusing and ineffective.

Some header shifts, however, are more subtle. In the above scene, the bold **INT.** and **EXT.** header introductions must shift as the action shifts from the interior of the car to the exterior countryside, and back again. Similarly, the **CONT.** (CONTINUOUS) abbreviations signal the reader that this is a sequence of brief, connected scenes as Laura's car moves across the countryside.

Let's return to our story as Laura drives into the small town she suspects may be connected in some way to her own mysterious past.

THE SINS OF RACHEL SIMS (SCENE 2)

EXT. POINT TYSON'S MAIN STREET – DAY

LAURA'S car moves slowly down the Main Street of a Midwestern small town. The car stops next to an ELDERLY MAN walking his dog.

INT. LAURA'S CAR – CONT.

LAURA rolls down the window.

>LAURA
>Can you tell me how I can get to Sutter Street?

>ELDERLY MAN
>Straight ahead. Two blocks.

Laura studies the street signs as she continues to drive down Main Street.

She spots a YOUNG GIRL sitting on the curb with her dog. Laura stares at the girl, and it seems to bring back a distant memory.

FLASHBACK BEGINS

Another YOUNG GIRL, dressed in faded, worn clothing sits on the same curb. Behind her, the stores on Main Street look the way they might have looked thirty years earlier.

BACK TO SCENE

When Laura looks back at the curb, the girl is gone. The Main Street stores are again more modern in appearance. She is puzzled, not certain what she has just seen.

She sees the sign for "Sutter Street" and pulls up to an old house that seems to be abandoned.

EXT. AN ABANDONED HOME – CONT.

LAURA gets out of the car and looks up and down the street. Then she stares at the sun-bleached curtains that cover the front windows.

She walks up to the front door and KNOCKS. She waits and then KNOCKS again. When no one answers, she walks around the house to the backyard.

The side windows are also covered with faded curtains, except for one window.

Laura tries to see through that dust-covered window, but cannot.

She continues to walk toward the backyard, but turns when she HEARS SOMETHING behind her.

FLASHBACK BEGINS

The YOUNG GIRL she had seen sitting on the curb on Main Street is now staring at her from behind the dust-covered window.

BACK TO SCENE

Laura closes her eyes briefly and then looks back at the window. The young girl is no longer there.

FLASHBACKS

When there is a short flashback or flashbacks within the same scene, they should be designated "FLASHBACK BEGINS" and "BACK TO SCENE" or "FLASHBACK ENDS." If there are several continuous flashbacks in a screenplay, they are often treated as a montage. The brief scenes in the montage can usually be numbered or simply listed in the order in which they appear.

The following is an example of how a montage might be introduced into Laura's search for her elusive past.

THE SINS OF RACHEL SIMS (SCENE 3)

INT. LAURA'S MOTEL ROOM - NIGHT

LAURA lies on the bed, apparently pondering something that is troubling her. She reminisces about the places she has visited in the small town.

She sees herself:

MONTAGE BEGINS

Walking past the aging gravestones in the city cemetery.
Returning several times to the defunct newspaper office.
Visiting the last surviving member of a church outside of town.
Almost being run off the road by a truck.

Driving back to the cemetery and wandering among the graves again. Sitting on an embankment and gazing downriver.

MONTAGE ENDS

INT. LAURA'S MOTEL ROOM – MORNING

LAURA wakes up and doesn't seem to know where she is. Her demeanor suggests that the reminiscences had turned into troubled dreams after she fell asleep.

>   LAURA
>   (to herself)
>   What were they trying to tell me?

MONTAGES

I have bolded the montage headings in the above scene for quick reference, but that is not necessary in the screenplay itself. It is enough to mark where the "MONTAGE BEGINS" and where the "MONTAGE ENDS."

What is the reason for the montage in this scene? During Laura's search to uncover the secrets of her mysterious past, the screenwriter might want to shorten some of the events and compress them into a few seconds or minutes of film time. This is frequently done to recreate a series of experiences or to allow the main character to reflect on previous experiences, as is the case in this scene. A montage thus provides a quick backstory.

When we return to Laura's story, she is moving deeper into the world of mystery and intrigue that surrounds her early childhood. She is still a long way from finding the truth about her parentage, but she has learned that whatever happened to her when she was very young is probably connected to other mysterious events in the small town's history. Some of those events might even include a string of murders that were staged to look like accidents.

THE SINS OF RACHEL SIMS (SCENE 4)

INT. OLD VICTORIAN HOME – DAY

LAURA sits alone at a table in an older refurbished home that has been converted into a small town historical society. An elderly FEMALE EMPLOYEE places some old newspapers on the table.

> FEMALE EMPLOYEE
> Here are the articles on Norbert Samuelson's death you were looking for.

> LAURA
> Thank you.

Laura starts to page through the newspapers. She stops suddenly and looks up when she hears VOICES in an adjacent room.

> FIRST MALE VOICE (O.S.)
> That was a very sad day in this town.

> SECOND MALE VOICE (O.S.)
> Yes, it was.

> FIRST MALE VOICE (O.S.)
> Good man, Norbert Samuelson. Did a lot for Point Tyson.

SECOND MALE VOICE (O.S.)
It was a shame about that boating accident.

Laura stands and walks over to the archway separating the two rooms. She sees TWO ELDERLY MEN sitting at a table with newspapers scattered across the top.

The men give every impression that they are a couple of old timers who often frequent the historical society to reminisce about the past.

LAURA
I'm sorry, but I heard you talking about Norbert Samuelson. I was just reading some articles about his boating accident. It's really none of my business, but I was wondering why you were talking about it, too.

FIRST OLD MAN
We heard you ask the librarian for those newspaper articles.

SECOND OLD MAN
Brought back a lot of old memories.

FIRST OLD MAN
A *lot* of memories!

LAURA
Think it happened the way it was described in the newspapers?

FIRST OLD MAN
What do you mean?

LAURA
Is it possible someone wanted him dead, and made it look like an accident?

FIRST OLD MAN
Nah. Not Norbert. He had no enemies.

LAURA
All politicians have some enemies.

FIRST OLD MAN
Not Norbert.

Laura turns and walks back to the table in the adjacent room. She sits down and is reading through the newspapers when she hears the two men's VOICES again.

SECOND OLD MAN (**O.S.**)
You know, I always wondered about that too.

FIRST OLD MAN (**O.S.**)
About what?

SECOND OLD MAN (**O.S.**)
The way Norbert died. Didn't seem like him to be so careless.

FIRST OLD MAN (**O.S.**)
Accidents happen.

OFF SCREEN

The bolded (**O.S.**) in the previous scene indicate that a character or characters can be heard speaking, but they are not visible in the scene. It is commonly used in screenplays when people are speaking from adjacent locations, talking on the telephone, and other such circumstances.

Returning to our story, Laura begins to realize her own past may be connected to the many mysterious events that occurred on a place called Hodges Island a few miles outside of town. She decides to visit the island to see if it brings back any distant memories from her childhood.

Once she is alone on the island, the screenwriter is confronted with one of the biggest challenges in writing a film script: *a character in isolation.* Since there is no dialogue and no dramatic conflict between characters, the screenwriter must find other ways to bring the scene to life. One way to do this is by utilizing screenwriting techniques that create a more cinematic effect, especially in the action descriptions.

THE SINS OF RACHEL SIMS (SCENE 5)

EXT. HODGES ISLAND – DAY

LAURA is walking on a narrow dirt road that leads to the center of the island. She hears the MUFFLED CHORTLE of the BIRDS nesting in the branches of the tall trees high overhead.

WIDER ANGLE of the clouds drifting in from the north and blocking out much of the sunlight, making it seem like early evening.

ANGLE ON Laura as she walks deeper into the interior of the island.

In the distance there is the steady rumble of THUNDER.

Laura stops dead in her tracks, startled by the sight of a DEAD RABBIT lying on the dirt road.

CLOSE SHOT of the rabbit reveals that it has been gutted, and FLIES hover around its entrails and bloody carcass. The handle of a hunting knife is visible in the middle of the carcass.

> LAURA
> (looking around the area)
> Another warning!

WIDER ANGLE as a STRANGE SILENCE envelopes the island. Even the winds have died. Nothing is moving. Every living thing seems to have disappeared into its shelter or burrow.

The branches in the tall trees suddenly begin to wave frantically as a strong gust of WIND ROARS out of the sky. A cloud of leaves tears loose from the branches and showers the island.

ANGLE ON Laura as she struggles to maintain her balance. There is a LOUD SNAPPING SOUND high overhead. A large tree branch CRASHES on the ground near where she is standing.

ANGLE ON an opening in the thick canopy of leaves reveals a black tornado twisting sinisterly across the sky.

Laura turns and races back to the riverbed. All around her trees and bushes toss violently in the increasingly ferocious winds.

More tree BRANCHES SNAP and CRASH to the ground. Rain pours out of the sky.

Laura dives for cover behind a fallen tree trunk. She keeps her face pressed to the ground as she listens to the TORNADO ROAR and SCREECH across the sky.

ANGLES AND CLOSE SHOTS

Is this overdone? Probably. I condensed a lot of examples into a short scene just to illustrate how these techniques can create a number of different cinematic effects. If it were an actual reading script, the screenwriter would be wise to use them more sparingly because they lose their effect when they are overused. Still, they do illustrate how a little manipulation of ANGLE ON, WIDER ANGLE, and CLOSE SHOT can breathe considerable life into what might otherwise be a rather mundane, listless description of violent weather patterns and the threat they pose to our main character.

As the story progresses, Laura begins to remember more events from earlier in her life, long before she could even have fully developed memories. They seem to be "emotional memories" that are struggling to enter the more conscious levels of her mind. Eventually she visits an abandoned farm where she believes she lived as a young girl. As she wanders around the property and enters the farmhouse, she has a number of sustained flashbacks that should be treated as a "Flashback Sequence."

THE SINS OF RACHEL SIMS (SCENE 6)

EXT. AN ABANDONED FARM – AFTERNOON

LAURA's car turns onto a weed-infested driveway. The charred remains of a barn are evident on the edge of the farmyard.

A horse-drawn plow with long wooden handles leans against the trunk of a dead tree. Some wooden posts and rails from a split-wood fence lean awkwardly in the grass and weeds.

INT. LAURA'S CAR – CONT.

LAURA surveys the abandoned items in the farmyard as she pulls up to the house.

EXT. THE FARMYARD – CONT.

LAURA gets out of the car and looks all around. The only structure that remains is the house, which has turned a pale ghostly gray.

A frayed rope dangles from the limb of a dead tree near the house.

Laura walks over to what remains of the porch. The front door is gone and most of the windows are missing.

She steps cautiously onto the porch. On the other side of the doorway, sunlight and shadows intermingle on the wooden floor.

INT. THE FARMHOUSE – CONT.

LAURA walks into the house and sees dust particles drifting gently across the sunlight that pours in through the holes in the roof and broken windows.

She walks among the various rooms and studies the debris that has drifted into the house over the years.

EXT. THE FARMHOUSE – CONT.

LAURA soon steps outside and walks over to the dead tree with the frayed rope hanging from one limb. A piece of wood with two holes at opposite ends lies on the ground near the rope.

Laura picks up the piece of wood and runs her fingertips gently across the surface.

FLASHBACK SEQUENCE BEGINS

EXT. THE FARMYARD – MANY YEARS EARLIER

A YOUNG GIRL is on the swing, and she is being propelled higher and higher into the air by an UNSEEN PERSON who is pushing her from behind.

> WOMAN'S VOICE (O.S.)
> When you are older, my sweet. When you are older.
> Then you can swing as high as the clouds in the sky.
> But not yet, my precious. Not yet.

EXT. THE FARMYARD – A FEW YEARS LATER

The YOUNG GIRL in the previous flashback scene is older and seemingly more aware of her surroundings. She stands in the driveway next to a small suitcase.

Two arms from an UNSEEN PERSON reach out and guide her into a waiting car. The suitcase is tossed in behind her, and the door slams shut.

The young girl stands on the car seat and looks out the back window at a tall, BEARDED MAN who is waving at her. He seems to be struggling to hold back the tears.

As the car speeds away, the dust kicked up by the back tires blots out the figure of the bearded man waving at her from the driveway.

>   ANOTHER WOMAN'S VOICE (O.S.)
> Everything will be okay, Anna. Everything will be okay. It will just take some time.

The young girl reaches her hands out to the bearded man, but the dust cloud completely envelopes him.

She starts to CRY and cannot stop.

FLASHBACK SEQUENCE ENDS

LAURA still stands by the tree with the rope dangling from the limb. She clutches the piece of wood with two holes in opposite ends which was once the seat for the rope swing. She holds it tightly to her chest as she cries softly.

FLASHBACK SEQUENCE

If there are several scenes in a flashback, they should be labelled "FLASHBACK SEQUENCE BEGINS" and "FLASHBACK SEQUENCE ENDS." Otherwise the reader will struggle to distinguish between scenes in the current story and scenes from the backstory. These distinctions are clearly designated in Scene 6 of *Sins of Rachel Sims*, thus enabling the reader to savor the interplay between past and present events. They also enable the reader to understand the connections between these events.

There was a time when flashbacks and flashback sequences were discouraged in reading scripts. The advice from professional screenwriters and film producers was to "keep the storyline strictly linear." It was probably sound advice at the time. As films became more sophisticated, however, scripts readers and others in the industry began to realize that flashbacks could add a whole new dimension to storylines. Past and present events could be juxtaposed and strengthened through their mutual interactions. Like every other screenwriting technique, flashbacks should not be overused. But they should also not be avoided. The rich juxtaposition between past and present events often strengthens the dramatic intensity of the storyline.

Conclusions about Screenplay Terms and Techniques

There is a thin line between using screenplay terms and techniques too much or too little. Used strategically, they can create a vivid cinematic effect in the storyline. Thus, they help the script reader to bridge the distance between the verbal description of the screenplay story and the pictures that will eventually appear on the screen if it is made into a film. In that sense, these technical terms help the reader answer the most important question during any reading of a speculative script: *How will this screenplay actually work and look as a film?* Still, in the end it is the story that will or will not sell the screenplay. A few well-chosen technical terms might help the film possibilities emerge from the words in the script. It is, however, highly unlikely that a clutter of technical terms thrown in to impress the reader will make it a more marketable script. A well-crafted storyline will do much more to capture the attention of a film producer or book publisher.

EXERCISES

1. Short stories are excellent sources for learning the screenplay terms discussed in this chapter. Choose any short story and identify precisely where ANGLE ON, ANOTHER ANGLE, CUT TO and other screenwriting terms might be used if the story were transformed into a screenplay. Also identify the screenwriting terms that probably should be avoided in this short story, albeit they might seem appropriate.
2. Project Gutenberg has the complete texts of many literary classics. Select a short scene from one of those literary works and convert it into a screenplay scene, using the appropriate formatting terms. <http://www.gutenberg.org/wiki/Main_Page>
3. Scenes from plays are ideal for this kind of exercise because the dialogue and brief action descriptions are already formatted much like screenplays. Select several scenes from one of your favorite plays and complete the transition to screenplay form by utilizing the appropriate screenwriting terms to create cinematic effects.
4. Select a song or poem that tells a story. Read and reread it several times until you have a clear, visual image of the action. If you were to transform the song or poem into a screenplay, where would you use some of the screenwriting terms listed at the beginning of this chapter? What would these screenwriting terms do to enhance the cinematic effects?
5. In your own screenplay, select any scene in which you have used the screenwriting terms discussed in this chapter. Then rewrite that scene, deleting many of those technical terms and focusing instead on character development and plot. Which of the two scenes is more effective in developing the storyline?

CHAPTER 9

SCENES AND SEQUENCES

Introduction

Scenes and sequences are essential elements in all screenplays. A scene is generally an action or series of actions that take place in a specific location and during a specific time. A sequence is a combination of scenes that develops a subplot or substantial part of the plot of the story as a whole. Sequences are like chapters in a novel. They unite individual scenes into coherent wholes that create shorter stories within longer stories.

Most of the principles regarding scenes and sequences apply to both screenwriting and novel writing. When to get into and out of scenes, how to juxtapose individual scenes, how to determine the relative merit and developmental length of each scene in the sequence—these are important concerns in all forms of storytelling. The great advantage of the lean, stripped-down style of screenplay form is that it makes it much easier for the writer to see these relationships more clearly, and then to manipulate, cut, and develop scenes and sequences for maximum dramatic effect. This is one of the major reasons why screenplays make such excellent first drafts or outlines for novels. (See Chapter 11, "From Screenwriting to Novel Writing," for a more detailed discussion of how a screenplay can function as a first draft/outline for a novel.)

Another literary classic, Edith Wharton's *The Age of Innocence*, provides some excellent examples of how scenes and sequences work in all stories. The novel is set in New York's upper class society in the 1870s. Newland Archer, the main character, becomes trapped in a loveless marriage to the beautiful, but unexciting May Welland. When May's cousin, Countess Ellen Olenska, arrives from Europe, Newland falls passionately in love with her. He is torn between remaining in a loveless, unexciting marriage to May or following Ellen back to Europe. After much soul searching and many encounters with Ellen, he finally decides to stay with May, although Ellen remains his true love throughout his life.

Twenty-five years later, after May's death, Newland returns to Europe with his son Dallas, who has learned from his mother that Ellen was his father's true love. While they are in their hotel room, Dallas reveals to Newland what his mother told him, and he compares his father's love for Ellen to his own love for Fanny, the young woman in his life. As Newland stares out the hotel window, he expresses considerable surprise that May knew he had always loved Ellen.

The final sequence (three scenes and a general summary of the fourth scene), illustrates the way individual scenes blend together to create a story within a story. It also illustrates when writers should enter and exit scenes, and what criteria they should use in prioritizing the length and development of each scene. The scenes in the sequence from Wharton's novel are numbered to highlight the shifts from location to location. This novel sequence is then followed by the same sequence of scenes in a screenplay adaptation of *The Age of Innocence.*

Scene 1 in a Novel Sequence

Newland Archer, looking out of his hotel window at the stately gaiety of the Paris streets, felt his heart beating with the confusion and eagerness of youth.

It was long since it had thus plunged and reared under his widening waistcoat, leaving him, the next minute, with an empty breast and hot temples. He wondered if it was thus that his son's conducted itself in the presence of Miss Fanny Beaufort—and decided that it was not. "It functions as actively, no doubt, but the rhythm is different," he reflected, recalling the cool composure with which the young man had announced his engagement, and taken for granted that his family would approve.

"The difference is that these young people take it for granted that they're going to get whatever they want, and that we almost always took it for granted that we shouldn't. Only, I wonder—the thing one's so certain of in advance: can it ever make one's heart beat as wildly?"

It was the day after their arrival in Paris, and the spring sunshine held Archer in his open window above the wide silvery prospect of the Place Vendome. One of the things he had stipulated—almost the only one—when he had agreed to come abroad with Dallas, was that, in Paris, he shouldn't be made to go to one of the new-fangled "palaces."

"Oh, all right—of course," Dallas good-naturedly agreed. "I'll take you to some jolly old-fashioned place—the Bristol say—" leaving his father speechless at hearing that the century-long home of kings and emperors was now spoken of as an old-fashioned inn, where one went for its quaint inconveniences and lingering local color.

Archer had pictured often enough, in the first impatient years, the scene of his return to Paris; then the personal vision had faded, and he had simply tried to see the city as the setting of Madame Olenska's life. Sitting alone at night in his library, after the household had gone to bed, he had evoked the radiant outbreak of spring down the avenues of horse-chestnuts, the flowers and statues in the public gardens, the whiff of lilacs from the flower-carts, the majestic roll of the river under the great bridges, and the life of art and study and pleasure that filled each mighty artery to bursting. Now the spectacle was before him in its glory, and as he looked out on it he felt shy, old-fashioned, inadequate: a mere gray speck of a man compared with the ruthless magnificent fellow he had dreamed of being . . .

Dallas's hand came down cheerily on his shoulder. "Hullo, Father: this is something like, isn't it?" They stood for a while looking out in silence, and then the young man continued: "By the way, I've got a message for you: the Countess Olenska expects us both at half-past five."

He said it lightly, carelessly, as he might have imparted any casual item of information, such as the hour at which their train was to leave for Florence the next evening. Archer looked at him, and thought he saw in his gay young eyes a gleam of his great-grandmother Mingott's malice.

"Oh, didn't I tell you?" Dallas pursued. "Fanny made me swear to do three things while I was in Paris: get her the score of the last Debussy songs, go to the Grand-Guignol and see Madame Olennska. You know she was awfully good to Fanny when Mr. Beaufort sent her over from Buenos Aires to the Assumption. Fanny hadn't any friends in Paris, and Madame Olenska used to be kind to her and trot her about on holidays.

I believe she was a great friend of the first Mrs. Beaufort's. And she's our cousin, of course. So I rang her up this morning, before I went out, and told her you and I were here for two days and wanted to see her."

Archer continued to stare at him. "You told her I was here?"

"Of course—why not?" Dallas's eyebrows went up whimsically. Then, getting no answer, he slipped his arm through his father's with a confidential pressure.

"I say, Father: what was she like?"

Archer felt his color rise under his son's unabashed gaze. "Come, own up: you and she were great pals, weren't you? Wasn't she most awfully lovely?"

"Lovely? I don't know. She was different."

"Ah—there you have it! That's what it always comes to, doesn't it? When she comes, she's different—and one doesn't know why. It's exactly what I feel about Fanny."

His father drew back a step, releasing his arm. "About Fanny? But, my dear fellow—I should hope so! Only I don't see—"

"Dash it, Dad, don't be prehistoric! Wasn't she—once—your Fanny?"

Dallas belonged body and soul to the new generation. He was the first-born of Newland and May Archer, yet it had never been possible to inculcate in him even the rudiments of reserve. "What's the use of making mysteries? It only makes people want to nose 'em out," he always objected when enjoined to discretion. But Archer, meeting his eyes, saw the filial light under their banter.

"My Fanny—?"

"Well, the woman you'd have chucked everything for: only you didn't," continued his surprising son.

"I didn't," echoed Archer with a kind of solemnity.

"No: you date, you see, dear old boy. But mother said—"

"Your mother?"

"Yes: the day before she died. It was when she sent for me alone—you remember? She said she knew we were safe with you, and always would be, because once, when she asked you to, you'd given up the thing you most wanted."

Archer received this strange communication in silence. His eyes remained unseeingly fixed on the thronged sun-lit square below the window. At length he said in a low voice: "She never asked me."

"No. I forgot. You never did ask each other anything, did you? And you never told each other anything. You just sat and watched each other, and guessed at what was going on underneath. A deaf-and-dumb asylum, in fact! Well, I back your generation for knowing more about each other's private thoughts than we ever have time to find out about our own. I say, Dad," Dallas broke off, "you're not angry with me? If you are, let's make it up and go and lunch at Henri's. I've got to rush out to Versailles afterward."

Scene 2 in a Novel Sequence

Archer did not accompany his son to Versailles. He preferred to spend the afternoon in solitary roamings through Paris. He had to deal all at once with the packed regrets and stifled memories of an inarticulate lifetime.

After a little while he did not regret Dallas's indiscretion. It seemed to take an iron band from his heart to know that, after all, someone had guessed and pitied . . . And that it should have been his wife moved him indescribably. Dallas, for all his affectionate insight, would not have understood that. To the boy, no doubt, the episode was only a pathetic instance of vain frustration, of wasted forces. But was it really no more? For a long time Archer sat on a bench in the Champs Elysees and wondered, while the stream of life rolled by . . .

A few streets away, a few hours away, Ellen Olenska waited. She had never gone back to her husband, and when he had died, some years before, she had made no change in her way of living. There was nothing now to keep her and Archer apart—and that afternoon he was to see her.

He got up and walked across the Place de la Concorde and the Tuileries gardens to the Louvre. She had once told him that she often went there, and he had a fancy to spend the intervening time in a place where he could think of her as perhaps having lately been.

Scene 3 in a Novel Sequence

For an hour or more he wandered from gallery to gallery through the dazzle of afternoon light, and one by one the pictures burst on him in their half-forgotten splendor, filling his soul with the long echoes of beauty. After all, his life had been too starved . . .

Suddenly, before an effulgent Titian, he found himself saying: "But I'm only fifty-seven—" and then he turned away. For such summer dreams it was too late; but surely not for a quiet harvest of friendship, of comradeship in the blessed hush of her nearness.

Scene 4 in a Novel Sequence

He went back to the hotel, where he and Dallas were to meet; and together they walked again across the Place de la Concorde and over the bridge that leads to the Chamber of Deputies . . .[43]

(Scene 4 in the sequence is much too long to reproduce in its entirety. Here is a quick summary: Newland and Dallas wander through the streets of Paris, reminiscing and gradually making their way over to Countess Olenska's apartment. Once there,

---

43 Edith Wharton, *The Age of Innocence* (The Project Gutenberg Etext of *The Age of Innocence*) 213-18. <www.gutenberg.org>

Newland must decide whether or not he will accompany Dallas when his son visits Countess Olenska, the woman Newland has loved all of his life even though he was married to May.)

Screenplay Sequence from *The Age of Innocence*

If the four scenes from *The Age of Innocence* were converted into screenplay form, there would be many cuts, but the focus should be on preserving the inner spirit of the sequence. This inner spirit involves Newland Archer's many conflicting motives when he returns to Paris, perhaps for the last time, and is forced to reevaluate his feelings for both Ellen and his wife May. The screenplay sequence below is followed by a discussion of some of the general principles regarding scenes and sequences that are illustrated in the adaptation and that apply to most forms of storytelling.

INT. A HOTEL IN PARIS - DAY

NEWLAND ARCHER is standing by a window, looking down at the streets of Paris. His son DALLAS approaches and stands next to him. They look out the window together.

> DALLAS
> I say, father, what was she like?

> NEWLAND
> Countess Olenska?

> DALLAS
> Come, own up. You and she were great pals, weren't you? Wasn't she most awfully lovely?

NEWLAND
Lovely? I don't know. She was different.

DALLAS
Dash it, Dad, don't be prehistoric! Wasn't she— once— your Fanny?

NEWLAND
My Fanny?

DALLAS
Well, the woman you'd have chucked everything for. Only you didn't.

NEWLAND
(solemnly)
I didn't.

DALLAS
No, you date, you see, dear old boy. But mother said—

NEWLAND
Your mother?

DALLAS
Yes, the day before she died. It was when she sent for me alone—you remember? She said she knew we were safe with you, and always would be, because once, when she asked you to, you'd given up the thing you most wanted.

Newland remains SILENT, his eyes unseeingly fixed on the thronged sunlit square below the window.

NEWLAND
She never asked me.

DALLAS
No. I forgot. You never did ask each other anything, did you? And you never told each other anything. You just sat and watched each other, and guessed at what was going on underneath. A deaf-and-dumb asylum, in fact! Well, I back your generation for knowing more about each other's private thoughts than we ever have time to find out about our own.

The two men continue to stand SILENTLY, looking out the window. Dallas appears to be uneasy, as though he has intruded on his father's privacy.

DALLAS
I say, Dad, you're not angry with me? If you are, let's make it up and go and lunch at Henri's. I've got to rush out to Versailles afterward.

Newland nods. He continues to stand at the window long after Dallas has left the room.

EXT. STREETS OF PARIS - DAY

NEWLAND is roaming through the streets of Paris, lost in his thoughts. He walks across the Place de la Concorde and the

Tuileries gardens to the Louvre. He is oblivious to his surroundings. His mind is fixed on other thoughts and other memories.

INT. PARIS ART GALLERIES - DAY

NEWLAND wanders from gallery to gallery. He is mesmerized by the beautiful paintings. They seem to fill his soul with the long echoes of beauty and remind him of the many voids in his own life.

>NEWLAND
>(oblivious to what he is saying)
>But I'm only fifty-seven—

EXT. STREETS OF PARIS - DAY

NEWLAND and DALLAS walk again across the Place de la Concorde and over the bridge that leads to the Chamber of Deputies. Newland is deeply lost in his thoughts.

Dallas pauses abruptly and grasps his father's arm.

>DALLAS
>Oh, by jove, Countess Ellen lives around here.

Newland nods knowingly but does not speak. The two men walk into a square radiating from the Invalides. The day is fading and the square is almost abandoned. Dallas stops, looks up and grasps his father's arm.

>DALLAS (CONT.)
>It must be here.

Storytelling as Art and Craftsmanship

ANGLE ON a modern building, without distinctive character, but many-windowed, and pleasantly balconied up its wide cream-colored front. On one of the upper balconies, which hung well above the rounded tops of the horse-chestnuts in the square, the awnings were still lowered, as though the sun had just left it.

ANGLE ON Newland and Dallas as they stare at the building

>DALLAS (CONT.)
>I wonder which floor? The fifth. It must be the one with the awnings.

Newland remains motionless, gazing at the upper windows.

>DALLAS (CONT.)
>I say, you know, it's nearly six.

Newland glances at an empty bench under the trees.

>NEWLAND
>I believe I'll sit there a moment.

>DALLAS
>Why? Aren't you well?

>NEWLAND
>Oh, perfectly. But I should like you, please, to go up without me.

Dallas is visibly bewildered.

                    DALLAS
But, I say, Dad. Do you mean you won't come up at all?

                    NEWLAND
  (slowly)
I don't know.

                    DALLAS
If you don't, she won't understand.

                    NEWLAND
Go, my boy. Perhaps I shall follow you.

Dallas gives his father a long look through the twilight.

                    DALLAS
But what on earth shall I say?

                    NEWLAND
  (smiling)
My dear fellow, don't you always know what to say?

                    DALLAS
Very well. I shall say you're old-fashioned, and prefer walking up the five flights because you don't like lifts.

                    NEWLAND
Say I'm old-fashioned. That's enough.

Dallas is incredulous. He clearly does not comprehend how his father could have come so far to reunite with the woman he had loved all his life, and then decide instead to sit on a bench outside her apartment.

Dallas leaves and Newland sits down on the bench and gazes at the awninged balcony.

SERIES OF ANGLES of Newland, sitting on the bench. His eyes remain fixed on the balcony.

> NEWLAND (CONT.)
> (softly, gently)
> It's more real to me here than if I went up.

Newland sits for a long time on the bench in the thickening dusk. His eyes never turn from the balcony. A light shines through the windows, and a MAN-SERVANT comes out on the balcony, draws up the awnings, and closes the shutters.

As if it had been the signal he waited for, Newland gets up slowly and walks back alone to his hotel.

Tips on Developing Effective Scenes and Sequences

- **It is not necessary, even counterproductive, to develop each scene from beginning to middle to end.** A rule of thumb with many scenes is to get in late, get out early. This keeps the story moving. For example, in the opening scene in this sequence, Newland and Dallas are already in the hotel room, and Newland is staring out the window at the streets of Paris. There is no need to have the two men open the door of the hotel room, take off their coats, open their valises, and attend to everything people do when they enter a hotel room. Those actions serve no dramatic purpose. They simply clutter up the scene. Having Newland already standing by the window, looking out at the streets of Paris, starts the scene at a particularly poignant moment when he is obviously thinking about Countess Ellen Olenska.

- **End many scenes early.** This scene ends with Newland still standing by the window, which is where it should end. The events in the hotel room after Dallas has left do not have to include Newland leaving the window, dressing to go outside, and closing the door behind him. These are all mundane, unnecessary actions that do nothing to advance the storyline. Instead, the action shifts immediately to the streets of Paris where Newland is walking and apparently continuing to reminisce about the past. Exiting the scene early enables the sequence to continue to build in dramatic and emotional intensity, rather than become cluttered with mundane actions of no real value to the storyline.

- **Some scenes can be summarized quickly.** For example, the scenes in the art galleries speak to the many emotional voids in Newland's life, but the point does not need to be belabored. It is probably more effective when it is subtly implied in the way he gazes longingly at the many beautiful paintings. Varying scenes of different lengths also keeps the pacing and movement of the storyline from becoming tediously predictable.

- **Whether a scene is developed in its entirety or in part depends on how important the scene is to the sequence or the story as a whole.** The scene with Newland and Dallas in the hotel is crucial to developing their relationship and the generational gap between father and son. Hence, it is developed in some detail. Similarly, the scene on the streets of Paris, near the Ellen's apartment, is arguably the most important scene in the story. In this scene, the reader/viewer learns whether Newland will take advantage of one final opportunity to consummate his love for Ellen. Hence, this scene also deserves to be developed in some detail.

- **Every scene, regardless of length, needs to make at least one major contribution to the plot.** Even the brief scene in the art gallery, while Newland is surrounded by "beauty," reveals that his soul longs to live the remaining years of his life with the beautiful Countess Ellen Olenska, although he eventually decides not to see her again.
- **Some scenes can be cleverly written so they serve several purposes simultaneously.** The opening scene in the hotel room develops three major threads in the storyline: Newland has loved Ellen all of his married life; his son Dallas is part of a new generation that does not feel so constrained by society or conscience to keep those forbidden subjects private; and Newland learns that his rather dull, unexciting wife May might not have been so dull and unexciting after all. May always knew her husband loved another woman, and yet she remained devoted and faithful to him throughout their marriage. Behind every scene in the sequence is not only the sense that Newland is constantly reevaluating his love for Ellen, but also his marriage to May. She was able to love a man and remain devoted to him throughout her life, even though he did not have the same feelings for her. This had to be in the back of Newland's mind throughout this sequence, even

as Dallas ignores that possibility and only conjectures rather superficially that his father must want to reconnect with Ellen now that he is back in Paris.

- **Sequences often develop smaller stories within bigger stories.** This sequence also develops the deep, loving bond between Newland and his son. Although Newland may have felt trapped at times in a loveless marriage, he realizes May gave him two children who cared deeply for their father. Newland's loving bond with his son certainly has to weigh on his mind as another of the many gifts May bestowed upon him in spite of his emotional distance from her. This father-son bond is a smaller story within the larger story of Newland's love for Ellen and some pangs of conscience he must feel that he should have done more to show May he loved her while she was still alive.

- **Every sequence should have threads that connect it to the previous sequence and the sequence that is to follow.** No sequence can exist in isolation from the rest of the story. This final sequence concludes Newland's love affair with Ellen, the central plot in the story, while simultaneously preparing the reader for the new generation that will take over once the "Age of Innocence" has passed.

- **Sequences sometimes connect beginning and ending scenes in the same way opening and closing scenes are often connected in the story as a whole.** After Newland learns in the opening scene that May was always aware of his deep love for Ellen, his motives for acting as he does for the rest of the sequence are open to speculation and different interpretations. Indeed, the final scene is a testimonial to the ability of ambiguity to create a richer, more powerful ending to a story. Undoubtedly, Newland ponders Dallas's revelations regarding May, albeit those emotions are often disguised behind his deeply felt love for Ellen. Perhaps Newland's real motive for leaving without seeing Ellen is not to preserve his memory of her in all of its youthful, romantic purity, as many readers have suggested. Perhaps it is the gradual realization that he was never a fully committed husband to May that explains his decision not to go up to see Ellen. Maybe he feels he owes it to May's memory, after what he learned from his son, to forego any kind of relationship with Ellen even after his wife's death.

Pacing Scenes in a Sequence: *Cat Ballou*

Individual scenes must be timed and paced to establish the relative importance of each scene to the sequence in which it appears. Timing is important in all films: In comedies, it is essential. Comedies are dependent on precise timing of individual scenes if they are to work at all.

Cat Ballou (1965), the film comedy that launched both Lee Marvin and Jane Fonda to stardom, is a little classic of comic timing. The plot and characters would be readily identifiable to anyone familiar with the western genre in films, novels, and short stories. There are also some delightful twists on the western genre, some so clever and imaginative that they earned Walter Newman and Frank Pierson an Oscar nomination for their screenplay adaptation of a novel by Roy Chanslor.

The plot involves Catherine Ballou (Jane Fonda), who has been in the civilized east studying to be a schoolteacher. When she travels by train to visit her rancher father in Wolf City, Wyoming, she meets two charming con men, Clay Boone (Michael Callan) and Jed (Dwayne Hickman), who will become her sidekicks and accomplices in subsequent adventures. In Wolf City, Cat learns that the Wolf City Development Corporation is doing everything in its power to take her father's ranch away from him. They have hired Tim Strawn (Lee Marvin), a comically malevolent gunfighter with a tin nose, to intimidate her father into turning over his ranch to them. Cat quickly learns that the Wolf City Development Corporation and Tim Strawn are too much for her to take on with her sidekicks. She decides instead to hire her own gunfighter, Kid Shelleen (also played by Lee Marvin), to protect her father and the ranch.

The individual scenes in this sequence, starting with Cat's decision to send for Kid Shelleen, are summarized below, along with the rationale for the film time each scene is allotted. Sometimes it is helpful to time and compare individual scenes in a sequence to determine why the screenwriter, director, and/or film editors paced the story as they did. This sequence runs approximately 13 minutes and 30 seconds. Since every page in a screenplay translates into a minute of playing time, this entire sequence would occupy approximately 13 ½ pages of the script.

(Note: Each scene would have an individual header. However, I have designated them differently for quick reference.)

First scene in the sequence (5 minutes, 5 seconds): Cat is in her bedroom on her father's ranch, getting ready for bed. She does not know that Clay has concealed himself in the covers on the other side of the bed. As Cat closes her eyes, Clay reveals his presence and seductive motives for being in the bedroom. As they talk, it becomes clear that Clay is a cad, but he also seems to be sincerely concerned about Cat's safety because he tells her maybe she should get her own gunfighter. After Clay finally leaves, Cat spots a Western Dime Novel on the nightstand. She picks it up and walks over to a writing desk. She starts her letter to Kid Shelleen

Storytelling as Art and Craftsmanship

as the angle falls on the dime novel. A highly glamorized, idealized portrait of a western gunfighter is faintly visible on the cover.

Rationale: This is a fairly long scene because it develops several important elements in the plot. It hints at a possible love relationship between Clay and Cat, albeit Cat does not yet trust him. Clay's comments regarding the world she has wandered into, and her need for a gunfighter, strengthens the antagonist (Tim Strawn) in the story and makes him more formidable. Most importantly, at the end of the scene the Western Dime Novel introduces Kid Shelleen, the most important character in the film.

Second scene in the sequence (1 minute, 40 seconds): Nat King Cole and Stubby Kaye, the western troubadours who interrupt the action periodically like some Greek Chorus, summarize the action up to this point in the plot. The angle then shifts to Cat and her motley crew as they stand on the streets of Wolf City, waiting for a stagecoach. As the passengers depart, a tall, muscular man, dressed immaculately in a dark suit and wearing pearl-handled revolvers in a fancy holster, steps out of the stagecoach. Cat's eyes light up as she gazes at the person she believes to be the legendary Kid Shelleen from the Western Dime Novel. Moments later, a woman and several children rush over and surround the man. Cat quickly realizes that this is not the gunfighter she has sent for. The stagecoach drivers then walk to the back of the stagecoach, lift a leather tarp, and roll the drunken Kid Shelleen onto the street. Kid Shelleen is in an alcoholic haze and sprawls face down in the dirt.

Rationale: There is no need to show Cat and her accomplices traveling to Wolf City. It serves no dramatic purpose. It is enough to have them standing on the street when the scene opens. Nonetheless, this scene is important because it introduces the most important character in the film. Although the film is named after Cat Ballou, Kid Shelleen dominates every scene in which he appears. He needs to make a timely entrance that is appropriately memorable for his central role in the film.

Third scene in the sequence (6 minutes, 40 seconds): The logical third scene in the sequence would have been the trip back to the Ballou ranch. However, the screenwriter, director, or film editor cut it for the same reason the trip to town was cut. Neither scene served any real purpose in the development of the storyline. Instead, there is a quick cut to the ranch. The same characters are gathered in the yard next to the barn, trying to decide what to do with the drunken gunfighter they have hired. Frankie Ballou, Cat's father, decides to test Kid Shelleen to determine if he has any gun fighting ability whatsoever. This is by far the longest scene in the sequence—and for good reason. The character of Kid Shelleen, who will dominate the film, is fleshed out considerably in this scene. We witness Cat's sense of despair as her gunfighter turns out to be a hopeless drunk. We watch Cat's father express his complete and total disgust with the gunfighter his daughter has hired to protect him and his ranch. Most importantly, we learn that Kid Shelleen, although he cannot hit the broad side of a barn when he is sober, can shoot tin cans out of the air when he is primed with whisky. When he reaches the point where he has had too much to drink, however, he is again totally inept as a gunfighter. Shelleen is so compromised by his alcoholic binges that he cannot pull his gun out of its holster without tearing off his pants. The comic irony is that the people Kid Shelleen has come to Wolf City to rescue may have to rescue him instead.

Rationale: This scene develops the character of Kid Shelleen, fleshes out Cat's dilemma, and establishes the comic premise that will function throughout the film. Shelleen is worthless as a gunfighter when he is either sober or completely inebriated, but he has uncanny gun fighting skills during the few lucid moments after he has had a few drinks. We know there is something authentic about Kid Shelleen, albeit it is buried somewhere beneath his thirst for whiskey. This scene must be developed in its entirety to reveal all of Kid Shelleen's subtleties and nuances as a comic character who will be the primary source of the humor for the remainder of the film.

A Final Note Regarding Scenes and Sequences

I have worked with many editors over the past four decades. The writing projects included novels, creative nonfiction, screenplays, textbooks, newspaper op-eds, and a newspaper column. All of these editors taught me something about writing and revising for publication. Perhaps they did not achieve the legendary status of Maxwell Perkins, the legendary editor for Ernest Hemingway and F. Scott Fitzgerald, but they were certainly professionals in every sense of the word. The most important lessons they taught me were how to make cuts and tighten up a manuscript. The best of these editors seemed to have an uncanny ability to recognize what needed to be cut, condensed, or expanded. I did not have that skill, at least earlier in my career, so these editors helped me develop it.

It was not until I started to work with screenplay form, however, that I began to develop a better sense of what these editors already knew regarding ways to cut and tighten up a manuscript and storyline for publication. When I began to think in terms of screenwriting techniques, even in the many diverse genres cited throughout this book, I started to see these issues more clearly. This was especially true when I began to apply the strategies discussed in this chapter.

Dennis M. Clausen

Today, many publishing companies require writers to become better editors of their own writing projects. Personally, I think every writer needs an editor. However, the realities are that we writers must become better editors of our own writing because not all publishers are going to do it for us. Screenwriting strategies, especially when applied to works of fiction, are invaluable resources for achieving these essential skills.

Storytelling as Art and Craftsmanship

EXERCISES

1. Chose any short story and block it off into individual scenes to be transformed into a screenplay. Then list each of the scene headings using the conventions that were described in Chapter 8. Next, under each header describe whether the scene should be fully developed, partially developed, quickly summarized, or eliminated. Finally, indicate where you, as the screenwriter, would choose to enter and exit each scene.
2. Choose a scene from one of your favorite movies and identify the connecting threads that unite the scene to the sequence in which it appears and to the film as a whole. Conversely, identify a scene in a movie that is not connected to a sequence or the film as a whole. Can we generalize that these connecting threads are usually found in superior screenwriting, but not in less effective screenwriting?
3. Put a stopwatch to the individual scenes in any sequence from one of your favorite movies. Then explain why the screenwriter, director, and/or film editor decided to devote less time to developing some scenes and more time to developing others.
4. Some song lyrics demonstrate how writers can create concise character descriptions, action sequences, and compelling plots using very few words. One such song is Kenny Rogers' "Lucille," which creates three very strong characters and an emotionally packed dramatic situation in less than forty lines. The characters could have stepped right out of a film: the wandering drifter with a conscience; the farm wife tired of living in bone-crushing poverty and desperate for a little fun and laughter; and a weather-beaten, muscular farmer who must care for four hungry children and harvest his crops

after his wife leaves him. We know these three characters as well as we would if they had been developed over several pages in a novel. Locate the lyrics for the song "Lucille" at www.musicsonglyrics.com or some other internet source, and then block off the various scenes in screenplay form with the designated headers "INT." and "EXT." Then describe whether in the context of the story each scene should be developed briefly or in some detail. Also describe when each scene should begin and end to maximize the dramatic impact. (In Chapter 11, "Writing Dialogue," one exercise will ask you to provide appropriate dialogue for the three characters in this story.)

5. Project Gutenberg www.gutenberg.org has the complete text of *The Age of Innocence.* Select any series of scenes that tell a story within the larger story, and convert those scenes into a screenplay sequence. Be prepared to explain why you developed some scenes more fully than others. Also be prepared to explain why some scenes in the sequence could be omitted, summarized quickly, or entered much later than they are in the novel.

6. Select any sequence in your own screenplay and time the individual scenes. (Remember that one page in a screenplay is approximately one minute of film time.) Is the time allotted for each scene in the sequence consistent with the principles of sequencing illustrated in *The Age of Innocence* and *Cat Ballou*? Also, explain the reasons for how you chose to enter and exit the individual scenes in the sequence.

CHAPTER 10

WRITING DIALOGUE

Introduction

Some of the great movie one-liners look rather inconspicuous on the printed page:

Butch Cassidy and the Sundance Kid: "Who are those guys?"
Cool Hand Luke: "What we've got here is . . . failure to communicate."
Chinatown: "Forget it, Jake, it's Chinatown."
The Godfather: "I'll make him an offer he can't refuse."
Grand Hotel: "I vant to be alone."
Gone With the Wind: "Frankly, my dear, I don't give a damn."
Casablanca: "Here's looking at you, kid."
On the Waterfront: "I coulda been a contender."
Gone With the Wind: "After all, tomorrow is another day."
The Graduate: "Mrs. Robinson, you're trying to seduce me."

Network: "I'm mad as hell, and I'm not going to take this anymore."
Love Story: "Love means never having to say you're sorry."

Most of these famous movie lines consist of no more than four to eight very common words. There is nothing magical about those words, either individually or collectively. Yet, they have been transformed into magical moments for everyone who has ever heard them on the silver screen.

This transformation reflects both the power of screen dialogue and the frustrations many screenwriters experience when they try to write it. It is highly unlikely that the screenwriters who wrote these lines anticipated that someday film audiences everywhere would remember them. Yet, something in those common words made them legendary.

In one respect, writing effective dialogue is a gift. America has produced many writers who have the musical equivalent of perfect pitch. When they hear dialects or unique dialogue, these writers seem to be able to reproduce what they have heard almost effortlessly on the printed page. The master of dialogue in our literary canon is, of course, Samuel Clemens, alias Mark Twain. Literary critics have identified numerous regional dialects in Mark Twain's *The Adventures of Huckleberry Finn*, each one flawlessly reproduced. Novelist Sinclair Lewis had a similar skill. In *Main Street*, Lewis accurately reproduced many different Midwestern dialects, including the speech patterns of European-born, small town characters who were in various stages of learning English. Not to be outdone by her male counterparts, Willa Cather wrote several magnificent novels, including *My Antonia* and *O Pioneers!*, that reflected her uncanny ability to reproduce on the printed page the dialects she had first heard as a young girl when her family moved from Virginia to Red Cloud, Nebraska.

Does this mean a screenwriter has to be born with this gift to write effective dialogue? Fortunately, the answer to this question is, "No!" Otherwise, we would not have so many great films with superb dialogue. There would never be enough screenwriters with perfect pitch to write them.

Movie *dialogue* is not the same as the *dialects* reproduced in novels, although they have much in common and are both the products of a skillfully trained ear. Indeed, one of the keys to writing effective screenplay dialogue is to remember that writing dialogue is an auditory, not a visual or conceptual skill. *A good rule of thumb is to write action descriptions for the eye, dialogue for the ear.*

My screenwriting students often ask me, "How can I write more effective dialogue?" Unfortunately, I do not have an easy answer for them, and they sometimes think I am being evasive or unresponsive when I say, "Writing effective dialogue comes through experience. The more you write dialogue, the better you will become at writing it." There are some strategies to improve dialogue, and they will be discussed throughout this chapter. However, writing effective dialogue is one of those skills that comes mostly through practice.

This touches on an essential lesson for all students who are learning to write screenplays. Screenplays are not written: They are rewritten—over and over again. Every rewrite makes the characters more alive in the writer's imagination, and characters who start to look and act like real people will also start to sound like real people when they speak. Until screenwriters really know their characters and think of them as real people, it is difficult to find appropriate speech patterns for them.

Screenplay dialogue is certainly not formal English prose of the type students practice in their English classes whenever they are required to write an expository essay. Formal English prose is the kiss of death in most screenplays and other forms of creative writing. However, most screenplay dialogue usually does not go to the other extreme: human talk as we might hear it on the streets. Screenplay dialogue has much in common with real-life human speech patterns, but it is generally a refined version of human talk as we might hear it in real-life situations. The rest is up to the actors to interpret and bring it to life.

What is Bad Dialogue?

What is bad dialogue? Let's look at someone who wrote a lot of it: James Fenimore Cooper, author of *The Leatherstocking Tales* (1823-1841). Cooper contributed much to American literature. He introduced several major literary genres to our national literature, created the Leatherstocking character who is the surrogate father of countless literary and film characters (including Butch Cassidy and the Sundance Kid), and wrote splendid descriptions of the pristine, almost Edenic American wilderness.

In spite of these accomplishments, few would argue that Cooper wrote good dialogue. He had a tin ear, and he violated just about every principle of writing effective dialogue. All writers would be wise to avoid just about everything Cooper did when he wrote dialogue. This is evident in the following exchange between two frontiersmen in *The Deerslayer* (1841). Deerslayer (Leatherstocking) and Hurry Harry have just stepped into a small clearing in the wilderness after what has apparently been a long trip. They immediately engage in a rather subjective philosophical discussion of the types of laws regarding ownership and property rights that apply and don't apply on the American frontier:

Dialogue Scene: *The Deerslayer*

"What! Did you never find a fellow thieving among your traps and skins, and do the law on him, with your own hands, by way of saving the magistrates trouble, in the settlements, and the rogue himself the costs of the suit?"

"I am no trapper, Hurry," returned the young man proudly. "I live by the rifle, a we'pon at which I will not turn my back on any man of my years, atween the Hudson and the St. Lawrence. I never offer a skin, that has not a hole in its head, besides them which natur' made to see with, or to breathe through. "

"Ay, ay, this is all very well, in the animal way, though it makes but a poor figure alongside of scalps and and-bushes. Shooting an Indian from an and-bush is acting up to his own principles, and now we have what you call a lawful war on our hands, the sooner you wipe that disgrace off your character, the sounder will be your sleep; if it only come from knowing there is one inimy the less prowling in the woods. I shall not frequent your society long, friend Natty, unless you look higher than four-footed beasts to practyse your rifle on."

"Our journey is nearly ended you say, Master March, and we can part to-night, if you see occasion. I have a fri'nd waiting for me, who will think it no disgrace to consort with a fellow-creatur' that has never yet slain his kind."

"I wish I knew what has brought that skulking Delaware into this part of the country so early in the season," muttered Hurry to himself, in a way to show equally distrust and a recklessness of its betrayal. "Where did you say the young chief was to give you the meeting?"

"At a small round rock, near the foot of the lake, where, they tell me, the tribes are given to resorting to make their treaties, and to bury the hatchets. This rock have I often heard the Delawares mention, though lake and rock are equally strangers to me. The country is claimed by both Mingos and Mohicans, and is a sort of common territory to fish and hunt through, in time of peace, though what it may become in wartime, the Lord only knows!"

"Common territory!" exclaimed Hurry, laughing aloud. "I should like to know what Floating Tom Hutter would say to that? He claims the lake as his own property, in virtue of fifteen years' possession, and will not be likely to give it up to either Mingo or Delaware without a battle for it."

"And what will the colony say to such a quarrel? All this country must have some owner, the gentry pushing their cravings into the wilderness, even where they never dare to ventur', in their own persons, to look at the land they own."[44]

This scene, with long exchanges of dialogue that often sound like alternating monologues between the two speakers, goes on for several pages. Here are some of the problems with this kind of dialogue:

- **There is no dramatic tension in this scene**. Furthermore, the entire scene is a long, rambling digression from the plot. A scene that has no dramatic tension and is largely irrelevant to the plot will inevitably create unnecessary, irrelevant dialogue.
- **The dialogue is not appropriate** for these two uneducated, semi-literate frontiersmen. At times, they sound like philosophers of the forest, and at other times like country bumpkins. The dialogue must be consistently compatible with the characters who are speaking it.
- **Sentence structures are too formal**, with some superficial attempts to rough up the spellings of a few words to create

---

44 James Fenimore Cooper, *The Deerslayer* (New York: The C. T. Brainard Publishing Co., 1910) 19-20.

an ineffective imitation of the vernacular. Cooper appears to be writing dialogue more for the eye than the ear.
- **Dialogue is too long** for the paucity of information it conveys. Furthermore, these exchanges need some variety. These long chunks of alternating dialogue between the two speakers, running on for several pages, become exceedingly tedious and irrelevant to the storyline. If this were a screenplay, it would destroy the storyline and any semblance of dramatic tension.
- **Cooper ignores the context** that should generate an appropriate dialogue. Two frontiersmen who have traveled for miles are probably more likely to talk about finding something to eat and drink. They are highly unlikely to engage in a debate about the laws that govern property rights on the American frontier.
- **The two frontiersmen do nothing for much too long**. A long, run-on scene with absolutely no action will need some powerful dialogue to sustain the reader's interest.

What is Effective Dialogue?

Mark Twain, one of the greatest writers of dialogue and dialect in all of American literature, would agree with this assessment of Cooper's dialogue. Twain wrote a blistering satire of Cooper's artistic and stylistic failings. In the satire, titled "Fenimore Cooper's Literary Offences," Twain claims Cooper violated eighteen of the nineteen rules that govern fiction. According to Twain, several of these rules pertain to the writing of dialogue, including: "They require that when the personage of a tale deal in conversation, the talk shall sound like human talk, and be talk such as human beings would be likely to talk in the given circumstances . . . and be interesting to the reader, and help out the tale, and stop when the people cannot think of anything more to say."[45]

Twain came into the world with an obsessive curiosity about the way people speak. He would visit the slave quarters on his uncle's farm and listen for hours to the slaves tell their stories in fractured, uneducated English. He found these stories, and the way the slaves told them, to be far more effective than stories told with the more proper English language we had inherited from Great Britain. Throughout his life, Twain gave those slaves considerable credit for teaching him that the *manner* of telling the story is far more important than the *matter* of the story.[46] There is even considerable evidence that the voice of Huckleberry Finn, which Ernest Hemingway believed liberated our national literary canon from the British tradition, came from the speech patterns of a young African-American boy Twain met later in life.[47]

Twain was also a stage performer who quickly learned that writing performance dialogue created far more authentic dialogue than merely writing it for the printed page. He trained his ear in every way to listen to the slight changes in accents or syllables that distinguished authentic dialogue from ineffective dialogue. He read virtually everything out loud to friends and relatives to judge how a real human audiences would react to his word choices, inflections, accents, and other speech patterns. Eventually, he would say, "The difference between the almost right word and the right word is really a large matter. It's the difference between

---

45 Mark Twain, "Fenimore Cooper's Literary Offences," *The Norton Anthology of American Literature.* Short. 5th ed. (New York: W. W. Norton and Company, 1999) 1457-58.

46 "Jim's Journey," The Huck Finn Freedom Center <jimsjourney.org/danielquarles>

47 Depalma, Anthony, "A Scholar Finds Huck Finn's Voice in Twain's Writing About a Black Youth," New York Times, July 7, 1992.

the lightning bug and the lightning."⁴⁸ He saw all of the failures of writing poor, ineffective dialogue in James Fenimore Cooper's *The Leatherstocking Tales*, and he was deeply offended when two scholars and a literary critic declared Cooper to be the best novelist our nation had produced.⁴⁹

We can easily demonstrate the differences between Twain's mastery of dialect and dialogue, and Cooper's inept attempts to rough up formal English in a weak attempt to make his dialogue sound like authentic frontier speech. In the following scene from *The Adventures of Huckleberry Finn* (1884), a drunken lower-class character named Boggs confronts and challenges Colonel Sherburne, a cold-hearted, unflappable member of a much higher social class. Twain uses Huck Finn as his literary persona to narrate this scene in flawless semi-literate prose:

Dialogue Scene: *The Adventures of Huckleberry Finn*

Boggs comes a-tearing along on his horse, whooping and yelling like an Injun, and singing out—

"Cler the track, thar. I'm on the waw-path, and the price uv coffins is a gwyne to raise."

He was drunk, and weaving about in his saddle; he was over fifty year old, and had a very red face. Everybody yelled at him, and laughed at him, and sassed him, and he sassed back, and said he'd attend to them and lay them out in their regular turns, but he couldn't wait now, because he'd come to town to kill old Colonel Sherburn, and his motto was, "meat first, and spoon vittles to top off on."

He see me, and rode up and says—

"Whar'd you come f'm, boy? You prepared to die?"

---

48 www.twainquotes.com
49 Mark Twain, "Fenimore Cooper's Literary Offences," 1457.

Then he rode on. I was scared; but a man says—

"He don't mean nothing; he's always a carryin' on like that, when he's drunk. He's the best-naturedest old fool in Arkansaw—never hurt nobody, drunk nor sober."

Boggs rode up before the biggest store in town and bent his head down so he could see under the curtain of the awning, and yells—

"Come out here, Sherburn! Come out and meet the man you've swindled. You're the houn' I'm after, and I'm a gwyne to have you, too!"

And so he went on, calling Sherburn everything he could lay his tongue to, and the whole street packed with people listening and laughing and going on. By-and-by a proud-looking man about fifty-five—and he was a heap the best dressed man in that town, too—steps out of the store, and the crowd drops back on each side to let him come. He says to Boggs, mighty ca'm and slow—he says:

"I'm tired of this; but I'll endure it till one o'clock. Till one o'clock, mind—no longer. If you open your mouth against me once, after that time, you can't travel so far but I will find you."

Then he turns and goes in. The crowd looked mighty sober; nobody stirred, and there warn't no more laughing.[50]

Unfortunately, Boggs does not shut up, and Sherburne steps out of the store at one o'clock and shoots him dead. The point, however, is that Twain blends dialogue masterfully with action to make this confrontation come alive for the reader. The scene illustrates several other guidelines for writing effective dialogue:

- **The scene has considerable dramatic tension** and is essential to Huck's initiation into the darker side of human

---

50 Mark Twain, *The Adventures of Huckleberry Finn* (The Project Gutenberg Etext of Huckleberry Finn) 100. www.gutenberg.org

nature. As a result, the dialogue has something important to contribute to the plot.
- **Twain knows his characters**, which is the foundation of all effective dialogue. Huck's distinctive narrative voice is that of a young, semi-literate adolescent who is new to the area. The people on the street are lower class townspeople who also speak in fractured, semi-literate English, but with a greater understanding of Boggs's drunken rampages. Boggs's speech reflects his own lower class, semi-literate background, but his word choices and speech patterns are also affected by his inebriated condition. Sherburne, a member of a more educated upper class, speaks in a language that is more formal and appropriate for his position in society.
- **Twain avoids slightly roughed up formal sentences** that *look* like vernacular speech and writes these sentences instead so they *sound* the way these people would speak (i. e., he is writing dialogue for the ear, not the eye.)
- **Twain varies the dialogue** so it doesn't become one long speech after another long speech—as was the case in the Cooper scene. As a result, Twain's dialogue sounds far more authentic, and the livelier verbal interplay between characters reinforces the dramatic tension.
- **The dialogue is appropriate because Twain has a clear sense of the context** in which it is used. People gathered in a small frontier town to watch a possible life-threatening confrontation between two members of their community would probably utter precisely these kinds of observations.
- **The characters are all involved in some action**: Boggs is a whirling dervish of action; Huck's life has been threatened and he is fearful; the townspeople are busy reassuring the newcomer that he has nothing to fear; and Sherburne

steps menacingly out of the store, makes his threat and walks back into the store.

Mark Twain's Principles Regarding Dialogue

The dialogue from Cooper's *Deerslayer* would not convert well to screenplay form. Most of it would end up on the cutting room floor. The scene from Twain's novel, however, could be transformed into a scene from a screenplay without sacrificing very much. The dialogue is so authentic and appropriate that it would be relatively unchanged.

The general principles regarding dialogue that Twain articulates in "Fenimore Cooper's Literary Offences" and practices in *The Adventures of Huckleberry Finn* all apply to screenwriting and novel writing:

- **Context creates dialogue.** A battle scene will create a different kind of dialogue than a courtroom scene or a scene in a church.
- **A scene without dramatic tension** will usually produce bad dialogue.
- **A scene that is not clearly connected to the plot** will produce bad dialogue.
- **Dialogue must be appropriate** to a character's social position, education, and standing in life.
- **Writing effective dialogue is primarily an auditory**, not a visual skill.
- **Long, alternating speeches seldom work.** Writers need to vary the length of these verbal exchanges so there is more dramatic interplay between characters.
- **Writers need to know their characters** as well as they know the members of their own families. All effective

dialogue evolves from a deeply intuitive knowledge of their characters.
- **Writers also need to know what their characters are doing** in a scene so the dialogue is compatible with those actions
- **Dialogue should reinforce and complement actions in a scene,** not exist independent of those actions.
- **Characters often interrupt one another, play off the other person's word choices, and do not always respond directly** to what someone else has said. They have their own agendas, and they frequently hear only what they want to hear.

Dialogue in Stage Plays

The best dialogue in the literary arts is often to be found in stage plays because they are written as performance dialogue. If the dialogue in the text doesn't work on stage, the actors will know very quickly by the audience's reactions. Screenwriters and novelists can learn much by reading the text of a play, and then attending the live performance; or, better yet, watch the play with text in hand. Once the written dialogue of the script is turned into performance dialogue on the stage, the importance of individual words, syllables, accents, and the other nuances and subtleties of language become immediately clear.

Arthur Miller's classic play, ***The Crucible*** (1953), provided some seemingly insurmountable challenges for any playwright. The language of the play had to be appropriate for both the late-seventeenth century, when the Salem Witch Trials took place; but it also had to reflect the language of mid-twentieth century America, when the House Un-American Activities Committee was engaged in a more contemporary witch hunt during the McCarthy Hearings. Miller somehow had to find a way to connect an event that occurred in 1692 with the troubling political events occurring during his own lifetime in 1953. He first wrote the play in verse that imitated seventeenth century speech patterns, but he realized that grounded the plot too much in the historic past. He decided instead to write the dialogue in speech patterns that were more contemporary, but with words and phrases that were grounded in the seventeenth century. This hybrid use of stage dialogue kept both past and current events clearly in the audience's minds throughout the play's performances. It is a tour-de-force manipulation of dialogue and dialects from two eras separated by almost three hundred years, and both the text and the performance of the play are musts for any writer seriously interested in writing better dialogue.[51]

Thornton Wilder's *Our Town* (1938) provided another unique challenge involving regional dialects and dialogue. All of the characters in the play speak in a common New English dialect that grounds the action in Grover's Corners, New Hampshire. The dialogue and dialects, however, could not be the same for each character, or the play would become tediously, even monotonously repetitive. The challenge facing Wilder, then, was to have all the characters speak in the same New England dialects, but with subtle differences to differentiate them from one another. The Stage Manager, thus, speaks in the most prominent New England dialect, one that is sprinkled with clichés and other trite expressions that are uniformly shared by others in Grover's Corners. Professor Willard speaks in a more educated, albeit exceedingly pretentious academic language. Mr. Webb also speaks in a more educated language, one befitting the owner of a small town newspaper, but his vocabulary is much less pretentious and academic than Willard's. Emily and George, the star-crossed lovers,

---

51 Miller, Arthur, *The Crucible* (New York: Penguin Books, 2003), xxi.

speak in dialogue that reflects their mutual need to determine what their true feelings are for one another. All of the characters in the play are differentiated through speech patterns as much as by what they say or do. There are subtle differences in their speech patterns and everyday concerns, but the foundational New England dialect is evident just below the surface in everything they say and how they say it.[52]

Susan Glasell's play *Trifles* (1916) reflects yet another playwriting challenge involving dialogue. The plot involves five characters who visit an isolated Iowa farmhouse to try to determine how John Wright had been murdered. They are also confronted by the task of determining whether his wife or an intruder was responsible for killing him. The men in the play—a sheriff, county attorney, and neighboring farmer—are convinced that Minnie Wright killed her husband. They are only interested in any kind of evidence that will help them prove her guilt to a jury. However, Mrs. Peters and Mrs. Hale, the two women who accompany the men to the farmhouse, become convinced that Minnie killed her husband because she was the victim of domestic violence and abuse—and she finally snapped. Once Mrs. Peters and Mrs. Hale come to that conclusion, their motive is to try to hide any incriminating evidence from the men who represent all the male authority figures in their community. The two groups of characters thus have antithetical motives for being in the farmhouse, and this is reflected in everything they do, say, or whisper to one another. All of the characters use words, dialects, and speech patterns that reflect their small town Midwestern backgrounds. However, since the women identify more closely with Minnie, their language is filled with expressions of grief, empathy, shock, dismay, and outright determination to protect an

---

52 Wilder, Thornton, *Our Town* (New York: Perennial Classics, 1965).

abused farmwife whose life on the isolated farm had turned into a nightmare. The men in the play never waiver from the more formal, almost official language one might hear in a small town courtroom or jail when authorities are trying to convict someone they are convinced is guilty of a serious crime. The motives for both the men and women in the play thus power the dialogue in terms of word choices, accents, speech patterns, and all the other elements of spoken language.[53]

Dialogue from Classic Films

Writing screenplay dialogue may not be quite as challenging as writing dialogue for novels or plays—or is it? Since screenplay dialogue exchanges are often brief, every word and every syllable counts, as we shall see in the examples below.

The legendary one-liners quoted at the beginning of this chapter all appeared in movies that are now considered classics. Sometimes, it is revealing to place these lines back in the context of the scenes in which they appeared, so we can try to understand why the dialogue worked so splendidly and memorably.

The following are excerpts from two scenes that created memorable dialogue that transcended the films in which they appeared and became part of American popular culture. These excerpts are from shooting scripts written much earlier in the evolution of screenplay form, so the formatting is different than the more modern reading scripts we have discussed in previous chapters. Also, these excerpts are in the middle of the scenes so the headers are not included, and some action descriptions are italicized as per earlier screenplay conventions.

---

53 "Plays by Susan Glaspell," <www.gutenberg.org>

Dialogue Scene: *Butch Cassidy and the Sundance Kid*

BUTCH. He stands, stretches.

                BUTCH

I haven't rode so much since I quit rustling. That's a miserable occupation; dusk to dawn, dusk to dawn, no sleep, rotten food—*(and suddenly his tone changes)*—Hey!!

              SUNDANCE
       (as Butch crouches down beside him)

I see it.

                  CUT TO

A LONG SHOT OF THE DEEP WOOD through which they have just come. And now, for the first time, the SUPERPOSSE begins to take on an almost phantom quality. For what we see, very faintly in the distance, is a slowly moving glow. The glow never stops moving. It never moves fast, but it keeps moving toward them.

        BUTCH'S VOICE (off-screen)
             (whispering)

Torches, you think?

       SUNDANCE'S VOICE (off-screen)

Maybe. Maybe lanterns.

        BUTCH'S VOICE (off-screen)

That's our path they're following.

       SUNDANCE'S VOICE (off-screen)

Dead on it.

> BUTCH'S VOICE (off-screen)
> I couldn't do that. Could you do that? How can they do that?
>
> CUT TO
>
> *BUTCH: CLOSE UP. Worried.*
>
> BUTCH
> (the first mention of what will become a litany)
> Who are those guys?[54]

Starting from when Butch and Sundance recognize the "superposse" advancing in their direction, there are a total of thirty-one words of dialogue, four of which are the legendary, "Who are those guys?" It is also important to note that the screenplay does not abandon action even in a scene where the characters are relatively static. Butch and Sundance act like two cornered animals who have been flushed out of their lair and are being hunted down.

If this movie is an accurate reflection of superb screenplay dialogue that blends with action descriptions—and it is—then we can conclude that simplicity, not complexity, should be the guiding principle for writing screenplay dialogue. Put another way, screenwriters are on safer ground by underwriting than overwriting. Overwriting dialogue can bring many screenplays to a grinding halt.

Perhaps a better analogy is that screenplay dialogue is the tip of an iceberg. On the surface it should appear relatively simple, while simultaneously evoking subterranean depths and powerful emotions just below the surface. However, it is the director's and

---

54 William Goldman, *Four Screenplays* (New York: Applause Books, 1995) 63-64.

Storytelling as Art and Craftsmanship

actors' jobs, not the screenwriter's job, to explore all of those subterranean depths and make them work in the film.

What are the subterranean depths that are reflected in these thirty-one words of screenplay dialogue? William Goldman, who wrote the original screenplay, has revealed in these few words one of the most important themes in all of American popular culture, literature, and history: the forces of civilization encroaching on the lawless old West. The "phantom superposse" in the distance is a brilliant symbol of the relentless forces of civilization, especially the law, that are slowly, inevitably cornering and destroying rebels like Butch and Sundance. The legendary line, "Who are those guys?," summarizes in four words the befuddlement every lawless renegade in the old West must have felt when confronted by powerful forces of civilization that were beyond his comprehension.

Yes, the dialogue is simple, but behind the dialogue there are powerful, complex themes and emotions that affected film audiences at some deep, subliminal level that made this scene from *Butch Cassidy and the Sundance Kid* unforgettable.

Dialogue Scene: *Casablanca*

Casablanca, often at the top of lists of the greatest movies ever made, also has more memorable lines than any other film. Most film historians could easily cite several lines from Casablanca that are some of the most memorable dialogue in movie history, including Humphrey Bogart's "Here's looking at you, kid."

The following excerpt from *Casablanca*, where Bogart's line appears, is formatted with names, dialogue, and action descriptions aligned with the left margin. This was a screenplay form that preceded the modern formatting with characters' names and dialogue in the center of the page, and action descriptions aligned with the left margin. Like the previous scene in *Butch Cassidy*

and the Sundance Kid, action descriptions are also italicized as per earlier screenplay formatting conventions.

The words in this flashback scene are kept to the absolute minimum. The dialogue consists of a series of brief exchanges between Rick and Ilsa. In a scene with relatively little action, these brief, fragmented exchanges between the characters nonetheless sustain the dramatic tension:

Inside Rick's Paris apartment, Ilsa fixes flowers at the window. Rick opens champagne. Ilsa joins him.

RICK

Who are you really? And what were you before? What did you do and what did you think? Huh?

ILSA

We said "no questions."

RICK

Here's looking at you, kid.

They drink.

Inside a swank Paris café, Rick and Ilsa dance.

ILSA

A franc for your thoughts.

RICK

In America they'd bring only a penny. I guess that's about all they're worth.

ILSA

I'm willing to be overcharged. Tell me.

RICK

I was wondering.

ILSA

Yes?

RICK

Why I'm so lucky. Why I should find you waiting for me to come along.

ILSA

Why there is no other man in my life?

RICK

Uh huh.

ILSA

That's easy. There was. He's dead.

RICK

Um. Sorry for asking. I forgot, we said no questions.

ILSA

Well, only one answer can take care of all our questions.

She kisses him.[55]

Screenwriters Julius J. Epstein, Philip G. Epstein, and Howard Koch accomplish so much with a few well-chosen words of dialogue. Behind the simple words in this flashback scene, film audiences sensed a brief peaceful prelude to a war-torn world that would soon be reeling in uncertainty; fascism in Germany and Italy would unleash its horrors on the human race; and the love affair between Rick and Ilsa would be doomed.

The legendary line, "Here's looking at you, kid," appears to be a casual toast over a glass of champagne, but it also reflects their inevitable fate. In the war-torn world that will soon envelope them, all Rick will be able to do is look at Ilsa. He can never have her in any other way. The screenwriters could have expressed this in several sentences, and they would never have had the emotional impact of, "Here's looking at you, kid."

---

55 Howard Koch, *Casablanca Script and Legend* (New York: The Overlook Press, 1992) 110-113.

Write Dialogue with the Ear

Certainly, not every writer can produce a legendary line or an entire screenplay that will be honored as a classic for all time. Nor can they write the kind of dialogue that turns good films into classics. However, there are some things all writers can do to improve the dialogue they write. None of these tips is the magic elixir that will immediately transform poor or mediocre dialogue into one-liners that become classic moments in films. They will, however, teach writers how to learn, over time, to write better screen dialogue.

The most important skill writers need to develop to write more effective dialogue is to write with the ear. Some writers like Mark Twain, Sinclair Lewis and Willa Cather come into the world with a gift that enabled them to write this way the first time they put pen to paper. The rest of us mere mortals have to develop and refine this auditory skill.

Years ago, I read an article about an author who turned off all the lights and wrote his novels in the dark on an ancient typewriter. He explained that he wanted to remove all distractions so he would be completely immersed in his stories. He explained that he found it was much easier to write dialogue in the dark because he had no choice but to write with the ear. The eyes were nullified and could not be part of the writing process.

What this writer discovered is useful advice for all writers. Anything they can do to force themselves to refine their auditory skills and write with the ear will probably strengthen their dialogue.

Write When You Are Not Writing

Many amateur writers think of writing as something they do only when they are sitting in front of their computers. Certainly, much of what we write has to be produced under these conditions.

However, this concept of what constitutes writing often denies writers the best times to write dialogue.

The best dialogue is often produced under other conditions. The myth that great plays, novels, or screenplays are only written in small rooms with computers and crumpled paper scattered across the floor has to go. Creative writers should always be writing, regardless of what they are doing.

Writers need to be sensitive to the internal dialogues all of us carry on with ourselves every minute of our lives. Writers must allow their characters to speak to them when they are taking a walk or driving to school or work. The more writers think of their characters as real people who exist in their imaginations, and not just on the printed page, the more these characters will start to sound authentic. Their words, whereas they might not become the classic one-liners quoted earlier in this chapter, will also become more authentic dialogue.

Freewriting Dialogue

Anything a writer can do in the early drafts to avoid an overly cerebral approach to writing dialogue will probably produce more authentic speech patterns. In subsequent drafts, writers can more deliberately refine and shape their words, but in the early stages of writing dialogue, an overly conscious cerebral approach tends to produce stilted, unconvincing speech patterns.

To avoid this, I encourage my students to *freewrite their dialogue* in the early drafts. Many of them have told me later that it was some of the best advice they received about writing dialogue. The idea is very simple. I encourage them to sit down with a pencil or pen and a legal- or letter-sized tablet and just let the dialogue between the characters flow quickly, spontaneously, and without pause. I tell them not to write in the characters' full

Storytelling as Art and Craftsmanship

names (just the initials), action descriptions, or visual images. All of those elements can be added later. Just concentrate on writing the dialogue without any interruptions of any kind.

For example, if the writer is trying to simulate a dialogue exchange between Peter and Mary in the days before their divorce is final, a freewrite of their last argument might unfold like this:

P: I never said it was me.
M: Are you kidding? It was always you.
P: How can you say that?
M. Because it's true.
P. The truth is something you never understood.
M. And I suppose you did?
P. I'm not saying that.
M: Then what are you saying?
P: Does it really matter?
M: Yes, it does matter.
P: Why does it matter?
M: Because we're getting a divorce. That's why it matters.
P: It never seemed to matter to you before.
M: How can you say that?
P: Because it's true.
M: You wouldn't know the truth if it bit you on the nose.
P: I suppose you would.
M: I would at least know there is something called the truth. You never will.

Is it perfect? Of course not. Will it have to be revised and refined? Yes, it certainly will—perhaps many times. However, by making these early drafts of dialogue flow quickly and spontaneously, writers tend to avoid the stilted prose style that befouls so much dialogue. The simple experience of putting pen to paper, because it requires a little more effort than word processing, also tends to keep the dialogue exchanges shorter and more direct.

My experiences with students over many years is that this forces them to tap into some deeper level of where they write—and this produces more natural dialogue.

Sometimes People Just Don't Communicate

Often we do not hear what somewhat else is trying to tell us. So instead of having meaningful conversations, we speak around the issues or get sidetracked onto irrelevant issues. In the brief freewrite above, for example, Paul and Mary start to obsess about the meanings of the words *true, truth,* and *matters.* As a result, their conversation goes nowhere, which is often the case in human dialogue exchanges.

Don't think that just because a character is communicating an idea to someone else, the other character will hear what is being said. That character may often interpret what is being said in a totally different way than it was intended. Such exchanges have an air of authenticity because we have all been involved in just these kinds of conversations where much is said, but little is actually communicated.

Avoid Long, Complete Sentences

Most dialogue is not written in long, complete sentences, primarily because this is not the way people communicate with one another. Also, the dramatic tension between characters can be lost if they respond to one another in alternating complete sentences or monologues. Shorter sentences and fragments generally create more dramatic interplay between actors.

There are exceptions, of course, when longer, more elaborate sentences and long monologues work splendidly in screenplays and films. *A Man for All Seasons* is one such film. Sir Thomas More (Paul Scofield) often responds to the court that is seeking to execute him with beautifully complete, elaborate English prose that is mesmerizing. The same is true for other movies with long courtroom scenes, including *JFK* and *Primal Fear* that are discussed elsewhere in this book. One of the most famous long monologues in film history is Howard Beale's rant in the movie, *Network*. Beale's insane diatribe against some amorphous adversary is the scene most film viewers still identify with the movie, and the reason why they returned to theaters to see it a second time.

Another famous long monologue is General George Patton's opening speech in the film, *Patton*. Patton, played by George C. Scott, is dressed in full military regalia, complete with a chest full of metals as he strides on stage in a huge auditorium and tells the unseen enlisted men seated below what war is really like. It is a brilliant and memorable opening to this Oscar winning film, and yet it was also one of the reasons why screenwriter Francis Ford Coppola was fired from the film. Later, he received an academy award for the film script. This entire incident, however, illustrates how wary film producers are of long speeches or monologues in films.[56]

Sometimes long speeches or monologues work. Sometime they don't. The key is the appropriateness of the dialogue to the character and the scene he or she is in at the time. No one, not even the producers who fired Coppola, would want to remove any of these monologues from their respective films.

---

56 Francis Ford Coppola, "Introduction," *Patton* (Cinema Classics Collection, 2006).

Other Tips for Writing Dialogue

Some film critics have argued that screenplay dialogue has become overly dependent on the "f-word." They point out that in many films, regardless of context, every exchange between characters contains at least one and often several repetitions of this word. An older generation of writers would see this as a lame attempt to conceal the fact that the dialogue is poorly written. To them, this kind of dialogue might be appropriate to street gangs, but it is not appropriate in all the contexts in which it is currently being used in films. They would urge students who aspire to learn the craft of screenwriting to sharpen their ear for dialogue that reveals the more subtle nuances of human interactions.

Screenwriters should also develop collaborative relationships with other screenwriters. Dialogue is meant to be read out loud, and these collaborative relationships enable writers to listen to what they have written while they are addressing another audience. This almost always sharpens the ear for developing appropriate dialogue.

Finally, if screenwriters carefully analyze some of the examples in this chapter, they will see that none of the dialogue is human speech precisely as we hear it every day. It is a refined form of human speech, but it is not the real thing—nor should it be. It is much more than that. It is a few well-chosen words that blend with action descriptions and sound authentic to keep the story moving, while occasionally creating unforgettable moments like, "What we've got here is … failure to communicate" (**Cool Hand Luke**, 1967).

EXERCISES

1. Katharine Anne Porter's short story, "Rope," is written almost exclusively as alternating stream of consciousness ruminations between a young farm couple as they struggle to understand one another after the husband has forgotten to purchase the coffee his wife sent him to town to buy. Convert this stream of consciousness scene into a dialogue scene. What changes in tone, word choices, and other elements of dialogue did you make to communicate the same tensions that were conveyed in the short story through the stream of consciousness technique? Also, how does the dialogue you have written capture the fact that this husband and wife are talking to one another, but they are not communicating?
2. Select one entry in each of the columns below and create a brief dialogue scene out of the characters, circumstance, and setting. Then do the same with another selection. You might even change the circumstances or settings for either of your selections (i.e., the student reveals domestic violence in the home while reading an essay "during class"; the two angry politicians extend their debate into "an adjacent room"; the two female adversaries confront one another "in the restroom," and so on.) Afterwards, compare the way dialogue is shaped by different characters, circumstances, and settings.

Characters	Circumstances	Settings
Young married couple	Lovers quarrel	Library
Elderly couple	At bingo game	Retirement home
Gay couple	About to meet Marine Corps drill instructor father of one of the men	Front stoop
Two female adversaries	Wearing same dress at wedding	Inside church
Two angry politicians	After debate, not knowing microphone is still on	On stage
Teacher and student	Student's essay reveals domestic violence in home	After class

3. Write a brief dialogue scene using exchanges of no more than eight words for each speaker. The point is not that all dialogue scenes should be similarly short, fragment exchanges. Context creates the appropriateness of the dialogue. However, exercises that require screenwriters to underwrite, rather than overwrite, dialogue scenes teach economy of statement—a crucial skill for all screenwriters. In most scenes, these shorter, more fragmented exchanges create more dramatic tension between characters.

4. The following is a scene in which the dialogue is kept to the bare minimum. Rewrite the dialogue, using alternating statements of no more than six words to create a more antagonistic relationship between the two detectives. Then, using the same six-word limitation, rewrite the dialogue to create a more mutually supportive relationship between the two detectives.

Storytelling as Art and Craftsmanship

Sample Dialogue Scene

A YOUNG DETECTIVE approaches an overweight, more STREET-WISE DETECTIVE who is examining the body of a WOMAN that is sprawled across the pavement in the back alley of a large city.

> DETECTIVE ONE
> Another one?

> DETECTIVE TWO
> Looks like it.

> DETECTIVE ONE
> Anyone know her?

> DETECTIVE TWO
> Nope.

The younger detective points at some coins that are lying next to the body.

> DETECTIVE ONE
> Same three coins?

> DETECTIVE TWO
> (shaking his head)
> They're nickels. Not pennies.

> DETECTIVE ONE
> What does that mean?

DETECTIVE TWO
Damned if I know.

5. Alfred Hitchcock once said that the sound and dialogue in a motion picture could be muted, and the audience should still be able to follow the plot. His comment is a testimonial to the power of the visual images on the silver screen. In the hierarchy of film techniques, it also relegates dialogue to a lesser role than graphic visual images. As an experiment, mute the sound for several minutes in any film, including some of Hitchcock's masterpieces, and try to determine if you can follow the plot. Then replay the film with sound and dialogue. What does this teach us about the relationship between dialogue and the images on the screen? Also, can you cite and play some films that might prove Hitchcock wrong?

6. Record as accurately as you can a short conversation between two or more people. Afterwards, write the dialogue and format it on the printed page as though it were a scene from a screenplay. What changes would you have to make in the spoken dialogue during real conversations to make it work in screenplay form? What does this teach us about the differences between screenplay dialogue and real human talk that we hear every day?

7. In Robert Browning's dramatic monologue, "My Last Duchess," the envoy representing the new Duchess is not very well defined. We can only guess at his reactions to the Duke's explanations for why he had the last Duchess executed. After developing the character of the envoy more fully, convert this poem into a screenplay dialogue scene. Be sure to focus on establishing an appropriate dialogue between the two characters. Afterwards, be prepared to explain how the dramatic

situation and the Duke's intimidating, menacing presence motivated the envoy to respond to the Duke as he does.

8. Robert Frost's poem, "Home Burial," involves a husband and wife who confront one another after the death and home burial of their newborn baby. At a time when they desperately need each other's support, they are unable to communicate and comfort one another. Instead, they engage in angry recriminations, each accusing the other of being insensitive and selfish. Read the poem out loud several times to "hear" the rhythms and tones in the dialogue Frost has created. Then convert the poem into a screenplay scene, making whatever cuts seem necessary. Be prepared to explain why some of the existing dialogue and action descriptions are essential to the screenplay scene, and others are not.

9. Write appropriate screenplay dialogue for the three characters in the Kenny Rogers' song, "Lucille," which was discussed in the previous chapter. The drifter's manner of speaking is well established in the song's lyrics. The challenge will be to develop suitable and appropriate dialogue for the weather-beaten farmer and his disillusioned wife. Be prepared to explain how the specific dramatic situation caused the three characters to speak as they do.

10. Record or take notes on a scene from a film that you believe overuses the F-word as a crutch for poorly written dialogue. Rewrite the dialogue using different word choices to convey the same emotions and tensions.

11. Read a dialogue scene you have written to your classmates or friends. What changes would you make in the dialogue after reading the scene to an audience? What did you learn about the dialogue by *hearing* it rather than just *seeing* it on the printed page? Does this reinforce the idea that writing dialogue is primarily an auditory skill?

CHAPTER 11

FROM SCREENWRITING TO NOVEL WRITING

Introduction

The primary purpose of a screenplay is to create a film. However, writers should also know how useful screenwriting techniques are for writing other types of fiction. As demonstrated previously, there are differences between screenwriting and other forms of creative writing, but there is also a symbiotic relationship between them. Joseph Campbell made that clear when he argued in *The Hero with a Thousand Faces* that most stories are grounded in the same "monomyth" and have similar character types and structural patterns.[57] If literature can teach us much about writing screenplays, screenplays can also teach us much about writing literature.

---

57 Joseph Campbell, *The Hero With A Thousand Faces* (New York: Princeton University Press, 1949) 36-37.

Storytelling as Art and Craftsmanship

Sue Grafton, the best-selling author of the alphabet series of mystery novels discussed briefly in the "Preface" and elsewhere in this book, did not have fond memories of the business side of her Hollywood screenwriting experiences. However, she was equally adamant that screenwriting taught her how to write dialogue and action scenes, get into and out of scenes, and structure a story.[58] Although Grafton refused to sell the film rights to her novels because she was apprehensive about what Hollywood might do to the storylines, she felt those screenwriting experiences and techniques enabled her to become a best-selling writer of mystery novels. The next logical step for the new generation of novelists would seem to be to learn to write their stories first as screenplays, and then convert them into novels. Although they might not have the same direct screenwriting experiences as Grafton, they can still learn how to use screenplays as outlines for novels.

Throughout *Storytelling as Art and Craftsmanship*, I have converted excerpts from novels and other literature to demonstrate the principles of screenwriting. This chapter will demonstrate the advantages of writing a story as a screenplay and then converting it into a novel. I will use as an example a screenplay I wrote and later converted into a mixed-genre (mystery/thriller/horror), best-selling, novel. (I would prefer to use another author's fictional work, but I would not be able to speak with the same degree of familiarity regarding cuts, additions, and other strategies during the actual compositional stages of another author's novel.)

One of my screenplays, which I had tentatively titled *The Locket* and later *The Search for Judd McCarthy*, received supportive letters from film producers who encouraged me to make some changes and resubmit it through my agent. I decided, instead, to use the screenplay as the outline for a novel. I learned rather

---

58 Macdonald, Moira. "With 'Y is for Yesterday,' Sue Grafton prepares for the alphabet series' end." The Seattle Times 10 September 2017.

quickly that using a screenplay as an outline involves neither a simple overlay of a novel on a screenplay format, nor is it a rigid, inflexible stifling of the writer's creativity and instinctive responses to the developing storyline. A screenplay provides a temporary scaffolding that supports the novel while the writer is searching for the organic flow of the story. The screenplay outline thus provides the necessary structure and support so the story does not wander down an irretrievable pathway and into the abyss of unsustainable endings.

As the novel evolved, I realized it was also challenging the modern genres (mostly thriller and horror) that had turned into literary blood feasts that described in vivid detail every slash of a knife on a victim's body, the gory details of disemboweling other victims, and a variety of ways to dismember and dispose of human corpses. From my own literary studies, I knew the contemporary horror genre had evolved from the much older Gothic tradition in literature. That tradition usually kept the violence on the edge of the action, or in the reader's imagination, where it was far more powerful and significantly less gory. The writers I admired the most who practiced this older Gothic tradition were Nathaniel Hawthorne, author of **The Scarlet Letter**, and Emily Bronte, author of **Wuthering Heights**. There was, to be sure, implied violence in both authors' literary works, but it was usually kept on the edge of the action. At the center of their stories were a love story, strong and compelling minor characters, complex literary symbolism, sophisticated plots, and the other elements of storytelling once practiced by master storytellers. I hoped to restore some semblance of that early Gothic storytelling tradition in the novel I would eventually title *The Search for Judd McCarthy* I was converting from a screenplay into a novel.

The story involves an itinerant laborer who disappears while he is transporting a company payroll between two Midwestern small towns in the autumn of 1926. Thirty-three years later, a man in a neighboring town suddenly starts to have nightmares that he is walking on a weed-infested railroad track, and he is very afraid. The nightmares become more vivid and horrifying, and he slowly takes on Judd McCarthy's personality. The rest of the story deals with a therapist's attempts to figure out what happened to Judd McCarthy, and why his memories continue to live on inside another man in the 1950s.

I quickly learned that the screenplay outline gave me a sense of purpose, control, and direction that were absent in my earlier attempts to write a novel. I also discovered that a screenplay is far superior to a conventional outline with Roman Numerals and other such mechanical designations. With the screenplay as my outline, I had already lived through the entire experience of the story. The screenplay brought the inner spirit and structure of the story to the surface before I had even written the first sentence of the novel. I knew the characters—their personalities, strengths, and weaknesses—as well as I knew the people in my own life. Those characters were already alive inside of me. Perhaps most importantly, I had a strong sense of my ending and how the various threads in the story came together at that precise point, albeit I kept an open mind regarding subtle changes in my ending. Knowing this, I could confidently provide foreshadowing and false foreshadowing to enrichen the plot.

The screenplay outline enhanced creativity and spontaneous decision making. It did not detract from them. I could allow my instincts greater freedom without losing control of the story. Since I had a preliminary scaffolding for the plot, I could concentrate my creative energies on finding the appropriate details to develop the characters, actions, and individual scenes. I also knew the inner spirit of the story and could use it in every scene to help me find the voice(s) of the story. I was completely in control.

Bantam Books published the novel in February of 1982. ***Publishers Weekly*** later described it as "an expertly written thriller, a kind of Steven King-Ross MacDonald hybrid (and in a class with either), that beautifully evokes the feeling of a small town dying—its buildings, its streets and, most of all, its lost souls."[59] Much to my surprise, according to the *Los Angeles Times* and other publications, the novel that Bantam renamed ***Ghost Lover*** became a best-selling paperback original.[60] The techniques of screenwriting, as I incorporated them into this novel, were the difference between my earlier attempts at novel writing and the novel about Judd McCarthy's disappearance, which held together as a complete story. It was the screenplay structure and strategies that enabled me to find the voice(s) of the story and transform it into a polished, professional story.[61]

The two excerpts below are from the screenplay and novel versions of the same story. The screenplay is somewhat wordy because I intended to convert the story into a novel. In the discussion after the second excerpt, I identify the specific screenplay strategies I used to write the novel.

---

59 *Publisher's Weekly Review* of Ghost Lover (February 12, 1982).
60 "The Book Review," *Los Angeles Times* (February 28, 1982)
61 There is a long history to this project. In screenplay form, it was titled *The Locket* and later *The Search for Judd McCarthy*. Bantam Books changed the title to *Ghost Lover* to acknowledge its hybrid status and appeal to a more widespread readership of the Gothic horror, thriller, and romance genres. Years later, when I reacquired the rights to the novel, I restored it to one of the original titles, *The Search for Judd McCarthy*. The novel is now available at Sunbury Press, Inc. under that title.

Screenplay Version: *The Search for Judd McCarthy*[62]

FADE IN

EXT. RAILROAD TRACKS - DAY

The date 1926 appears and slowly fades.

JUDD MCCARTHY, a huge man, well over six feet tall, tugs at the straps of a canvas bag marked "Hanley Brothers Construction" he carries over his shoulder.

ANGLE ON his dirty leather shoes as they CRUNCH through the gravel and small rocks on the railroad embankment.

OTHER ANGLES. A leather holster with a revolver and a large hunting knife are strapped around his waist. The brim of a floppy black hat tilts awkwardly over his forehead. McCarthy's eyes constantly scan the surrounding terrain. His eyes betray a gentleness and sensitivity that contradict his otherwise menacing appearance.

WIDER ANGLE. Signs of Indian summer are all around him. Dead leaves, propelled by steady autumn breezes, hop and skip across newly plowed fields.

McCarthy pauses to watch a flock of GEESE as the V-formation slowly opens and closes high overhead. Their LOUD HONKING ECHOES across the Midwestern prairies.

---

62 Dennis M. Clausen, *The Search for Judd McCarthy* (screenplay), 1-5.

MCCARTHY

Damn, if me soul don't feel like going south like that. But Kate said it's time to do somethin' else with me life. And she's right.

McCarthy reaches into his overalls and pulls out a small golden locket. The tiny piece of jewelry almost disappears in his huge callused palm. McCarthy smiles as he admires the locket.

MCCARTHY
(laughing, reminiscing)
Ah, Tobin. Ya ugly Norwegian. Ya jus ain't no match for an Irishman, lad. But I thank ya for the money to buy a locket for me Lady Kate. I made a promise to ya, Kate, an I mean to keep it. Above all else, Judd McCarthy means ta keep that promise.

McCarthy places the locket in his pants pocket, and again his dirty leather shoes CRUNCH through the gravel and small rocks.

MCCARTHY
(singing)
Got a locket for me darlin', for me darlin' Lady Kate.

Suddenly McCarthy sees something ahead of him. He stops instantly, his right hand drawing the revolver out of the leather holster.

MCCARTHY
(yelling)
Who be it there? If ya be waitin' for me, ya best come out or get yur head blown off.

The dried reeds sway slowly back and forth on the edge of the marshland.

McCarthy kneels down and picks up a rock.

> MCCARTHY
> I be warnin' ya. If ya don't come out, ya'll be a mighty sore lad!

There are a few moments of SILENCE. Then McCarthy fires the rock into the brush, and a SHRILL SCREECH pierces the autumn air.

ANGLE ON the marsh. There is a brief flurry of movement where the rock entered the brush. Then there is stillness and SILENCE.

ANGLE ON McCarthy. He creeps over to the marsh and slowly, cautiously parts the reeds with his huge hands. A rooster PHEASANT lies in the brush.

> MCCARTHY
> Ah, no, me beauty. I only meant ta scare ya, not ta kill ya.

McCarthy gently strokes the pheasant. The pheasant shudders, breathes its last breath and dies.

> MCCARTHY
> (softly, sadly)
> I only meant ta scare ya, lad.

McCarthy kneels by the dead pheasant while the crickets CHIRP in the tall grass. He digs a hole in the dark black soil with his hunting knife and places the bird in it. Then he piles dirt and weeds over the dead pheasant and walks back to the railroad embankment.

The sun is dipping into the western horizon.

McCarthy pauses to watch the sun cast its shadows across the stubble of the wheat fields. He looks at a river curling southwards across the prairie. He starts walking faster.

Moments later, McCarthy comes to an abrupt halt. He sees something in the shadows of a small clump of trees. A sudden gust of wind causes the dead autumn leaves to wave wildly in the thicket and tumble out into the prairie.

McCarthy reaches instinctively for the revolver. He takes two cautious steps in that direction.

IMMEDIATE FADE TO BLACK. There are STRANGE SOUNDS in the darkness, like tiny muffled feet running across a floor. There is HEAVY BREATHING and the sound of someone POUNDING on a wooden surface.

A soft, deep MOAN is followed by a SCREAM that builds in intensity.

CUT TO

INT. HAMPTON HOME - 33 YEARS LATER

The date 1959 appears and slowly fades.

JOEL HAMPTON sits straight up in bed, his body drenched in a feverish sweat. His wife SUSAN is staring down at him, looking puzzled and frightened. She has apparently been shaking him by his shoulder.

JOEL

Huh?

Joel's eyes open slowly, then close.

SUSAN

Joel, wake up! You're having that nightmare again.

JOEL

Nightmare?

Joel does not seem to comprehend the meaning of the word.

SUSAN

You're dreaming again. And talking in your sleep. God, Joel, you scared me half to death.

JOEL

I'm sorry. What did I say?

SUSAN

Nothing that I could understand. You just started to sweat and then you began to scream. Joel—

JOEL

Yes, honey?

SUSAN
You've got to stop working so hard. I know it's your first year in the law firm and you feel you have to prove something to the others. But you can't kill yourself in the process. You're just trying to do too much.

JOEL
It isn't my job, Susan. I've been having that nightmare ever since I was a boy. I'm out in the country. Somewhere. It seems like autumn. Everything is fine. And then—

SUSAN
What happens?

JOEL
I don't know. It's (BEAT) It's something terrible. But I don't know what it is.

SUSAN
Did your mother and father ever know what caused that dream?

JOEL
No. It was like I came into the world with it.

Storytelling as Art and Craftsmanship

Novel Version: *The Search for Judd McCarthy*[63]

Chapter One

I

October, 1926

Judd McCarthy tugged at the straps of the huge canvas bag he carried across his shoulders and looked down at his dirty leather shoes as they crunched through the gravel and small rocks on the railroad embankment. A leather holster and a large hunting knife were strapped around his waist, and the brim of a floppy black hat tilted awkwardly over his forehead. His right hand moved back and forth between the straps of the canvas bag and the .45 caliber Smith and Wesson revolver that protruded out of the holster. His eyes constantly scanned the surrounding terrain, searching for any movement in the brush and clumps of trees on both sides of the railroad tracks.

Earlier in the day he had been sent to Carson to bring the Hanley Brothers Construction Company payroll back to Danvers. He was now within a few miles of the construction camp, but the sun was bending into the western horizon. He knew if an attempt was to be made on his life, it would probably be at dusk in the marshland just ahead of him.

It had occurred to McCarthy that there was something strange in Fred Hanley's decision to send him for the company payroll on a day when the trains were not running. Normally two or three heavily armed men went to Carson to accompany the payroll back by railroad car.

---

63   Dennis M. Clausen, *The Search for Judd McCarthy* (Mechanicsburg, PA: Sunbury Press, Inc.) *1-8.*

"The men are getting nervous about not being paid," Fred Hanley had said. "We can't wait for a day when the train's be runnin'. Besides, Mac, with your reputation no one'll mess with ya."

Judd McCarthy had the reputation of being one of the most violent men in Carver County. It was a reputation he had earned in numerous bar fights and wrestling matches, during his two years as a laborer for the Hanley Brothers Construction Company.

He was a huge man, well over six feet tall, and his wide muscular shoulders easily bore the weight of the canvas payroll bag. His hands were large and callused from years of hard labor in heavy construction projects. Only his eyes betrayed a gentleness and sensitivity that contradicted his otherwise menacing appearance. There was a twinkle of life and good humor in his large brown eyes, even as they moved apprehensively over the surrounding terrain.

Signs of Indian summer were all around him. The stubble of recently harvested wheat fields poked out of the parched earth. Dead leaves, propelled by steady autumn breezes, hopped and skipped across newly plowed fields. Hen pheasants clucked contentedly in the nearby brush, while an occasional rooster pheasant emitted a shrill mating call that echoed across the desolate Midwestern landscape. In nearby sloughs and ponds, muskrats busily stockpiled reeds and fallen branches. And overhead a V-shaped formation of Canadian geese flew gracefully southwards.

McCarthy paused briefly to watch the geese as the V-formation slowly opened and closed high overhead. Their loud honking echoed across the Midwestern prairies.

"Damn, if me soul don't feel like going south like that," McCarthy blurted out in a thick Irish accent. "But Kate said it's time to do somethin' else with me life. An' she's right."

The thought of Kate reminded him of the present he had brought back from Carson, and he reached into the front pocket of his canvas overalls and pulled out a small golden locket. The tiny piece of jewelry almost disappeared in his huge, callused palm.

As he admired the golden locket, he remembered the wrestling match in Carson. While he was waiting for the payroll to arrive, Farmer Tobin had challenged him to a wrestling match, winner take all. Tobin was the strongest man in Carver County, stronger and bigger even than McCarthy. But McCarthy had managed to stay out of Tobin's hammerlock long enough to wear him out. When it was over, Tobin was flat on his back, unable to move.

"Ah, Tobin," McCarthy laughed to himself as he admired the golden locket, "Ya ugly Norwegian. Ya jus ain't no match for an Irishman, lad. But I thank ya for the money to buy a locket for me Lady Kate." The thought of Kate brought the gentleness back into McCarthy's brown eyes. "I made a promise to ya, Kate, an I mean to keep it. Above all else, Judd McCarthy means ta keep that promise. I loves ya, lass, more'n anything else in the world."

He carefully placed the small locket back into his pants pocket, and again his dirty leather shoes crunched through the gravel and small rocks alongside the railroad embankment. Ahead of him, on both sides of the railroad tracks, was the last marshland he would have to pass through before reaching the wheatfields just outside of Danvers. He was almost home. He knew that Kate was waiting for him farther south, by the banks of the Little Sioux River, but first he would have to leave the payroll with the company paymaster and collect his wages. Then he was free.

"Got a locket for me darlin', for me darlin' Lady Kate." He sang the chorus of an old Irish folk ballad and then suddenly stopped as he entered the fringes of the marshland. The railroad company had been negligent in caring for the Little Sioux Line, and the weeds and brush grew almost to the edge of the railroad trestles. McCarthy proceeded cautiously, his right hand never more than a few inches from the .45caliber revolver.

Suddenly there was a movement in the brush ahead of him. McCarthy stopped instantly, his right hand drawing the revolver out of the leather holster.

"Who be it there?" he yelled into the reeds and brush. "If ya be waitin' for me, ya best come out or get yur head blown off."

The dried reeds swayed slowly back and forth on the fringe of the marshland, but there was no response to McCarthy's challenge. Slowly he knelt on the edge of the railroad embankment, his eyes never leaving the dried brush where he had spotted the movement. He picked up a huge rock and stood back up to his full height.

"I be warnin' ya. If ya don't come out, ya'll be a mighty sore lad!" he yelled again into the marsh.

Still there was no response. Suddenly McCarthy fired the rock into the brush and a shrill screech pierced the autumn air. There was a brief flurry of movement where the rock had entered the brush. Then there was again stillness and silence.

McCarthy crept up to the edge of the marsh and slowly, cautiously parted the reeds with his huge hands. In the middle of the dried vegetation a rooster pheasant lay prone on the ground, its neck broken from the impact of the rock. The pheasant's eyes blinked twice, then remained open.

"Ah, no, me beauty. I only meant ta scare ya, not ta kill ya." McCarthy lay the revolver down on the ground and gently stroked the beautiful red and brown feathers of the rooster pheasant. Beneath his hand he felt a convulsive movement in the animal's chest, then a shutter as the pheasant breathed its last and died.

"I only meant ta scare ya, lad," McCarthy repeated softly and sadly as he felt the bird stiffen and die beneath the stroke of his huge hand.

A few yards away, in the waters of the marshland, the early evening crickets began to chirp contentedly and a frog leaped off a fallen log and splashed into the shallow slough. McCarthy heard these sounds as he stroked the dead body of the rooster pheasant.

McCarthy dug out a hole in the dark black soil with his sharp hunting knife and placed the bird in it. Then he piled dirt and weeds over the dead pheasant, picked up the revolver and canvas bag, and walked back to the railroad embankment.

The sun was dipping into the western horizon when McCarthy stepped out of the marsh and entered the wheatfields a few miles outside of Danvers. He paused briefly to watch the sun cast its shadows across the stubble of the wheatfields. In the distance, the Little Sioux River was curling southwards across the prairie. He remembered that Kate was waiting for him down by the river, and he walked faster in the direction of Danvers.

It was then that he saw something in the shadows of a small clump of trees a few hundred feet to the east of the railroad embankment. As McCarthy looked in that direction, a sudden gust of wind caused the dead autumn leaves to wave wildly in the thicket and tumble out into the prairie.

McCarthy's hand reached instinctively for the handle of the .45caliber Smith and Wesson revolver. Something was hiding in the shadows of the trees. As McCarthy drew the revolver out of the leather holster and pointed it in the direction of the clump of trees, a human figure stepped out of the shadows and waved to him. McCarthy recognized who it was immediately, and he replaced the pistol.

He walked down the railroad embankment, entered the stubble of the wheatfield, and approached the figure. . . .

But it did not end there. It was days later. Maybe weeks. Maybe even months. It did not matter. Surrounded by the impenetrable darkness, time ceased to exist. Except as measured by his failing strength, his dying will.

At first he lashed out frantically, until the blade of the hunting knife shattered. When that failed he fired the revolver into the darkness. He watched the orange flames spit out of the barrel as the muffled gunshots echoed harmlessly all around him. Still it did not end.

And each time he fell, the rats would scurry over to sniff at his mildewed clothing. Bolder they became with the passage of time, until he would lash out with the butt end of the knife, sending them scurrying back into the darkness. But always they came back. Relentlessly. And he grew weaker.

Sometime, near the end, he heard the scream. Loud and shrill, it echoed in the darkness. First in anger, then in agony. Growing weaker as his strength failed him. When it too failed, he again heard the soft padding of tiny feet scurrying about in the darkness. Moving ceaselessly. Relentlessly.

When the end came, he was lying face down. The rats sensed that he had lost his will, his strength. He heard them padding softly across the ground to where he lay. They sniffed at his clothing and brushed against his cheek. Then a sharp pain tore through his arm like a thousand needles penetrating the flesh. But he was too weak to care. And he lay there, enduring the pain until it turned into a moist numbness.

As the life poured out of his body, he was filled with rage at the horror of how he had been duped. And even as his life yielded to the darkness that surrounded him, his soul held firm against the night and refused to accept what had been left undone.

It was then that he thought of the locket. He reached towards his pocket to see if it was still there. But the numbness had spread over his entire body and his arm would not move...

II

When Judd McCarthy failed to return to Danvers with the payroll, the Hanley Brothers Construction Company sent a search team out after him. At first they assumed McCarthy was the victim of foul play, but when no body was found alongside the Little Sioux Railroad, they concluded he had fled into the Dakotas with the payroll. A reward of $5000 was posted and McCarthy became a wanted man.

To the men who worked for Fred Hanley, McCarthy's disappearance was not exactly unexpected. He was a drifter, a man who lived for the moment, and it was not surprising that he would seize an opportunity to become wealthy beyond their wildest dreams. The men on the construction crew cursed him because his disappearance with the company payroll meant they would not be paid for three months of work, but they also felt that Fred Hanley should have known better than to send a man with McCarthy's reputation after the payroll.

Within weeks after McCarthy's disappearance, the Hanley Brothers Construction Company abandoned the Little Sioux Water Reclamation Project. Fred Hanley moved to the East Coast, where he retired and lived for the next ten years until his death in 1936. Ben Hanley simply disappeared somewhere in Florida. Some of the construction workers stayed around Carver County for several weeks, hoping that McCarthy might yet return with the long overdue payroll. Then they too drifted away. Soon the memory of Judd McCarthy faded and his disappearance was forgotten by all except a few of the men who had worked for Fred Hanley and decided to stay in the Danvers area after the company folded. The mystery of McCarthy's disappearance became only a minor footnote in the larger history of Carver County.

The Little Sioux Railroad line that connected Danvers and Carson was abandoned in 1927. As the seasons changed and the years passed, the vegetation alongside the railroad embankment crept steadily towards the railroad tracks. By 1930 the vegetation had buried the rusty tracks.

For thirty-three years the seasons passed with monotonous regularity. In winter the wheat fields were buried beneath the glistening white snows. In spring the waters of the Little Sioux River would break free from the ice-covered lakes farther north and drift slowly southwards towards the Mississippi River and the Great Sea beyond. In summer the tiny heads, of grain would dance playfully above the wheat fields that now grew almost to the very edge of the abandoned Little Sioux Railroad Line. And in late fall, Indian summer would settle over the marshlands and newly harvested fields of wheat and corn, and the Canadian geese would fly overhead in V-formation on their annual pilgrimages southwards.

The Great Depression of the 1930s wiped out most of the farmers along both sides of the Little Sioux River, forcing entire families to abandon their farms to follow their shattered dreams westwards to California and Oregon. World War II and the Korean War came and went, and, by October of 1959, so much history had passed through Carver County that the name Judd McCarthy was buried in the memories of all but a few of the old timers.

Like the thousands upon thousands of itinerant laborers who had passed through the Midwest in the 1920s and 1930s, Judd McCarthy and his mysterious disappearance became a forgotten issue, another of the eternal secrets buried beneath the prairie soil. Certainly his life carried with it no special significance for most of those who continued to live in Carver County into the middle of the twentieth century.

But Judd McCarthy had made a promise in October of 1926 before he journeyed from Danvers to Carson. And, more than anything else, Judd McCarthy meant to keep that promise.

Chapter Two
I

October, 1959

When Joel Hampton awoke his body was drenched in a feverish sweat and his wife, looking puzzled and frightened, was staring down at him. She was shaking him by his shoulder.

"Huh?" he managed to whisper through dried lips. His eyelids were sleepy and heavy. They opened, then slowly closed again.

"Joel, wake up!" Susan insisted. She seemed to be calling to him from far away, pulling him out of the darkness. "You're having that nightmare again."

"Nightmare?" The word itself was only faintly recognizable to him.

"You're talking in your sleep."

Slowly he pushed himself up to a sitting position. His eyelids blinked twice, then remained open. "The nightmare?" He was beginning to remember.

"Yes," Susan said, the concern evident in her voice.

"Did I do it again?"

"Yes, Joel. God, you scared me half to death."

He knew then why she was afraid. He had been having the same nightmare since he was a boy. It had stopped during the years that he was in high school and college, but as soon as he became a junior partner in the law firm the nightmares started again. It was always the same. He was walking alone, somewhere out in the country. It was autumn and colorful leaves waved in the wind and blew out into the empty fields. He was happy, but he was also apprehensive about something. Something that was lurking in the shadows of a group of trees. Then he took a step out into an empty wheat field and suddenly he was surrounded by darkness. There were strange noises in the darkness, strange and threatening noises that he did not understand. Then he felt pain and fear and he heard the scream as his body grew numb. The scream grew louder and louder and . . .

As a boy he would awaken to look up into the eyes of his mother. She would be staring down at him, looking puzzled and frightened. Now it was his wife who had pulled him out of the darkness.

"I'm sorry," he said to Susan gently as he looked into his wife's dark eyes. "What did I say?"

"You didn't say anything. You just started to sweat and then you began to scream. Joel . . ." Susan Hampton paused to sit up on the edge of the bed.

"Yes honey?"

"You've got to stop working so hard," she said wearily. "I know it's your first year in the firm and you feel you have to prove something to the others. But you can't kill yourself in the process. You're just trying to do too much."

"It isn't the firm, Susan. I've been having that nightmare for years, ever since I was a boy."

"Then I think it's time you see someone about it. Someone who can help you figure out what it means and why it keeps coming back to you."

"What are you suggesting?"

"I don't know. . ."

Screenwriting Strategies Used To Write the Novel

The following are some of the strategies discussed in *Storytelling as Art and Craftsmanship* that were used to write the novel version of this story:

- *My one-sentence summary or logline was*: "The story involves a young man in 1959 who gradually assumes the identity of an itinerant labor who disappeared under mysterious circumstances in 1926 while walking on the railroad tracks between two small towns in the Midwest."

- *After reviewing the screenplay in its entirety, and before writing the novel, I cut several scenes that clearly did not work.* I also made other cuts in the screenplay outline to enter some scenes late and exit them early to improve the pacing and movement of the story. I was able to do this quite effortlessly because the plot of the story was on the surface of the screenplay treatment, not buried in the descriptive and expository prose of a novel.
- *The hook and setup in both the screenplay and novel occur when Judd McCarthy disappears without a trace,* and the reader knows that something terrible happened to him. The rest of the story will answer three questions: What happened to Judd McCarthy on that autumn day in 1926 when he disappeared? Who was responsible for his disappearance? And why does someone else thirty-three years later apparently share McCarthy's identity and memories?
- *McCarthy is identified by certain physical anomalies*: his size, huge muscular arms, menacing appearance—and yet his gentle, sensitive eyes.
- *Certain objects* like the knife, revolver, floppy black hat, and especially the locket and migrating flock of geese also shape and define McCarthy's character and foreshadow actions that will occur later.
- *McCarthy has weaknesses and flaws as well as strengths.* His reputation as a brawler and ruffian, perhaps even a dangerously violent man, are evidence of his many flaws and weaknesses. Yet, the episode with the rooster pheasant reveals him to be a very complex man, one who is also capable of great tenderness and kindness.

- *The antagonist is very powerful.* Whatever or whoever caused McCarthy to disappear is apparently something or someone with enormous power. This antagonist was capable of subjugating a man of legendary strength and size.
- *There is a strong sense of place in both the screenplay and the novel.* I choose the rural Midwest during Indian summer because I had lived there for two decades, and I was emotionally connected to both that place and time of year. I also learned of some abandoned Midwestern railroad lines that would be convenient substitutes for the fictional railroad line the main character Judd McCarthy was walking on when he disappeared. To strengthen the sense of place in the novel, I walked some of those railroad lines while I pondered the subtleties of the story I was writing.
- *The dramatic tension (hook) developed early in the screenplay is replicated early in the novel.* Although McCarthy is alone in the opening scene, he is always active and there are potential threats (antagonists) everywhere. He is also struggling with his own internal tensions, specifically his rowdy and irresponsible temperament, which threatens his relationship with Kate. When the action shifts to 1959, the tension is sustained through Joel Hampton's reoccurring nightmares that are undermining his relationship with his wife and slowly consuming his identity.
- *The dialogue was improved by first writing it as screenplay dialogue and then converting and expanding it to novel dialogue.* Screenplay dialogue is performance dialogue. It is meant to be heard. Novel dialogue is meant to be read, usually silently. When I wrote the dialogue for this story, I *listened* to what I was writing and how a reader would *hear* it. This was made much easier by writing the dialogue in screenplay form and then expanding it in the novel.

- *The dialogue was also shaped by the characters' backgrounds and their specific circumstances in each scene.* McCarthy is an uneducated, itinerant Irish laborer, and his speech patterns reflect this background. Joel and his wife are more educated, and their dialogue is more elevated and refined, although in the opening scene Joel has just woken up and is not fully in control of his thought process or speech patterns. Practice in writing screenplay dialogue sensitized my own ear to all of these considerations.
- *The Screenplay descriptions also improved the descriptions in the novel.* Although screenplays must be written in a lean, sparse style and without lengthy, overly detailed descriptions, the action descriptions must nonetheless be written to appeal to the senses—especially the visual and auditory. Thus the principle of *showing* not *telling* was already deeply engrained in the screenplay before I even started writing the novel.
- *The screenplay developed the opening scenes primarily through vivid descriptions and dialogue.* The novel uses descriptions and dialogue, but also exposition, stream of consciousness, and other literary techniques. Consequently, some information can be communicated in the novel that cannot be communicated in the screenplay unless the screenwriter decides to use flashbacks, inserts, voice over, and other screenwriting techniques. For example, the novel directly addresses McCarthy's reputation as a "violent man." The screenplay can only suggest this through the description of his "menacing appearance." Through exposition, the novel incorporates other information that could not appear in the screenplay: the description of McCarthy's wrestling match with Tobin prior to his disappearance; the newspaper account of his

disappearance; the fact that he is planning to meet Kate after he delivers the company payroll; a glance into the future that suggests he was alive for some time after he disappeared; the fact that he was rumored to have fled into the Dakotas; and virtually all of Chapter One, Part II.

- *Screenwriting enabled me to think in pictures.* Using what I learned from screenwriting, I tried to recreate vivid images and compliment them with the sounds that surrounded McCarthy as he walked along the railroad tracks.
- *The novel and screenplay are both structured on the "The Classical Film Paradigm"* that is illustrated in Chapter 4 of this book. The setup, plot point I, confrontation, plot point II, and resolution are the loom on which this story is structured and developed:

The Setup: Judd McCarthy disappears in 1926 and thirty-three years later Joel Hampton has memories that could only belong to McCarthy.

Plot Point I: Joel Hampton's wife consults psychiatrist Ned Finley, and shortly thereafter Joel becomes so violent that he is institutionalized.

Confrontation: Ned Finley journeys to the county where Judd McCarthy disappeared and learns that the threat is still there. Joel also battles with his own demons in the mental institution.

Plot Point II: Joel Hampton escapes from the mental institution and makes his way back to the county where McCarthy disappeared.

Resolution: Ned Finley has learned enough about McCarthy's disappearance to speculate where Joel is heading. He finds Joel and puts the final pieces of the puzzle together.

After I wrote *The Search for Judd McCarthy* as a screenplay using the classical structural paradigm discussed by Syd Field in his book, I was able to weave a much more complex and sophisticated plot without losing control of my story. I was also able to develop more sophisticated and organically developed character relationships, symbolism, structural devices, and the other elements of storytelling.

- *The place became the story when I realized the "dying small town" was also a main character*—perhaps even the most important main character—and it needed to take center stage and be developed at length. This was a departure from my original conception regarding the structure and spirit of the novel, but, according to many reviewers and readers, it was also a decision that distinguished the story from others in this genre.
- *The minor characters came to the forefront more than I expected.* I believe this is because I had a structural paradigm in place, and my creative energies could devote more attention to what are normally considered minor elements in a novel. (I should quickly point out that many authors and critics believe the ultimate test of a novel is the strength of the minor characters.) As a result, the minor characters had fertile soil in which to grow and proliferate. It probably also accounts for the *Publisher's Weekly* review that stated the novel "beautifully evokes the feeling of a small town dying . . . and, most of all, its lost souls."
- *Individual scenes throughout the novel make at least one, and often several major contributions to the plot.* For

example, the opening scene when McCarthy is walking on the railroad tracks establishes his relationship to Kate, the Hanley Brothers, and Farmer Tobin—all of whom will be important later in the story. The first scene in the Hampton's bedroom develops Joel's fragile relationship with his wife and hints at his mysterious connection to Judd McCarthy.

- *The chapters of the novel are based on the sequences in the screenplay.* For example, the sequence that follows the scene in the Hampton's bedroom creates a story within the larger story. At the end of this sequence, Joel will fully assume the identity of Judd McCarthy and must be institutionalized because he poses a threat to everyone around him.
- *There is a great deal of false foreshadowing* that leads the reader to expect one ending, while other potential endings have been hidden just beneath the surface of the storyline. Because I know where the knot (ending) is tied at the end of the rope, I have the creative freedom to unravel the individual threads in various and creative ways.
- *In both the screenplay and the novel, I wrote the tentative ending shortly after I completed the opening scenes* on the railroad tracks and in the Hampton's bedroom. Once the knot (ending) was tied, I wrote several scenes just prior to the final scene of the novel. Then I returned to the scene in the Hampton's bedroom and moved the story forward again. Everything was in place to foreshadow and falsely foreshadow the ending of the story, although I kept an open mind to potential changes in my anticipated ending. Most importantly, it enabled me to be constantly thinking of potential endings behind the ending.

Storytelling as Art and Craftsmanship

- *Another ending behind the ending emerged from out of the shadows of the creative process.* That ending revealed the relationship between Judd McCarthy "Kate" to be more complicated than I had envisioned. Yet, in retrospect, I realized it provided the final explanation and resolution for many of the events that occurred earlier in the story. It reinforced in my mind that an early anticipation of the final ending is more preparatory than final, and it has doors behind it with rooms that still need to be explored. However, without the early anticipated ending, those doors would probably remain locked. Once again, I was convinced the moderately structured environment of a preliminary screenplay outline enhances, not represses the creative process of storytelling.

- *With a screenplay outline, it was much easier to integrate and coordinate three voices throughout the story* because I was not distracted by overwhelming structural issues. One voice, which is most evident in "Chapter One, Part I," utilizes the five senses and adheres to the principles of *showing* not *telling* to recreate the actual details of the scene prior to McCarthy's disappearance. These apparently minor details are elements of foreshadowing that will become more important as the story progresses. The second voice is the stream of consciousness point of view of McCarthy at the end of "Chapter One, Part I" and later in the novel as it gradually makes its presence felt in Joel Hampton's subconscious mind thirty-three years later. A third voice, which is evident in "Chapter One, Part II," is that of a more visible omniscient author who provides some historical perspective on what happened in the years after McCarthy disappeared. Coordinating these three voices, sometimes in the same scene or chapter, would have been extremely difficult, if not impossible, without the structural foundation of a screenplay outline.

To the best of my knowledge, when I wrote *The Search for Judd McCarthy* in the early 1980s, I was one of the first to experiment with using screenplay form and techniques to write novels. My ideas regarding this strategy have changed and evolved somewhat as I wrote and published several novels, a work of creative nonfiction, a memoir, two textbooks, and various other literary works. However, I have not lost faith in the strategy. To the contrary, I am even more convinced than I was almost forty years ago that it works.

I am compelled in part to accept the strategy because I have read too many student stories that fall apart at the end because there was little in the way of advanced planning. They had written with the hope that the many threads of their stories could somehow be tied together in the final scenes. But this seldom happens without some forethought.

The advantages of using a screenplay as an outline for a novel are readily apparent if we expand on an earlier analogy to medical science. A first-year medical student is not going to learn much about the skeletal structure of the human body by studying a living, breathing human being. The skeletal structure is too concealed in the body. Similarly, a finished novel conceals its skeletal structure behind the descriptions, exposition, stream of consciousness ruminations, and other literary techniques that are used to complete the story. It is, thus, difficult to teach structure in novels, which is probably why many teachers and professors only mention it in passing.

A screenplay strips away everything that conceals the structure of the story and displays it bare for the reader to see. An author who writes a screenplay first, and then converts it into a novel, has a complete x-ray of the anatomy of the story. It is much easier to flesh out fully developed character descriptions, the voice or voices of the story, scenes, actions, and the other elements of a novel with the screenplay as a structural foundation.

A screenplay outline for a novel is, thus, a very helpful tool to hold the elements of the story in place as the writer is gaining a clearer sense of how the plot is developing. Screenplay structure, however, should not be viewed as a convenient checklist for novelists to gauge their progress through the set-up, plot-points, and resolution of the story. If used this way, the story itself will become too mechanical and formulaic.

Perhaps a final analogy would be helpful, one from my undergraduate days as a college basketball player. A screenplay outline is like the game plans we developed long before we even stepped onto the basketball court. They are developed in the context of the challenges we expected to encounter once the game started. We even went through practices in which we played out the way we anticipated the game might develop. However, when the game starts, a player's instincts have to take over and work with the preconceived game plan, modify it, or, in some cases, abandon it altogether. Basketball is a very instinctive game, one that has an organic flow that develops as the two teams test one another's strengths and weaknesses.

Much of this is done instinctively as the game progresses. Instincts, after all, are intelligence that informs us at some deeper level of consciousness and creates a more organic flow to everything we do in life. Advanced planning and instinctive spontaneity are both necessary in a basketball game.

They are equally necessary in writing a novel.

FINAL EXERCISE

Choose any sequence from the screenplay you are writing and rewrite it as a chapter in a novel. Then compare the screenplay outline to any other outline you have ever used. Which gives you a better sense of control and direction, while unleashing the spirit of the story?

AFTERWORD

Students of screenwriting need to be realistic about their chances of breaking into the screenwriting market. They may not become professional screenwriters, although the thrill of producing their first screenplays will certainly get the adrenalin pumping enough to make many of them want to become screenwriters. Having said that, the chances of breaking into the screenwriting profession are greatly enhanced if the student concentrates on writing a good story rather than impressing readers with his or her knowledge of screenwriting jargon.

More to the point—and I stress this in my screenwriting classes—what students learn about screenwriting will make them better students of literature and better creative writers. Regardless of what they do with that knowledge, they will understand the art of storytelling in ways that may have eluded them in their traditional literature and creative writing courses. Students will also learn how to structure a story more effectively, write better dialogue, and create more vivid pictures with their writing, all of which are invaluable skills in every form of creative writing. If they decide to convert a screenplay into a novel or other work of fiction, it will be much easier for them to find the *voice* of the story because they will have already experienced the *spirit* of the story.

Personally, I never pursued a career in screenwriting after writing in that genre in the early 1980s. I decided instead to write fiction and nonfiction, often using screenplays as outlines. Screenplay structure helped me organize and develop many major writing projects, including four novels, a memoir, an award-winning book of creative nonfiction, and other published works. I even used screenplay structure when I wrote a newspaper column for several years. Nothing enabled me to see my own writing, and what I needed to do to improve it, better than my early attempts to write screenplays.

Students should always remember that their own efforts to learn screenwriting form should not be viewed as wasted efforts if they fail to become professional screenwriters or novel writers. What they learn about screenwriting will apply to everything they write in the future; and every time they view a film or read a novel, it will be a richer, more satisfying experience for them.

ABOUT THE AUTHOR

Dennis M. Clausen grew up in west central Minnesota. There, he gained a close, intimate knowledge of the small towns and the lives they harbored. They provided the inspiration for many of the novels and other books he has published with traditional publishing companies. These include Bantam Books, McGraw-Hill Book Company, Sunbury Press (Brown Posey Imprint), and other publishers. *The Search for Judd McCarthy* (2018), the story of an itinerant laborer who disappeared in 1920s-era Minnesota, was a best-selling paperback novel original when first published in 1982. *The Sins of Rachel Sims* (2018) is a novel inspired by both Nathaniel Hawthorne's *The Scarlet Letter* and one of Clausen's ancestors who bore her own stigma of shame when she gave birth to a child out of wedlock in an unforgiving church community. *The Accountant's Apprentice (2018)*, a novel that explores mysterious events that occurred in San Diego's homeless population in the mid-2010s, was the recipient of a "First Place" designation in the 2016 Chanticleer International Book Awards Competitions.

My Christmas Attic (2018) is the story of a young boy in the early 1950s who struggles with dyslexia and the loss of his father in the Korean War. Clausen is also the author of *Prairie Son* (1999), a book that was the winner of Mid-List Press's "First Series: Creative Nonfiction Award." This book recreates his father's struggles as an adopted child to survive the Great Depression in a farm home where he was treated more as a worker than a son. *Goodbye to Main Street* (2016), a memoir and sequel to *Prairie Son,* has received considerable attention in several national book competitions. It also earned a "First in Category" designation in the 2018 Chanticleer International Book Award Competitions. Clausen has also authored textbooks, including *The Concise Process Handbook* (1986) and *Screenwriting and Literature* (2009). For over forty years, he has taught literature and screenwriting courses at the University of San Diego.

Made in the USA
Las Vegas, NV
09 September 2024